Constructing and Reconstructing Gender

SUNY Series in Feminist Criticism and Theory
Edited by Michelle A. Massé

Constructing and Reconstructing Gender

The Links Among Communication, Language, and Gender

EDITED BY

Linda A.M. Perry
University of San Diego

Lynn H. Turner
Helen M. Sterk
Marquette University

STATE UNIVERSITY OF NEW YORK PRESS

Published by
State University of New York Press, Albany

©1992 State University of New York

Printed in the United States of America

Marketing by Dana E. Yanulavich
Production by Cathleen Collins

For information, address State University of New York Press,
State University Plaza, Albany, N.Y., 12246

Library of Congress Cataloging-in-Publication Data

Constructing and reconstructing gender : the links among
    communication, language, and gender / [edited by] Linda A.M. Perry,
    Lynn H. Turner, Helen M. Sterk.
        p.   cm. — (SUNY series in feminist criticism and theory)
    "Selected readings from the 10th and 11th Annual Meetings of the
    Organization for the Study of Communication, Language and Gender" —
    Includes bibliographical references and index.
    ISBN 0–7914–1009–9 — ISBN 0–7914–1010–2
    1. Communication—Sex differences.   2. Language and languages—Sex
differences.   I. Perry, Linda A.M., 1947–   .   II. Turner, Lynn H., 1946–
III. Sterk, Helen M., 1952–   .   IV. Organization for the Study of
Communication, Language, and Gender.   V. Series.
P96.S48C64   1992
306.4'4—dc20
                                                        91–29718
                                                           CIP

10   9   8   7   6   5   4   3   2   1

Contents

Section I
Constructing Gender
Unit I
Defining Gender

Unit II
Learning Gender

Acknowledgments

The chapters in this book are competitively selected readings from the 10th and 11th Annual Meetings of the Organization for the Study of Communication, Language, and Gender (OSCLG). We thank OSCLG, Marquette University, and the University of San Diego (where these conferences were held) for their support. Special thanks to Marquette University's College of Communication, Journalism, and Performing Arts Committee on Faculty Research Development and the University of San Diego's Faculty Research Grant Committee for research funding. Additional thanks to the University of San Diego for providing us with a transcript typist, Juli Jones-Busse, without whose amazing patience and talents we could not have brought this project to fruition. Thanks to Monica Wagner for her work on charts. Dawn Formo, a research assistant at USD, gave excellent help in editing a number of the chapters—we thank her for her contribution. Finally, we thank each of the authors for their original pieces and, especially, for their diligence in working with us throughout the project.

Introduction

Communication and language link people to their societies such that the concept of gender is constructed and reconstructed over time. Communication scholars grounded in both social scientific and humanities backgrounds have long been interested in gender and its construction. Early communication research in which gender was investigated did not, however, challenge the hegemonic worldview of white, male dominance. Studies often simply searched for the ways in which women differed from men in order to establish women's deviation from the norm. Research also tended to focus on women—that is, gender became a euphemism rather than a category including both males and females. "Gender" in this volume includes both female and male experiences.

The authors represented in this book create new, and test old, paradigms for researching gender. The essays are organized around two frameworks. The first, Constructing Gender, focuses on the relationship of gender to other cultural and social variables. The second, Reconstructing Gender, focuses on the interactions among a variety of contextual variables that affect gender.

In this way, the book is an effort to examine the interaction between individuals and society—an examination that is critical to an understanding of the process of gender acquisition and enactment. Both social hierarchy and individual agency are essential elements in feminist theory. Issues of social hierarchy define the problems of women's oppression whereas personal agency provides insights that can afford us solutions.

Section One is concerned with some of the ways gender is constructed. From an interactionist's perspective, gender definitions evolve as individuals interact within their environments. Further, gender may be seen as the product of psychological imprinting, social learning, and language. As gender definitions evolve, people learn what behaviors are afforded them according to the cultural mores for their particular gender. Finally, this gender role is expressed through language and behaviors of individuals. Several chapters in this section focus on the notion of gender as a linguistic construct, thus highlighting the ways males and females choose to express gender. In many ways some of these essays challenge earlier theoretical understandings of how gender operates within white Western culture. Previously, much feminist work within the area of communication glossed over the role of personal agency. The concern was more about ascertaining how women and men, as groups, were expected to act than about how individuals may have tested or even resisted gender-role expectations. The authors here explore new territory in feminist communication research, adding nuance and flexibility to areas once marked by rigidity.

Section Two of this volume looks at how gender roles can be reconstructed through one's interactions with power, culture, and audiences. There is a growing concern about whether interactional outcomes are gender related or power related. Authors in this section attempt to unravel this knot by looking at how gender and power interact in language, organizations, and personal constructs.

The role culture plays in gender formation has just begun to emerge as a research focus for feminist communication scholars. This new orientation has come about largely in response to the challenge presented to feminist theory in general by women of color. The universality of the white, middle-class women's experience was an unspoken assumption of early feminist writing. These writers were writing, as does every writer, out of their own experience. It was ironic that the people who so keenly felt what it was like for their experience to be suppressed were guilty of doing the same thing to others. Work is now being done to expand notions of gender and power by including race, ethnicity, and culture as important elements in the symbolic mix that produces gender identity and action. This section contains examples of just such work.

Finally, several authors in this volume address the negotiation of gender identity that takes place between speaker and audience. This perspective has been traditional in speech communication. The audience has long been assumed to exert influence on the message. The authors included here are breaking newer ground, however, when they take the position that the meaning of gender, like communication, evolves in an ongoing process. Thus, gender changes through transactions with others. In a real sense gender is the co-creation of speaker and audience. The chapters in this unit operate from an interactional perspective, positing that gender is an evolving construct. Gender changes as a result of perceived expectations and constraints emanating from an audience.

Each essay that we have included examines the intersection of communication, language, and gender from its own perspective. Our analytical framework of construction and reconstruction imposes an organizing principle on these essays. However, we recognize that the categories overlap each other—pointing to links among all the essays in this collection. Taken together, we believe the essays suggest the vital role communication plays in connecting the individual and society in the evolving process of gender construction.

Section I
Constructing Gender

Unit I
Defining Gender

Gender is constructed in various ways. In this section, the process of defining, learning, and expressing gender are delineated. Unit I is concerned with how gender comes to be defined. How gender is defined is of primary concern because the definition becomes the backdrop for people's perceptions and behaviors. In this unit, the authors take a close look at from where gender orientations evolve, how to recognize them, and with what methods to evaluate them. Dana Cloud begins this unit by arguing that novels can work as persuasive tools for supporting a particular gender orientation. We may, for example, define our gender according to the behaviors and/or beliefs of fictitious characters. T. Joan Fecteau, Jullane Jackson, and Kathryn Dindia argue that gender roles are altered over time and, as such, may not be appropriately measured by extant gender scales. To support their argument, they examine five psychological gender scales. In Chapter Three, Lisa Merrill explores how courses and texts in oral interpretation are politically slanted to represent only the white male view. She offers exercises from which students can learn to explore their own stereotypes of men and women of various races by adopting a cross-sex orientation for both the reader and the assumed audience. The final chapter of this unit explores the impact traditional rhetoric has had on limiting women's roles to biological functions. Lesley Di Mare argues that new forms of persuasion must be integrated into old forms in order for rhetoric to reflect both masculine and feminine perspectives.

CHAPTER 1

The Possibility of a Liberating Narrative: *Woman on the Edge of Time* as Radical, Mythic, Moral Argument

Dana L. Cloud
University of Iowa

In a recent conversation with a friend, I brought up Marge Piercy's utopian novel *Woman on the Edge of Time*. Her reaction was a surprise. "Oh, God. I hate that book," she said. "It's so didactic, it pounds you over the head. It's not literature." I worried over these statements, wondering where my own pleasure in reading this novel lies. How could I account for its success (in more than four printings)? Ultimately I agreed with my friend. This novel is not really literature—it is politics, and good politics at that. As such, it should be treated as explicit political rhetoric, and assessed according to the political and ethical standards of the critic's interpretive community.

Walter Fisher, Wayne Booth, and others have argued that narrative serves more than an aesthetic function. My argument is that this novel, like narratives of all types, makes public arguments about political, moral, and ethical questions. This process is akin to what philosopher Carl Wellman describes as "thought experimenting," the imaginary testing of hypotheses regarding ethics and values that attempts to convince an audience of the value of a particular way of living.

NARRATIVES AS ARGUMENT: IMAGINING A BETTER WORLD

Because narrative arguments personalize public debate, using emotional and ethical proofs and experientially based data and warrants in support of their claims, they are a unique vehicle for public moral or political argument. In the course of this paper, I will raise issues about the ways in which narratives argue, the efficacy of presenting radical or oppositional arguments in a literary format, and the role of the critic in evaluating these arguments.

To get at the question of how narratives argue, I want to explore Carl Wellman's notion of the "thought experiment." To put it simply, a thought experiment is the mental process in which a person asks others or herself, "What would the world be like if X happened?" or "What would it be like to live in a different kind of place?" or "What would it feel like to be this other kind of a person?" and finally, "Would it be right or good or valuable?" As Wellman puts it, a thought experiment is the testing out of an ethical hypothesis' implications (32). This process is not always a private one. On the contrary, when ethical matters arise in debate, the though experiment, a kind of imaginary induction, is one of the only methods of proof.

> *A thought experiment is an argument. The description of the test case is the premise or set of premises of the argument; the statement that the imagined object is good or the possible act is right is the conclusion. (41)*

An important characteristic of this kind of thinking is the use of imagery to concretize an ethical principle. Imaginative descriptions function as premises in the argument, providing reasons for the ethical conclusion (43–44).

In a fictional narrative, then, a proposition is set forth with evidence constituted by the experiences of the characters in the narrative and by the way these experiences are structured. MacCabe (as represented in Fiske) describes how the multiple discourses in any given narrative are structured to privilege one of them in a "hierarchy of discourses" (Fiske 25). Like other kinds of narrative, feminist utopian novels do exhibit hierarchies of discourses that privilege the discourses of specific political perspectives.

These novels do this in a way that could be characterized as oppositional myth. According to Fiske (after Lévi-Strauss, Barthes), mythic narrative puts opposed cultural values or groups into a dialogue in which the voice of the established order comes out on top (Fiske 132–33). The oppositions embodied in a myth are mediated by the mythic hero "with characteristics from both categories" (Fiske 133). Feminist utopian novels usually feature this kind of hero(ine). Here, however, this mythic strategy does not reinforce the dominant culture, but rather functions as a rhetorical/argumentative strategy that helps the reader to understand an *oppositional* set of values. The hero has just enough of the characteristics of the dominant set of values to facilitate reader identification and mediate between the known and the new. This mediation helps ease the reader into a new, radically challenging world.

Marge Piercy's novel is a mythic, argumentative, and potentially radical narrative that employs several rhetorical strategies—dialectical opposition of worldviews and values; the embodiment of public, sociopolitical and ethical issues in personal, experiential data; and an initiation strategy that allows the reader to become gradually integrated with the utopian society along with the story's protagonist—in support for its claims about the ideal world. After explicating the text, I will discuss these strategies and their goals in light of their fidelity to a socialist-feminist political agenda. If there can be such a thing as a radical narrative, is *Woman on the Edge of Time* an example? And what is the critic's role in evaluating such a narrative?

THE ARGUMENTATIVE STRATEGIES OF THE FEMINIST UTOPIAN NOVEL: *WOMAN ON THE EDGE OF TIME*

The genre of utopian fiction (from the Greek, meaning "no place," places of the imagination) includes depictions of alternative worlds and lives in both eutopias ("good places") and dystopias ("bad places"). So it follows that a feminist utopia, like all utopias, is basically a depiction of an alternative society that acts as a perspective on and critique of the structural oppression of our own society, targeting those aspects of our society directly related to the oppression of women.

Such novels sustain an intense dialectic between the personal and the political, the private and the public, undertaking the explicit negotiation of the relationship between an individual woman and the societies in which she lives—and could live. A utopian novel is explicitly didactic and political, designed to teach and to argue. Most critics see utopias as calls to action (Kessler 19). In my view, the primary rhetorical strategy of the feminist utopian novel is the presentation of political, public messages about the structure of society at large through the personal, private perspective of an individual woman.

The form of these novels, then, is simultaneously public and private, reinforcing the feminist political messages that our public and private lives are interrelated and that to live in a society based on the welfare of the collective is better than to live in one that is completely privatized. The dialectic between public and private is, in both content and structure, the underlying principle of Marge Piercy's novel *Woman on the Edge of Time.*

Woman on the Edge of Time is the story of Connie Ramos, a single, Chicana welfare mother. At the beginning of the story, she attacks her niece Dolly's pimp Geraldo in order to defend Dolly, whom he is beating. As a result, Connie is incarcerated in a mental hospital, where we learn she has been before as a result of a prolonged depression over the death of her imprisoned, black, blind, and utterly powerless lover Claud. During her period of grief, Connie had neglected her daughter Angelina, and she committed herself to the hospital in the hope of being healed. Her daughter has been adopted by a white family, and now Connie is once again imprisoned. While in the hospital, she is treated like an object. No one listens to her side of the story or tries to help her in any way. Instead, she is drugged and ignored—until she is selected for use in a frightening neurosurgical mind-control experiment.

Meanwhile, Connie has been contacted by Luciente, a woman from a eutopian future, and learns to project herself mentally into this future. Eventually she becomes intimate with the members of this society, which provides a critical perspective on her own, teaching her as the novel teaches the reader. The novel alternates among several different times. There is of course Connie's present and the eutopian future. The reader also has access to Connie's memories of her difficult life. In addition, a second future hinges on the thought-control experiments imposed on Connie, this one horribly dystopic. In her encounters with the people of Mattapoisett (Luciente's community), Connie learns that her present is a "crux time" that determines which of the futures will come to be.

An intense dialectic between public and private operates in this novel on several levels. First, Piercy is careful to draw clear connections between the individual private lives she documents and the impact on them by the structure of the society. Second, Luciente's community is just that—an integrated community with a rich public life, whereas Connie's version of the twentieth century is highly privatized, a place where people live in almost complete isolation from one another. The eutopian public world provides a point-by-point critique of the private one, with Connie as the link between the two. Finally, as discussed above, the interaction between the novel and the reader is simultaneously public and private. The text is a public call to action that is very persuasive insofar as the reader can identify with Connie and trust her voice and her interpretation of events.

To identify with Connie is to experience her world, and to engage in the first level of the public/private dialectic I have identified: the recognition that the private is public, that identity itself is socially constructed. Connie's world, symbolized by the isolation of the mental ward, is extremely privatized despite the fact that her activity is regulated by the state. In her private life, Connie faces an onslaught of sexism, racism, dehumanization, poverty, manipulation, and grief—all strands of the rope that binds her. In this world, the only sources of power and self-esteem a woman has are her sexuality, her ability to bear children, and her family. In a society where people compete for scarce and unequally distributed resources, individuals are forced into the isolation of the nuclear family, waging battles for power and control within its limits. This is what Geraldo, Dolly's pimp, does to Dolly.

Early on, Geraldo comes to represent all men (14–15), yet as Connie points out, he is the positive embodiment of twentieth-century masculine traits:

> *A man is supposed to be...strong, hold his liquor, attractive to women, able to beat out other men,...macho, we call it,* muy hombre....*to look out for number one...to make good money, well, to get ahead you step on people...you knuckle under to the big guys and you walk over the people underneath. (120)*

Here and throughout the book, Piercy links the personal, private abuses of women, as well as of other marginalized, alienated groups of people, to a key oppressive component of the basic structure of public society, namely, capitalism—the need to "look out for number one," to "make money," to "get ahead." Unfortunately, women are at the bottom of the competitive social hierarchy, the ultimate scapegoats and victims of the limitation of their personal power to the private realm.

As Geraldo represents all men, the mental institution itself and the manipulative techniques it employs are symbols of the larger society. Connie calls electroshock therapy "a little brain damage to jolt you into behaving right" (81). The "barbecue of the brain" (81) she experiences is the silencing of those on the fringe of society by those in its center, the "doctors and judges, caseworkers and social workers, probation officers, policy psychiatrists" (91) and other middle-class institutional representatives. Connie faces all these people in the center as she is screened for participation in a test of a brain implant (called a dialytrode). This implant would allow for complete social surveillance and control. Thus Connie's private experience and observations become metaphors for the cruelty of American society at large.

By contrast, Luciente, Connie's counterpart, lives in a socialist society where no one is victimized. There is no private property; the wealth of the community is earned by and distributed among all of its members. Everyone has access to good food, housing—all the basic necessities of life—and no one has more than anyone else. In fact, Luciente's definitions of ultimate evil "center around power and greed—taking from other people their food, their liberty, their health, their land, their customs, their pride" (139). Through a number of rich, culturally meaningful rituals, members of this community of Mattapoisett, Massachusetts, maintain a feeling of connection, kinship, and integration with each other. Whereas Connie conceives of power and wealth in terms of "I," Luciente and the rest of her community think almost always in terms of the collective "we." Luciente says, "The gift is in growing to care, to connect, to cooperate. Everything we learn aims to make us feel strong in ourselves, connected to all living at home" (248). The phrase "at home" is a telling one, reflecting the complete conjoining of public and private in Luciente's world. Here people are at home with the other members of their community, not in isolation from them. Action here is collective, with all participating in all major decisions (277). Here individuals are valued instead of alienated for their special gifts and characteristics, and Luciente, an educated, happy, successful, free woman, is the person Connie could be—given this context.

With Connie, the reader comes to know this world, but only gradually to accept it. Because the twentieth-century American reader is more or less a member of Connie's culture, it is easy to identify with Connie's difficulty in shifting from self-directed consciousness to other-directedness, from technological control of the environment to harmony with the natural order, from isolation and competition to cooperation and love. The novel's third-person limited point of view enhances the process of reader identification with Connie. At the beginning of the story, Connie (mis)interprets everything Luciente reveals to her from behind a twentieth-century screen. She cannot conceive of a viable collective, because, as she puts it, "Her life was thin in meaningful we's" (35). She first mistakes Luciente for a man because in her experience, women are not direct, assertive, or strong (40), and upon discovering that she was wrong, automatically labels Luciente a "dyke" (67). Because she cannot interpret outside her frame of reference, she struggles with the societal vision Luciente provides her. And because her frame of reference is also the reader's, so is her struggle.

Similarly, her first glimpse of pastoral Mattapoisett is one fraught with confusion:

> *What did I expect from the future...Pink skies? Robots on the march? Transistorized people? I guess we blew ourselves up and now we're back to the dark ages....She stood a moment weakened by a sadness she could not name. A better world for the children—that had always been the fantasy....But if Angelina had a child and that child a child, this was the world they would finally be born into....how different was it really from rural Mexico with its dusty villages rubbing their behinds into the dust? (73)*

Ironically, her expectations for a "better world" closely match the dystopic future that she encounters later in the novel, whereas the real eutopia is much like traditional societies of the past. She (and the reader) is not yet ready to see the possible dystopic future until she can realize the merits of Luciente's society. Until then, she would evaluate the dystopic future according to her own culture's criteria—and her evaluation would be positive. Throughout the novel, Connie must come to realize that Mattapoisett is "a better world for the children."

Although it is not perfect, Connie gradually comes to realize that Mattapoisett is a good place to live. She notices that the entire community is a sort of family (118). Working from her own experience, Connie begins to understand. In the same chapter, Connie sees a child, Dawn, who resembles her own Angelina, running, playing, and laughing. In an epiphanic moment, Connie sees how much better off the child is in this world than Angelina was—and is—in the twentieth century:

> *Suddenly she assented with all her soul to Angelina in Mattapoisett, to Angelina hidden forever one hundred fifty years into the future....For the first time, her heart assented to Luciente, to Bee, to Magdalena. Yes, you can have my child....I give her to Luciente to mother, with gladness I give her. She will never be broken as I was. She will be strange, but she will be glad and strong, and she will not be afraid. She will have enough. She will have pride. She will love her own brown skin and be loved for her strength and her good work. (141)*

This moment, reinforced by the pathos of the knowledge that Angelina will never really experience the life Connie imagines for her, is the culmination of Piercy's first argument. Given her association as a familiar guide, the reader can come to this realization, too. The reader is with Connie alternately in her own world, where Connie watches more and more of her friends become resigned and beaten, and in Luciente's world, where she sees a healthy community living, loving, and working out its problems together.

In this way, Connie—and through identification, the reader—share in the argument's gradual unfolding. By revealing the virtues of one societal structure over another through the personal experiences of individuals, Piercy is able to present her argument in the representation of dramatic thought, feeling, and action. This ability is the most significant manifestation of the public/private dialectic for this novel: The reader who has identified with Connie at this point can adhere with her to Piercy's claim that, despite its flaws, contradictions, and strangeness, Mattapoisett is a preferable society to her own.

From this alternative perspective, Luciente targets sexism, destruction of the environment, violence, hierarchical power structures, and especially the tragic isolation of individuals, that, in her view, result from unmitigated consumption and competition—that is, capitalism (see especially 42–55). This explicit identification of the widespread oppression and rape of the environment of twentieth-century America forms an obvious link between the abuses and excesses of Connie's time with its likely successor: a dystopia where all the worst tendencies of our world are projected much larger than life.

This dystopia is a surrealistic, nightmarish exaggeration and compression of all of the evils Luciente points out. Yet it is powerful, again because we know it not only in propositional terms but also through Connie's experience and the personal account of Gildina, whom Connie meets in this horrifying place. If Luciente is Connie's futuristic counterpart, Gildina is Dolly's. Like Dolly, she is a woman who accepts her place and uses her feminine "powers" to maintain dependent relationships with men. Like Dolly, she is a prostitute, in a world where contract sex has replaced marriage. She lives in New York, 127 floors up, isolated from an atmosphere clogged with filth and from the rest of humanity. Her only contact is the "Sense-all," the future of television, on which she views programs very much like today's most sadomasochistic pornography. In this society, people are owned by multi-national corporations that monitor their property via mind-control technology—the technology about to be tested on Connie in her own time.

This coincidence is an invitation to infer direct parallels between the two worlds, as is Connie's cheerless statement, "Men and women haven't changed so much" (294). The presentation of this dystopic future is the capstone of the novel's argument. Recall Connie's vision of the logical successor to her time: "Pink skies? Robots on the march? Transistorized people?" (73). Connie returns to the mental ward knowing this vision of the next "dark ages" is indeed a possibility. She decides to fight the power of the mental institution, enlisting herself—and the reader—in Luciente's war (338–76).

The hierarchy of values in this novel is explicit. By engaging socialism and feminism in a dialectical exchange with patriarchal capitalism and its consequences, by revealing the relations of domination within capitalism from the perspective of a marginalized, powerless, victimized woman, and by initiating the viewer into the socialist eutopia along with her, *Woman on the Edge of Time* argues that Mattapoisett or somewhere like it is where we want to be. In this way, the novel is a thought experiment in mythic form, an imaginative argument that is "designed to decide between competing theories" (Wellman 34). It remains, then, to evaluate its success.

ISSUES FOR CRITICS

For Wellman, a good argument invites challenge and critique with each new encounter. Different audiences bring different criteria to the text. For this reason, the critic's job is to decide who would find the text in question acceptable. This can be achieved by locating the narrative's implied audience (in this case marginalized women and socialist feminists) and its political values. But the critic must do two more things. First, s/he must assess the narrative's fidelity to those particular values, and second, s/he must look to her own community's criteria for acceptability in order to decide whether or not the narrative constitutes an ethical argument.

My task with Piercy's book is clear in this regard. Connie represents a community of extremely marginalized people who suffer from their subjection to the dominant capitalist, patriarchal ideology. Luciente's discourse is also privileged here, representing the ideals of socialist feminism. Because Connie's discourse becomes aligned with Luciente's by the end of the novel, I feel that the novel strongly endorses a socialist feminist perspective.

WOMAN ON THE EDGE OF TIME AND SOCIALIST FEMINISM

In her book *Feminist Politics and Human Nature,* Alison Jaggar outlines the major principles and strategies of socialist feminism, all of which are part of the foundation of *Woman on the Edge of Time.* Basically, socialist feminism relies on many of the analytical tools provided by Marxism, but adds and foregrounds the element of gender as a specific (i.e., not necessarily rooted in class stratification) source of oppression. Socialist feminism is careful, however, to articulate issues of gender in a larger context that includes issues of class, race, and ecology. People are constituted by their social relations along these axes in order to perpetuate unequal power relations (Jaggar 147).

A second major organizing principle of socialist feminism is that because gender distinctions are created to perpetuate male dominance, such distinctions must be erased. A corollary to this principle is that there should be no distinction in material or theoretical terms between public and private spheres. In addition, one's experiences of family, community, and self are variable depending on the larger "public" social structure. For socialist feminists, the larger public should be a version of the family and community.

As should be evident from the foregoing textual analysis, Piercy's eutopia incorporates these two ideals. The eutopian world inhabited by Luciente is a socialist community, a fully participatory democracy in which the fruits of production are shared equally by all. *Woman on the Edge of Time* provides an explicit comparison of a world in which the public/private distinction is enforced in order to maintain power relations and in which that distinction is erased to the benefit of all. And structurally, as I have already argued, the novel represents the interdependence and integration of private, personal experience with public ethical debate. What makes feminist utopian literature, and possibly all literature, ideal for political argument is the ability to embody the data, warrants, and claims of an argument in the experiences of characters.

To its credit, Piercy's novel hinges on exactly the issues targeted by socialist feminism. Capitalism and its results—competition, strict gender roles, and individual isolation—are the objects of critique, juxtaposed in stark contrast with the integrated community of Mattapoisett. Compulsory heterosexuality, ecology, the rights of children, community responsibility for education, transportation, food and shelter, health care, and every other basic human need are still other items on the socialist feminist agenda addressed carefully by Piercy. In short, Marge Piercy in 1976 helped to form a clear articulation of all the major issues in socialist feminism. Furthermore, Piercy achieves this goal in such a way as to overcome reader resistance.

But in addition to exhibiting all the assets of socialist feminism, *Woman on the Edge of Time* also suffers from its foremost problem: limited persuasive appeal. From a socialist feminist perspective, the novel receives a positive evaluation. The problem is that from other perspectives, the story is very likely going to seem tedious, heavy-handed, or just plain wrong. Connie's perspective is not one with which just anyone can identify.

In a sense, this paper has come full circle. *Woman on the Edge of Time* does engage in a kind of public moral argument, but it is not mainstream. Instead, it appeals to a limited audience. It tells a story about the world from a particular perspective, endorsing socialist-feminist values that challenge the status quo. For this reason, its acceptance depends heavily on its reaching a specific audience who can and will accept and learn from it.

Paradoxically, a less accessible narrative such as Piercy's meets John Fiske's definition of a successful radical text:

> *a critical interrogation of the dominant ideology and of the social system which it has produced and underpins; this entails an awareness of the inequalities and of the arbitrariness of late capitalism, which in turn produces the desire to hasten social change and the willingness to work for it. (33)*

A truly challenging text is necessarily limited in its mainstream appeal. However, it is important to mobilize the marginalized for whom this story would ring true to work for social change. For this reason, the limited rhetorical appeal of *Woman on the Edge of Time* is not the novel's failure—indeed, it is a significant strength. I do not advocate skepticism about the possibility of persuading a wide audience to accept marginal or radical ideas. My goal here is to endorse a critical perspective that can assess a text's worth on political grounds, so that narratives such as *Woman on the Edge of Time* might be celebrated as successful politics rather than dismissed as failed literature.

REFERENCES

Barr, Marleen, and Nicholas D. Smith. 1984. *Women and Utopia: Critical Interpretations.* Lanham, MD: University Press of America.

Belsey, Catherine. 1985. "Constructing the Subject: Deconstructing the Text." In *Feminist Criticism and Social Change,* edited by Judith Newton and Deborah Rosenfelt. New York: Methuen.

Booth, Wayne. 1974. *Modern Dogma and the Rhetoric of Assent.* Chicago: University of Chicago Press.

Fisher, Walter. 1987. *Human Communication as Narrative.* Columbia, SC: University of South Carolina Press.

———. 1984. "Narration as a Human Communication Paradigm: The Case of Public Moral Argument." *Communication Monographs* 51:1–22.

———. 1987. "Technical Logic, Rhetorical Logic, and Narrative Rationality." *Argumentation* 1:3–21.

Fiske, John. 1987. *Television Culture.* New York: Methuen.

Freibert, Lucy M. 1984 "World Views in Utopian Novels by Women." *Women and Utopia: Critical Interpretations,* edited by Marleen Barr and Nicholas D. Smith, 43–66. Lanham, MD: University Press of America.

Jaggar, Alison. 1983. *Feminist Politics and Human Nature.* Sussex, England: Harvester.

Kessler, Carol Farley. 1984. *Daring to Dream.* Boston: Pandora.

Piercy, Marge. 1976. *Woman on the Edge of Time.* New York: Fawcett Crest.

Roller, Judi M. 1986. *The Politics of the Feminist Novel.* New York: Greenwood Press.

Rosinsky, Natalie M. 1984. *Feminist Futures: Contemporary Women's Speculative Fiction.* Ann Arbor, MI: University of Michigan Research Press.

Wellman, Carl. 1971. *Challenge and Response; Justification in Ethics.* Carbondale, IL: Southern Illinois University Press.

CHAPTER 2

Gender Orientation Scales: An Empirical Assessment of Content Validity

*T. Joan Fecteau, Jullane Jackson,
and Kathryn Dindia*
University of Wisconsin, Milwaukee

In the field of communication, sex-role orientation has been studied in relationship to a number of communication variables including, but not limited to, communication apprehension (Greenblatt, Hasenauer, and Freimuth, 1980), communicator style (Warfel, 1984), communication competence (Wheeless and Duran, 1982) and self-disclosure (Greenblatt, Hasenauer, and Freimuth, 1980).

Over the years several scales have been developed to measure psychological gender orientation. Briefly, these scales were developed by generating items to represent masculinity and femininity, then selecting items by asking a small sample of subjects, usually students, to indicate which items they perceive as masculine or feminine. It has been almost ten years since the latest scale was developed. These items may no longer represent masculinity and femininity. Perceptions of what is masculine and feminine may have changed or disappeared such that particular personality traits may no longer be considered masculine or feminine. If so, it is possible that measures of psychological gender orientation that rely on traditional notions of masculinity and femininity may no longer predict gender-related attitudes and behaviors. The purpose of this study was to investigate whether masculinity-femininity (M-F) scales measure current perceptions of masculine and feminine traits.

PSYCHOLOGICAL GENDER ORIENTATION

The concept of psychological gender orientation is based on the assumption that psychological differences between men and women should be expected because males and females differ biologically (Freimuth and Hornstein, 1982). The majority of M-F scales focus on specific personality traits assumed to differentiate men from women. These traits are assumed to be inherent in each individual, have limited potential for change, and distinguish between males and females in attitudes and behavior (Constantinople, 1973).

Although it is assumed that there is an association between these personality traits and biological sex, it is not assumed that there is a one-to-one correspondence between biological sex and these traits. In other words, a male may possess feminine personality traits and a female may possess masculine personality traits. When a male possesses many masculine traits and few feminine traits, or a female possesses many feminine traits and few masculine traits, the individual is said to be "sex-typed," to possess a psychological gender orientation that consists of sex-appropriate traits (Bem, 1974, 1975; Spence, Helmreich and Stapp, 1974). If, however, a male possesses many feminine traits and few masculine traits, or a female possesses many masculine traits and few feminine traits, he or she is said to be "cross-typed," possessing a psychological gender orientation that is sex-inappropriate (Bem, 1974, 1975; Spence, Helmreich, and Stapp, 1974). Individuals who have many masculine and many feminine traits are labeled "androgynous" (Bem, 1974, 1976), while those who possess few masculine and few feminine traits are said to be undifferentiated (Spence, Helmreich, and Stapp, 1974). The latter two categories are necessary because masculinity and femininity are conceptualized as separate dimensions, rather than bipolar ends of a single dimension. Thus, individuals may possess both or neither sets of traits (Money and Erhardt, 1972; Bem, 1974, 1975; Spence and Helmreich, 1978).

GENDER ORIENTATION SCALES

Five scales predominantly are used to measure psychological gender: the Bem Sex-Role Inventory (BSRI; Bem, 1974), the Personal Attributes Questionnaire (PAQ; Spence, Helmreich, and Stapp, 1974), the MF scale of the Minnesota Multiphasic Personality Inventory (MMPI; Hathaway and McKinley, 1943), the masculinity-femininity scale (Heilbrun's ACL; Heilbrun, 1976) of the Adjective Check List (Gough and Heilbrun, 1965), and the Personality Research Form-Androgyny Scale (PRF-Andro; Berzins, Welling and

Wetter, 1978). The item pools for these scales were created in one of two ways: The researcher generated an item pool based on items he or she believed discriminated between males and females and/or the researcher utilized an existing scale as an item pool. Bem's (1974) item pool included items she believed logically differentiated the sexes. The MMPI MF scale (Hathaway and McKinley, 1943) item pool was developed in the same manner. Potential PAQ (Spence, Helmreich, and Stapp, 1974) items were taken from the Sex Role Stereotype Questionnaire (Rosenkrantz, Vogel, Bee, Broverman, and Broverman, 1968), whereas the ACL masculinity-femininity scale (Heilbrun, 1976) and the PRF-Andro scale (Berzins, Welling, and Wetter, 1978) item pools were taken from the Adjective Check List (Gough and Heilbrun, 1965) and the Personality Research Form (Jackson, 1967), respectively.

Once an item pool was created, items were selected in one of two ways. Students responded to the items according to (a) whether each trait applied to the subject or (b) whether each trait was more typical of men or women. Items for the BSRI (Bem, 1974) were selected if 100 college students considered them significantly more desirable in America for one sex than the other. PAQ (Spence, Helmreich, and Stapp, 1974) items were selected if groups of college students considered them to be ideal traits for either males or females and more typical of one sex than the other. Items for the PRF-Andro scale (Berzins, Welling, and Wetter, 1978) were rejected if they failed to discriminate between male and female college students responding to how self-descriptive each item was. Items were discarded from Heilbrun's ACL (Heilbrun, 1976) if they failed to discriminate between male college students who identified with a masculine father and female college students who identified with a feminine mother. Items for the MMPI MF scale (Hathaway and McKinley, 1943) were chosen if they discriminated male from female college students and if they discriminated 13 homosexuals and an unspecified number of men with high inversion scores on the Terman Inversion scales from 54 male heterosexual soldiers.

The BSRI, PAQ, ACL, MMPI, and PRF-Andro scales are reliable (Bem, 1974; Yanico, 1985; Spence, Helmreich, and Stapp, 1974; Wilson and Cook, 1984; Berzins, Welling, and Wetter, 1978). Tests of criterion-related validity have shown that the scales are moderately positively correlated with one another (Spence, Helmreich, and Stapp, 1974; Smith, 1983; Wilson and Cook, 1984; Heilbrun, 1976; Heilbrun and Bailey, 1986; Berzins, Welling, and Wetter, 1978). Tests of criterion-related validity indicate that these measures show good predictability for behaviors that required either assertive or nurturant behavior (Deaux, 1984). Contradictory results have been found when these measures were correlated with other classes of gender-related attitudes and behaviors (Spence and Helmreich, 1978).

In recent years gender orientation scales have been severely criticized for a lack of content validity and criterion-related validity (Banai, 1984; Belcher, 1981; Constantinople, 1973; Goodman, 1982; Herron, Goodman, and Herron, 1983; Morawski, 1982; Myers and Gonda, 1982; Pyke, 1982). Considerable research using the M-F scales point to two major flaws in these scales that need to be corrected (Baldwin, Catelli, Stevens, and Russell, 1986; Gergen, Hepburn, and Fisher, 1986; Morawski, 1982; Myers and Gonda, 1982; Orlofsky, 1981).

Temporal Considerations

The first of these flaws is a lack of consideration for changes in what is considered masculine and feminine gender traits and behaviors (Baldwin, Catelli, Stevens, and Russell, 1986; Constantinople, 1973; Deaux, 1984; Gergen, Hepburn, and Fisher, 1986; Locksley, Borgida, Brekke, and Hepburn, 1980; Morawski, 1982; Orlofsky, 1981). The passage of time and the changes in society's rules and roles that take place over time must be considered when dealing with gender scales (Morawski, 1982). The majority of M-F scales were constructed in the early or late seventies. As previously stated, item selection for each scale was based mainly on the ratings of a small sample of college students during the development of the scale more than ten years ago. Since then there has been only one independent test of content validity (Wheeless and Dierks-Stewart, 1981). Tests of content validity are needed to show that psychological gender scales measure current perceptions of masculine and feminine traits.

As noted by Kay Deaux (1984), M-F scales and theories rely "on traditional notions of masculinity and femininity." According to Deaux (1984) and others, gender orientation scales are not tapping masculinity and femininity *as they are conceptualized today.* Rather, they are measuring masculinity and femininity as defined and measured by how many instrumental/agency traits one possesses in relation to how many expressive/nurturant traits one possesses (Constantinople, 1973; Freimuth and Hornstein, 1982; Tellegen and Lubinski, 1983; Spence, 1983; Helmreich, Spence, and Holahan, 1979; Pyke, 1982; Pleck, 1975). It is possible that at the time of scale construction, instrumental/expressive traits were indicative of masculinity and femininity. However, instrumental/expressive traits may no longer be synonymous with masculinity-femininity.

Stereotypes, rules, roles, and norms for the sexes have changed considerably in the past ten years (Constantinople, 1973; Deaux, 1984; Heilbrun, 1986; Morawski, 1982; Pleck, 1975). The women's movement and the increase in the number of career-oriented women have changed prior norms of behavior so that behavior previously defined as masculine has become part of the feminine identity (Deaux, 1984; Duffy, 1986). The push for women to be career-oriented and independent has caused some traditional feminine behaviors (as measured by M-F scales) to be viewed as inappropriate traits for women (Duffy, 1986; Deaux and Ullman, 1983). Likewise, in a society that advocates movement away from traditional norms, men, as a whole, have adopted some traits previously categorized as feminine as part of the norm for masculine behavior.

This study will attempt to provide evidence that psychological gender orientation scales do not measure what are considered masculine and feminine traits in today's society.

Contextual Problems

The second flaw in these scales is the lack of contextual information in the items, which, if included, would guarantee that subjects are reporting on the same traits (Gergen, Hepburn, and Fisher, 1986). A study conducted by these researchers (1986) has shown that it is unwise to use statements devoid of context when measuring traits because one cannot be certain whether the subject is responding to the trait the researcher intended. Gergen et al. investigated subjects' responses to items on the Rotter Internal-External locus of control measure (Rotter, 1975). Their hypothesis, which was supported, was that if language users were sophisticated enough, they could argue that any response on a scale could realistically be interpreted as an indicator of virtually any common trait in the English language.

This problem is evident in the psychological gender orientation scales (Morawski, 1982; Banai, 1984). One subject's perception of an adjective does not always hold true for another subject. An example of this can be found in the BSRI (Bem, 1974) item "warm." Subject A interprets "warm" as being kind to everyone, consequently he or she responds to the item as self-descriptive. In contrast, subject B interprets "warm" as being kind and friendly only to people with whom he/she has close relationships, not to everyone, and responds to the item as being self-descriptive. Both report "warm" as self-descriptive, yet this choice may fail to predict behavior when the subjects are, for example, interacting with a stranger or acquaintance. It is the ambiguity inherent in adjectives that makes their use problematic for categorizing individuals into groups such as masculine or feminine. When an ambiguous and ungrounded adjective is given to a subject, the response tends to reflect what the subject believes he/she is being asked.

One alternative to the current form of scales is to provide more context (Constantinople, 1973; Gergen, Hepburn, and Fisher, 1986) by giving either specific meaning to words such as "warm" (i.e., what, when, where, why) or providing a detailed situation to which a subject can respond. Measurement of a particular trait may be more valid because context will, to a certain extent, ground the item so that less flexibility in interpretation may occur, thus insuring that the same question is being asked of each subject. Without context, M-F scales can only be thought of as measuring how subjects answer each item in accordance with their own connotative meanings and their own situations in which such behaviors and traits are manifested (Gergen, Hepburn, and Fisher, 1986).

This suggestion holds true for all the gender orientation scales, but the problem is more severe for adjective scales than for scales utilizing statements. When responding to a statement such as "I believe in giving friends lots of help and advice," instead of the adjective "helpful," there is less flexibility of interpretation. Thus, in addition to a test of content validity, this study will test whether the additional context provided by statement scales, the PRF-Andro scale (Berzins, Welling, and Wetter, 1978) and the MF scale of the MMPI (Hathaway and McKinley, 1943) yields items that are more likely to be perceived as masculine and feminine than the adjective scales (BSRI; Bem, 1974; PAQ; Spence et al., 1974; ACL; Heilbrun, 1976).

METHOD

Subjects

Six hundred subjects participated in this study. Most of the subjects were volunteers from communication courses at a large, urban, Midwestern university. Sixty-three percent of the subjects were female; 37 percent male. The subjects' average age was 21.65 years old (SD = 4.91). Most of the subjects were single (86%) and Caucasian (91%). Eighty-nine percent of the subjects were full-time students, the remaining were part-time students.

Procedures

Students completed surveys during class time or outside of class and returned them to the instructor. To assess the content validity of the items designed to measure psychological gender orientation, a questionnaire was developed containing all the items from the following scales: BSRI, PAQ, ACL, MF scale of the MMPI, and PRF-Andro. After redundant items were eliminated, the questionnaire contained 303 items, 116 statement items and 187 adjective items. The questionnaire contained the following number of items from each scale: BSRI, 40 items; PAQ, 54 items; ACL, 93 items; MF scale of the MMPI, 60 items; PRF-Andro, 56 items. Half of the questionnaires listed statement items first (MF scale of the MMPI, PRF-Andro), and half listed adjective items first (BSRI, ACL, PAQ).

Subjects were given instructions to rate each item according to their opinion of how masculine or feminine it was. Each item was rated on the following seven-point Likert-type scale: 1 (Very Masculine), 2 (Masculine), 3 (Slightly Masculine), 4 (Neither or Both Masculine and Feminine), 5 (Slightly Feminine), 6 (Feminine), 7 (Very Feminine). A neutral midpoint was chosen because the researchers did not want to force a subject to label an item as either masculine or feminine if the subject actually perceived the item as neither masculine nor feminine.

The selection of "Neither or Both Masculine and Feminine" rather than just "Neither Masculine nor Feminine" as the midpoint was the result of a pilot study. In the pilot study the questionnaire listed "Neither Masculine nor Feminine" as the midpoint. Feedback from pilot study participants indicated that some subjects perceived some items as masculine *and* feminine traits. Consequently, they didn't know how to classify these items. We assumed that items perceived as being masculine and feminine traits would be viewed as neither masculine nor feminine. However, the midpoint, "Neither Masculine nor Feminine," in the pilot study questionnaire elicited cognitive dissonance, or simply confusion, for some of the subjects. Thus, the revised questionnaire included "Neither or Both Masculine and Feminine" as the midpoint.

Data Analysis

T-tests were conducted to test the effect of order (i.e., adjective items followed by statement items versus statement items followed by adjective items) on perceptions of masculinity/ femininity for each of the 303 items in the questionnaire (alpha = .01, two-tailed tests). One-sample T-tests were conducted to test whether the means of the feminine items were significantly greater than the midpoint and the means of the masculine items were significantly less than the midpoint (one-tailed tests). As a more stringent test of content validity, we tested whether the means of the masculine items were significantly less than 3 (Slightly Masculine), and whether the means of the feminine items were significantly greater than 5 (Slightly Feminine) (one-tailed tests). With the exception of the order tests, T-tests were performed for each item for male and female subjects separately. To control for experiment-wise error rate, alpha was set at .01 for both male and female samples. Power was .75 for small effect sizes for males and .96 for small effect sizes for females, and greater than .995 for medium and large effects sizes for males and females. Power was calculated for one sample of "*n*" observations (see Cohen, 1977). The difference between the percentage of statement items that were significant and the percentage of adjective items that were significant was tested using McNemar's formula (1969) for testing whether two percentages are equal (alpha = .05, two-tailed test).

RESULTS

Only six of the 303 order tests were significant. The items that were significantly different appeared to be randomly distributed across the five questionnaires. Thus, the order in which subjects completed questionnaires was not retained as an independent variable in subsequent analyses.

The first research question dealt with whether the items on the psychological gender orientation scales were measuring current perceptions of masculinity and femininity. The majority of the items had a mean that was significantly different from the midpoint of the scale. Only 63 items were not significantly different from the midpoint for males and/or females. The means, standard deviations and t values for these items are reported in Table 1. Thus, the majority of the items were perceived as significantly different from "Neither or Both Masculine and Feminine." However, most of these items had means between 3 (Slightly Masculine) and 5 (Slightly Feminine).

Table 1. Items That Were NOT Significantly Different from "Neither or Both Masculine or Feminine."

Scale and Item	Females			Males		
	Mean	SD	t	Mean	SD	t
MMPI						
Childlike	4.01	1.22	−.29			
Defends own beliefs	3.91	.92	1.81			
Loyal				4.00	.91	−.07
PAQ						
Outgoing, very	4.06	.99	−1.23			
Intelligent, very	3.93	.72	1.69			
Tactful, very				4.06	.92	−1.06
Has strong conscience				4.10	.94	−1.73
ACL						
Good-natured				4.07	.74	−1.50
Natural	3.92	.88	1.73	3.92	.77	1.46
Shallow				3.88	1.02	1.73
Tense	4.07	1.00	−1.48			
Temperamental	4.09	1.17	−1.61			
Anxious				4.07	.85	−1.31

Table 1. continued

Scale and Item	Females			Males		
	Mean	SD	t	Mean	SD	t
High-strung	4.00	1.24	-.12			
ACL						
Impatient				3.94	1.01	.77
Thorough	4.07	.88	1.55			
Stable	3.94	.88	1.15			
Terse	4.05	.89	-1.32			
Practical	4.02	1.02	-.55	3.90	.96	1.56
Clear-thinking	3.95	.88	1.04			
Resourceful	3.90	.91	2.05			
Responsible				3.87	.83	2.35
Foresighted	4.08	.85	-1.86			
Talkative				4.18	1.12	-2.52
Outgoing	4.02	.89	-.57			
Unconventional	3.94	.80	1.40			
Idealistic				3.87	.83	2.22
Spontaneous	3.98	.88	.29			
Complicated	3.92	1.06	1.30	4.13	1.18	-1.72
Insightful				3.92	.84	1.4
Impulsive	4.10	1.06	-1.88	4.06	1.18	-.89
Irritable	3.90	1.04	1.77	4.04	1.11	-.65
Sociable				4.10	.83	-1.98
Enthusiastic				3.92	.82	1.43
Mannerly				4.00	.96	.14
Appreciative				4.13	.83	-2.51
Generous				4.01	.82	-.24
Polished				4.05	.99	-.79
Sophisticated				3.88	1.35	1.25
Witty	3.91	.90	1.76			
MMPI						
Likes to be tipped off				3.83	.94	2.59
Likes work of journalist	3.97	.55	.83	3.93	.72	1.35
Stands up for what is right	4.01	.82	-.37			
Believes in afterlife				4.04	.59	-1.21
Thoughts race ahead faster than can speak them				3.93	.84	1.24
Keeps mouth shut when in trouble				3.88	1.11	1.52
Doesn't like to be bothered about thoughts about sex	4.09	1.10	-1.71	4.13	1.09	-1.86
Daydreams very little				3.90	.82	1.83
Annoyed by family habits				4.01	.82	-.32

Table 1.   *continued*

Scale and Item	Females			Males		
	Mean	SD	t	Mean	SD	t
MMPI						
Believes in devil and hell	3.95	.59	1.47	3.95	.66	.98
Hands are not awkward or clumsy	3.97	1.04	.39			
Fear of being caught causes honesty	4.10	.89	−2.40	3.90	.81	1.68
Disappointed in love				4.16	1.04	−2.39
Has intense feelings				4.10	1.09	−1.49
Feels hate to family members	4.09	.72	−2.46	3.95	.74	.97
PRF						
Continue work on problem	3.92	.89	1.59			
Rarely argue				3.95	.94	.69
Give advice				4.15	.98	−2.38
Offer help				4.07	.96	−1.15
Ask to help				4.14	.89	−2.41
Unrealistic to believe the best				4.08	.75	−1.74
Good opinion of friend is reward				3.97	.75	.43
Praise inspires me	4.10	.94	−2.26	3.85	.85	2.54

NOTE: *Alpha = .01, two-tailed test. The PAQ, MMPI and PRF-Andro scales are copyrighted. Abbreviated versions of items from these scales are reported in table.*

Only a few items were significant when using the more stringent test of content validity, that is, that items be either significantly more feminine than "Slightly Feminine" or significantly more masculine than "Slightly Masculine." The means, standard deviations and t values for these items for males and females are reported in Table 2. Thus, the majority of items were not perceived as significantly more masculine than slightly masculine or significantly more feminine than slightly feminine on a seven-point scale.

Because the scales were designed to be used by men and women and are typically used for samples consisting of men and women, an item should represent males' and females' current perceptions of masculinity-femininity. Thus, although all the significant items are reported in Table 2, only items that were significant for males and females will be discussed.

Overall, only 24 of 303 items were perceived as significantly more masculine than slightly masculine or significantly more feminine than slightly

Table 2.   **Items That Were Significantly More Masculine than "Slightly Masculine" or Significantly More Feminine than "Slightly Feminine."**

	Females			Males		
Scale and Item	Mean	SD	t	Mean	SD	t
BSRI						
MASCULINE ITEMS						
Acts as leader	2.80	.96	3.21			
Aggressive	2.68	.91	5.18	2.82	.98	3.52
Dominant	2.70	1.07	4.13	2.84	1.07	2.84
Forceful	2.65	.91	5.73	2.61	.93	8.21
Masculine	1.80	.92	19.32	1.79	.94	24.68
FEMININE ITEMS						
Soft-spoken				5.13	1.02	−2.53
Does not use harsh language				5.30	1.09	−5.16
Eager to soothe hurt feelings				5.20	1.05	−3.79
Feminine	6.18	1.03	−16.84	6.30	.93	−27.08
PAQ						
MASCULINE ITEMS						
Good at sports, very	2.72	1.02	4.03			
Feels superior, very				2.72	1.13	4.78
Aggressive, very	2.78	.94	3.47	2.86	1.06	2.53
Dominant, very	2.67	1.12	4.38	2.78	1.02	4.14
Has mechanical aptitude	2.58	.90	6.86	2.56	.93	9.14
FEMININE ITEMS						
Emotional, very	5.15	1.09	−2.08	5.48	.98	−9.45
Needs approval				5.16	1.04	−3.03
Cries easily	5.48	1.02	−6.96	5.64	.90	−13.89
ACL						
MASCULINE ITEM						
Handsome	2.14	1.02	12.16	1.86	.96	22.95
MMPI						
MASCULINE ITEMS						
Forest Ranger	2.79	1.07	2.85	2.78	1.02	4.20
Hunting	2.15	.94	13.30	2.15	1.01	16.37
Soldier	2.30	1.02	10.10	2.21	1.03	14.70
Likes to report sporting news	2.44	.84	9.71	2.57	.96	8.72
Likes mechanical magazines	2.19	.86	13.95	2.03	.86	21.91
Building contractor	2.39	1.04	8.57	2.48	1.03	9.73

Table 2. *continued*

	Females			Males		
Scale and Item	Mean	SD	t	Mean	SD	t
MMPI						
MASCULINE ITEMS						
Enjoy a game if				2.77	1.08	4.04
betting on it						
Does not like dolls				2.74	1.56	3.20
FEMININE ITEMS						
Librarian	5.24	.99	−3.65	5.53	1.01	−10.04
Never regretted	5.17	1.34	−1.91	5.26	1.34	−3.69
being a girl						
Florist	5.18	.97	−2.72	5.25	1.04	−4.72
Nurse	5.20	1.08	−2.69	5.25	1.04	−4.60
Kept diary	5.31	.95	−4.81	5.65	.92	−11.55
Likes love stories	5.51	.91	−8.31	5.74	.94	−15.32
Collects plants/flowers				5.25	1.09	−4.49
PRF-ANDRO						
MASCULINE ITEMS						
Never passes up	2.79	.95	3.34			
something fun because						
it is hazardous						
Forceful leader in politics				2.83	1.08	2.98
FEMININE ITEMS						
Will ask to hold baby	5.38	1.05	−5.43	5.61	.97	−12.06
Would prefer to take				5.21	1.10	−3.72
care of sick child						
Try to get others				5.17	1.10	−2.95
to notice dress						

Alpha = .01, one-tailed test. The PAQ, MMPI and PRF-Andro scales are copyrighted.
Abbreviated versions of items from these scales are reported in table.

feminine for both males and females. Fourteen of the items were perceived as masculine, ten as feminine. The following items from each scale emerged as significant: BSRI, four masculine items and one feminine item; PAQ, three masculine items and two feminine items; ACL, one masculine item; MF scale of the MMPI, seven masculine items and six feminine items; PRF-Andro, one feminine item.

The second research question dealt with whether more statement items would emerge as significant than adjective items. Eighty percent (n = 93) of all statement items (MF scale of the MMPI, PRF-Andro) and 79 percent (n = 147) of all adjective items (BSRI, PAQ, ACL) were significantly different from the midpoint for males and females. The difference between these two percentages was not statistically significant. Eleven percent (n = 13) of all statement items and 6 percent (n = 11) of all adjective items were significantly more masculine than slightly masculine or significantly more feminine than slightly feminine for both males and females. Again, the difference between the two percentages was not statistically significant. However, 12 of the 13 statement items were from the MMPI MF scale. Thus, statements per se were not more likely to be significant than adjectives, but a number of items from the MF scale of the MMPI were perceived as significantly more masculine than slightly masculine or significantly more feminine than slightly feminine.

DISCUSSION

The results of this study indicate that the majority of the items from the BSRI, PAQ, ACL, MMPI MF scale, and PRF-Andro are perceived as significantly different from "Neither or Both Masculine and Feminine" but are not perceived as significantly more masculine than "Slightly Masculine" or significantly more feminine than "Slightly Feminine." Depending on the criterion one uses for content validity, one draws contradictory conclusions. When contrasting the means of subjects' perceptions of these items with the midpoint of the scale (4, or Neither or Both Masculine and Feminine), it would be concluded that most of these items tap current perceptions of masculinity and femininity for men and women. However, when contrasting the means of subjects' perceptions of the items with the "Slightly Masculine" and "Slightly Feminine" points on the scale, it would be concluded that most of these items do not tap males' and females' perceptions of masculinity and femininity. Although certain items from each scale represent current perceptions of masculinity and femininity, none of the scales does as a whole.

In our opinion, the less stringent test of content validity provides weak evidence of content validity. The majority of the items that were significant using this criterion had means between 3 (Slightly Masculine) and 5 (Slightly Feminine) on the scale. When using the more stringent criterion for content validity, the majority of the means of subjects' perceptions were not significantly less than 3 (Slightly Masculine) or significantly greater than 5 (Slightly Feminine). Clearly, the majority of the items on these measures of psychological gender orientation are not perceived as masculine or very masculine, feminine or very feminine. It is our opinion that an item designed to measure psychological gender orientation should be perceived as being more masculine than slightly masculine or more feminine than slightly feminine. Thus, we conclude that the majority of the items do not possess content validity as measures of psychological gender orientation.

However, some of the traditional notions of masculinity and femininity prevailed in this sample. Masculinity continues to be associated with aggressiveness and forcefulness. Even with the increase of females in traditionally male dominated careers, respondents in this study perceived professions such as building contracting and the military as masculine. Likewise, feminine individuals were perceived as emotional and as enjoying the work of librarians or florists.

Though some of the traditional stereotypes of masculinity and femininity prevailed, numerous other traditional stereotypes seem to have diminished. For example, the adjectives affectionate, gullible, yielding, forgiving, and thoughtful (feminine items) and resourceful, enterprising, independent, competitive, and stable (masculine items) were not perceived as masculine or feminine traits in this sample. These and numerous other items from the five scales were perceived by the respondents as representing traits and behaviors characteristic of neither or both masculine and feminine individuals, or slightly masculine or slightly feminine individuals. The results of this study provide some evidence that roles for men and women in our society may have become less sex-typed and more egalitarian.

All of the 24 items that were significantly more masculine than "Slightly Masculine" or significantly more feminine than "Slightly Feminine" were appropriately gender-typed. In other words, these masculine items were perceived as masculine and these feminine items were perceived as feminine.

Statement items were not more likely to be perceived as masculine or feminine than adjective items using either criterion for content validity. However, all but one of the significant statement items (using the more stringent test of content validity) were from the MMPI MF scale. Thus, statements versus adjectives per se was not the factor that explains why these items are more likely to be perceived as masculine or feminine. Some other factor, possibly the construction of the scale itself, influenced its content validity. Most of the significant items from the MMPI MF scale dealt with careers and hobbies (e.g., forest ranger, hunting). It appears that people still perceive some careers and hobbies as gender-specific. However, based on the results of this study, we cannot conclude that statement items are more likely to be perceived as masculine or feminine than adjective items. The other statement scale, the PRF-Andro, had only one significant item. If statement items were more valid than adjective items, there should have been more significant items from both the PRF-Andro scale and the MF scale of the MMPI, in comparison with the adjective scales.

Though some items from each scale were perceived as more masculine than slightly masculine or more feminine than slightly feminine, most were not. In addition, most of the items that were perceived as masculine or feminine were obvious items (masculine, feminine, never regretted being a girl), or stereotypes, such as stereotyped careers (florist, nurse, forest ranger, soldier, building contractor), stereotyped activities (cries easily, likes love stories, kept diary, holds baby, hunting, likes to report sporting news, likes mechanical magazines), stereotyped personality traits (aggressive, dominant, forceful, and emotional), and stereotyped physical appearance (handsome). These stereotypes apparently still exist, but will any subjects describe these stereotypes as applying to themselves when completing one of these measures? If not, the scales are useless.

The results of this study have important implications for researchers studying psychological gender orientation. Many researchers study gender as an independent variable, and the scales are believed to be valid and reliable measures of gender orientation. Our results indicate that, as a whole, these scales do not measure current perceptions of psychological gender orientation. If a researcher uses any of these scales to measure psychological gender orientation, and draws conclusions from the results, these conclusions may not be warranted. In addition, we do not know when these scales began to lose content validity. Perhaps gender scholars and researchers should be wary of conclusions drawn from research utilizing gender orientation scales. At a minimum, consideration should be given to using the MMPI MF scale rather than the BSRI, PAQ, ACL or PRF-Andro scales or eliminating items from the scales that were not significantly different from "neither or both masculine and feminine" (items in Table 1).

Based on the results of this study, we believe that the concept of psychological gender needs to be critically reexamined. Perhaps this concept is no longer theoretically relevant; a person's psychological gender orientation is not a good predictor of his/her attitudes and behavior. Similarly, if masculine and feminine traits and behaviors are becoming increasingly alike (most of the items were not significantly more masculine than slightly masculine or significantly more feminine than slightly feminine), attempting to differentiate between masculinity and femininity may serve little purpose.

On the other hand, it is possible that psychological gender orientation is a theoretically relevant concept but that current measures of it lack content validity, and new measures need to be developed. If this is the case, new scales based on current perceptions of masculinity and femininity could be developed. The items found to be significant using the more stringent criterion of content validity (items in Table 2) could be used to create new measures of psychological gender orientation and other similar items developed. If this path is taken, the content validity of these scales needs to be assessed regularly, as we have attempted to do in this study. Periodic assessments of content validity are necessary if researchers continue to measure psychological gender orientation.

We believe that researchers need to become less committed to discovering psychological gender differences and instead focus on whether gender is still a salient concept in our society. If it is thought that psychological gender orientation is a theoretically important variable (it is able to explain and predict gender-related attitudes and behaviors), researchers need to develop measures of psychological gender orientation that possess content validity as well as other types of validity, whether the measures are self-report or observational.

Additional examinations are necessary to replicate our results. Only in this way can researchers adequately address whether psychological gender orientation scales are valid representations of the concepts "masculinity" and "femininity."

REFERENCES

Babbie, E. 1986. *The Practice of Social Research,* 4th Edition. Belmont, CA: Wadsworth.

Baldwin, A., J.W. Catelli, L.C. Stevens, and S. Russell. 1986. "Androgyny and Sex Role Measurement: A Personal Construct Approach. *Journal of Personality and Social Psychology* 51:1081–88.

Banai, Y. 1984. "Thurstone Scales for the Measurement of Psychological Androgyny." *Dissertation Abstracts International,* 44:8 (Ms. No. 2539).

Bem, S.L. 1974. "The Measurement of Psychological Androgyny." *Journal of Consulting and Clinical Psychology* 42:155–62.

———. 1975. "Sex Role Adaptability: One Consequence of Psychological Androgyny." *Journal of Personality and Social Psychology* 31:634–43.

———. 1976. "Probing the Premise of Androgeny." In *Beyond Sex-Role Stereotype. Readings Toward a Psychology of Androgeny,* edited by A. Kaplan and J. Bean 47–62. Boston: Little, Brown and Co.

Belcher, M.J. 1981. "Factor Analysis in Assessing Validity: Applications to the Bem Sex-Role Inventory." *Dissertation Abstracts International* 42:6 (Ms. No. 8127414).

Berzins, J.I, M.A. Welling, and R.E. Wetter. 1978. "A New Measure of Psychological Androgyny Based on the Personality Research Form." *Journal of Consulting and Clinical Psychology* 46:126–38.

Cohen, J. 1977. *Statistical Power Analysis for the Behavioral Sciences.* New York: Academic Press.

Constantinople, A. 1973. "Masculinity-Femininity: An Exception to a Famous Dictum?" *Psychological Bulletin* 80:389–407.

Deaux, K. 1984. "From Individual Differences to Social Categories: Analysis of a Decade's Research on Gender." *American Psychologist* 39:105–16.

Deaux, K., and J.C. Ullman. 1983. *Women of Steel.* New York: Praeger.

Duffy, A. 1986. "Reformulating Power for Women." *Canadian Review of Sociology and Anthropology* 23:22–46.

Freimuth, M.J., and G.A. Hornstein. 1982. "A Critical Examination of the Concept of Gender." *Sex Roles* 8:515–31.

Gergen, K.J., A. Hepburn, and D.C. Fisher. 1986. "Hermeneutics of Personality Description." *Journal of Personality and Social Psychology* 50:1261–70.

Goodman, C.K. 1982. "The Comparability of Sex-Role Measures: A Validation Study." *Dissertation Abstracts International* 42:8 (Ms. No. 8201679).

Gough, M.G. and A.B. Heilbrun. 1965. *Manual for the Adjective Check List and the Need Scales for the ACL.* Palo Alto, CA: Consulting Psychologists Press.

Greenblatt, L., J.E. Hasenauer, and J.S. Freimuth. 1980. "Psychological Sex Type and Androgeny in the Study of Communication Variables: Self-Disclosure and Communication Apprehension. *Human Communication Research* 6:117–29.

Hathaway, S.R., and J.C. McKinley. 1943. *The Minnesota Multiphasic Personality Inventory.* New York: Psychological Corporation.

Heilbrun, A.B. 1976. "Measurement of Masculinity and Femininity Sex-Role Identities as Independent Dimensions." *Journal of Consulting and Clinical Psychology* 44:183–90.

Heilbrun, A.B., and B.A. Bailey. 1986. "Independence of Masculine and Feminine traits: Empirical Exploration of a Prevailing Assumption." *Sex Roles* 14:105–21.

Helmreich, R.L., J.T. Spence, and C.K. Holahan. 1979. "Psychological Androgyny and Sex Role Flexibility: A Test of Two Hypotheses." *Journal of Personality and Social Psychology* 37:1631–43.

Herron, W.G., G.K. Goodman, and M.J. Herron. 1983. "Comparability of Sex-Role Measures." *Psychological Reports* 53:1087–94.

Jackson, D.N. 1967. *Personality Research Form Manual.* Palo Alto, CA: Goshen.

Locksley, A., E. Borgida, N. Brekke, and C. Hepburn. 1980. "Sex Stereotypes and Social Judgment." *Journal of Personality and Social Psychology* 39:821–31.

McNemar, Q. 1969. *Psychological Statistics* 4th Edition. New York: Wiley.

Money, J., and A. Erhardt. 1972. *Man and Woman: Boy and Girl.* Baltimore, MD: Johns Hopkins University Press.

Morawski, J.G. 1982. "On Thinking About History as Social Psychology." *Personality and Social Psychology Bulletin* 8(3):393–401.

Myers, A.M., and G. Gonda. 1982. "Empirical Validation of the Bem Sex-Role Inventory." *Journal of Personality and Social Psychology* 43(2):304–18.

Orlofsky, J.L. 1981. "Relationship of Sex-Role Attitudes and Personality Traits and the Sex-Role Behavior Scale-1: A New Measure of Masculine and Feminine Role Behaviors and Interests." *Journal of Personality and Social Psychology* 40(5):927–40.

Pleck, J.H. 1975. "Masculinity-Femininity: Current and Alternative Paradigms." *Sex Roles* 1(2):161–78.

Pyke, S.W. 1982. "Confessions of a Reluctant Ideologist." *Canadian Psychology* 23(3):161–34.

Rosenkrantz, P.S., S.R. Vogel, H. Bee, I.K. Broverman, and D.M. Broverman. 1968. "Sex-Role Stereotypes and Self-Concepts in College Students. *Journal of Consulting and Clinical Psychology* 32: 287–95.

Rotter, J.B. 1975. "Some Problems and Misconceptions Related to the Construct of Internal Versus External Control of Reinforcement." *Journal of Consulting and Clinical Psychology* 43:56–67.

Smith, S.G. 1983. "A Comparison Among Three Measures of Social Sex-Role." *Journal of Homosexuality* 9(1): 99–107.

Spence, J.T. 1983. Comment on Lubinski, Tellegen, and Butcher's "Masculinity, Femininity and Androgyny Viewed and Assessed as Distinct Concepts." *Journal of Personality and Social Psychology* 44(2): 440–46.

Spence, J.T., and R. Helmreich. 1978. *Masculinity and Femininity: Their Psychological Dimensions, Correlates and Antecedents.* Austin, TX: University of Texas Press.

Spence, J.T., R.L. Helmreich, and J. Stapp. 1974. "The Personal Attribute Questionnaire: A Measure of Sex-Role Stereotypes and Masculinity and Femininity." *JSAS Catalog of Selected Documents in Psychology* 4:43–44 (Ms. No. 617).

Tellegen, A., and D. Lubinski. 1983. "Some Methodological Comments on Labels, Traits, Interaction and Types in the Study of 'femininity' and 'masculinity': Reply to Spence." *Journal of Personality and Social Psychology* 44(2):447–55.

Warfel, K.A. 1984. "Gender Schemas and Perceptions of Speech Style." *Communication Monographs* 51:253–67.

Wheeless, V.E., and K. Dierks-Stewart. 1981. "The Psychometric Properties of the BSRI: Questions Concerning Reliability and Validity." *Communication Quarterly* 29:173–86.

Wheeless, V.E., and R.L. Duran. 1982. "Gender Orientation as a Correlate of Communicative Competence." *The Southern Speech Communication Journal* 48:51–64.

Wilson, F.R., and E.P. Cook. 1984. "Concurrent Validity of Four Androgyny Instruments." *Sex Roles* 11(9/10):813–37.

Yanico, B.J. 1985. "BSRI Scores: Stability over Four Years for College Women. *Psychology of Women Quarterly* 9:277–83.

CHAPTER 3

Gender, Ethnicity, and the Politics of Oral Interpretation

Lisa Merrill
Hofstra University

More than twenty years ago, in an introductory text in oral interpretation, Wallace Bacon wrote, "All literature is in some sense conversation. There is always a speaker, and also a listener, whether clearly defined or not" (Bacon, 1966, 48). Thus, the discipline of interpretative reading or oral interpretation of literature shares with the fields of literary criticism, reader-response theory and semiotics some crucial questions. Each asks, "Who is the literary speaker or persona through whom we receive the words of a given text?" and "Who are the assumed silent readers or implied audience of a text?"

In oral interpretation of literature, the answers to these questions are embodied and personified by a performer who actualizes her or his response as a silent reader; performing the literary text as if he or she were the narrative persona speaking to a live audience. Thus, to some extent the analysis, rehearsal, and oral interpretative performance becomes a metacritical event.

Methods of applying constructs current in rhetoric and reader-response theory to the oral interpretation class will be explored in this chapter. Of particular concern will be the impact of gender and ethnicity upon a performer's response to and performance of a given literary text.

In an article entitled "Consciousness and Authenticity: Toward a Feminist Aesthetic," Marcia Holly writes:

> *The activity of literary criticism is no longer so simple as it was. Like most thoughtful communication, it has become a political act. (in Donovan, 45)*

I. ORAL INTERPRETATION AS A POLITICAL ACT

In oral interpretation, as in other analyses of communication inter-action, we may begin to examine the politics of the communicative act by defining our notion of speaker or narrator. As early as 1950, literary critic Walker Gibson noted that

> *It is now common in the classroom as well as in criticism to distinguish carefully between the author of a literary work of art and the fictitious speaker within the work of art...the speaker [is] the voice or disguise through which someone...communicates with us. (Gibson, 265)*

For many interpretation scholars, "the process of becoming or embodying [this fictitious speaker or] persona is the central matter in interpretation" (Yordon, 1982, 8).

Who is this fictitious speaker, and how may students learn to identify this persona? I have devised several exercises and assignments to aid in answering this question. Students may begin their exploration with first-person narratives by constructing a fictional autobiography of the persona based on the point of view they perceive in the text (see Long and Hopkins, 1982). As drama teachers know, there is no singular definitive performance of a given role. Similarly, when several students attempt to create fictional auto-biographies for the same narrative persona, it becomes clear that each is dif-ferent. The fictitious speaker is as much a construction of the reader/per-former as of the original author. What also becomes apparent are the myriad ways in which the fictitious speaker as written differs from the actual performer. As Judy E. Yordon (1982) instructs students in her text, *Roles in Interpretation:*

> *When you journey out from yourself—becoming the persona, rather than remaining yourself—your latent feelings, attitudes and perceptions become manifest. When you are asked to discover how another feels, you summon forth responses of which you may be unaware. (9)*

The tension between the feelings, attitudes, and perceptions of the fictive speaker and those of the actual performer is in no way more clear than when student performers are instructed to embody personas of opposite gender or different ethnicity. I have employed this technique for the past six years and would like to report on the theory that informs this assignment and on a selection of students' responses.

II. PERFORMING GENDER

In a 1971 article on "Women and the Literary Curriculum," Elaine Showalter remarked that women "are expected to identify with a masculine experience and perspective which is presented as the human one" (856). In an attempt to expose the politics implicit in this identification, I require students in oral interpretation classes to choose one selection in which they will speak as a persona of the opposite gender. Almost immediately the difference between male and female students' reactions to the assignment is evidenced. At first, the men in the class are visibly uncomfortable. Depending to some extent upon their own degree of homophobia or misogyny, the male students are discomfited at the notion of having to sound and act as if they were women; to speak a woman's words in a woman's voice in front of their peers.

Male students' first questions invariably reflect societal stereotypes. Will they have to employ an artificial falsetto voice, or walk with mincing steps to the podium? However, my assurances to the contrary are sometimes even more unsettling. If they are not to perform a "drag," stereotyped notion of a "woman," what *are* they to do? Embodying the words of a specific female character as written by an actual woman requires an empathic response that may feel far more threatening to male students. However, I find the exercises and the accompanying discussion consistently enlightening. To perform as a particular female persona necessitates both an awareness on the student's part of the degree to which that female persona is a construction of the specific male reader, therefore not unlike him, and an awareness of the limitations of our socially constructed notions of gender. In reading as a character of the opposite sex, the students are surprised to find resonances of the character's voice within themselves.

For female students faced with the assignment to read as a man, the responses are quite different. First comes the awareness that this is not difficult, because, in fact, women have been taught to read as men, to identify with the male persona who has been presented to them as an embodiment of neutral and "human" (rather than specifically "male") qualities. As Jonathan Culler (1982) notes in *On Deconstruction*, "Women do not always read or have not always read as women: they have been alienated from an experience appropriate to their condition as women" (50); "...to read as a woman is to avoid reading as a man, to identify the specific defenses and distortions of male readings and provide corrections" (54).

However, before a woman can read as a woman, she must recognize these distortions. Female students may begin to do this by first learning to recognize the extent to which they have been led to identify with male protagonists. As Sue-Ellen Case (1988) asserts in *Feminism in Theatre:*

> *The traditional subject has been the male subject with whom everyone must identify. Scanning the "masterpieces" of the theatre, with their focus on the male subject, one can see that women are called upon to identify with Hamlet, Oedipus, Faust and other male characters imbued with specifically male psychosexual anxieties. The idea that these are*

"universal" characters represses the gender inscription in the notion of the self." (121)

Judith Fetterly (1978) further believes that there is a psychological danger for women when "universality" is defined "in specifically male terms." Fetterly claims:

In such fictions the female reader is co-opted into participation in an experience from which she is explicitly excluded. She is asked to identify with a selfhood that defines itself in opposition to her; she is required to identify against herself. (xii)

Fetterly's text is entitled *The Resisting Reader;* I believe that before women may become resisting readers, they must recognize the extent to which they have been assenting readers. Therefore, an exercise that requires female students to recognize as specifically "male" those qualities which they have been led to consider neutral or universal, may be a first step toward what Fetterly calls "the process of exorcising the male mind that has been implanted in us" (xxii).

III. PERFORMING ETHNICITY

Socially constructed stereotypes of ethnicity and economic class may be confronted in the interpretative reading class as well. As with the gender exercise, I routinely require my students to read a selection written in the voice of a character of a different ethnicity than themselves. There are several things to be gained from this activity. First, (since I require the text to be written by a person of a different background from the performer) my predominantly white, middle-class university students are exposed (often for the first time) to literature written by persons of color. Once again, students are confronted with the need to overcome rigid and stereotypical notions of how members of a particular group speak, sound, gesture, and move. Rhythm, cadence, emphasis are explored. The connection between vocal stress and gesture is made manifest, for example, when a white, Anglo student attempts to perform a monologue from Ntzozake Shange's "For Colored Girls Who Have Considered Suicide/When the Rainbow is Enuf." Finally, the rehearsal and identification needed to speak empathically with the persona's voice has additional politicizing benefits. As Susan Willis (1985) explains when discussing black women writers' slave narratives:

If the slave narratives begin by positing the "I," they do so dramatically to wrest the individual black subject out of anonymity, inferiority and brutal disdain. The "I" stands against and negates the perception of the black person as indistinguishable from the mass, as slave, as animal. The "I" proclaims voice, subject and the right to history and place. (213)

Members of third-world cultures derive benefit from this activity as well. When examining the voice of a persona from a culture different from their own, but also not of the dominant white, Anglo-American tradition, the student may perceive similarities and allegiances between his or her own group and others. Further, the experience of hearing literature of her or his own culture embraced and validated through the respectful performance of others is frequently empowering. As Jonathan Culler (1982) notes:

> *The most insidious oppression alienates a group from its own interests as a group and encourages it to identify with the interests of its oppressors, so that political struggles must first awaken a group to its interests and its experience. (50n)*

When a student witnesses others' attempts to embody his/her experience through interpretation, the student's own repressed identification with her/his ethnic, cultural, or socioeconomic group may be awakened.

IV. THE LITERARY CANON— WHAT LITERATURE IS PERFORMED?

Implicit in the preceding discussion is a criticism of the established literary canon, or the selection of literary classics generally anthologized for performance in interpretative reading texts. Although some recent texts have begun to include literary works by women and people of color, these writers are still enormously underrepresented. Further, since this literature, the subjects it contains, and the personas who people it may be foreign to students, the performance assignment mentioned above provides teachers with an opportunity to discuss criteria for an appropriate performance selection and to contrast these criteria with those traditionally brought to bear on "great works." This discussion may, in itself, politicize the students. Gayle Greene and Coppelia Kahn (1985), in their discussion of "Feminist Scholarship and the Social Construction of Women," state:

> *The criteria that have created the literary canon have...excluded the accomplishments not only of women but of people of races, ethnic backgrounds and classes different from the politically dominant one. Feminist criticism questions the values implicit in the Great Works, investigating the tradition that canonized them and the interests it serves. It exposes the collusion between literature and ideology. It is alert to the omissions, gaps, partial truths and contradiction which ideology masks—it attends to the silences..." (22)*

Sue-Ellen Case (1988) further relates literature and ideology in her discussion of the etymology of the word "classic." Case claims that "the consonance of aesthetic criteria with economic ones becomes clear in the term itself" (12).

If a "classic," by virtue of the appellation, reifies the values of the dominant socioeconomic class, what are the responsibilities of the teacher, who chooses to introduce the classic to his or her students? I believe, along with Marcia Holly, that "the critic in her/his capacity as analyst and interpreter is responsible for admitting and understanding any biases she/he maintains." Holly (1975) claims that critics "often establish the limits of meaning for a work; that is, the critic and/or teacher can set the terms within which a work is questioned, thereby establishing the boundaries of potential response. It then takes a rare reader to pose questions outside those limits" (41).

V. THE ASSUMED AUDIENCE, OR, WHO IS LISTENING?

One of the questions with which I started this paper, (and which to some extent frames all the questions of pedagogical technique that emanate from this discussion) was, "Who is the assumed audience to a particular literary work?" It is to that question which I shall now return. Walker Gibson (1950) wrote not only of the fictitious speaker in a literary text, but also of the assumed or "mock reader" of the text.

Every text is written to an assumed reader; the listener to whom the narrator/person directs his/her remarks. Just as the fictitious narrator has a particular set of values and beliefs, so too does the assumed listener. Gibson believed that the teacher of literature should make students aware that "the literary experience is not just a relationship between themselves and an author, or even between themselves and a fictitious speaker, but a relation between such a speaker and a projection, a fictitious modification of themselves" (68). This projection Gibson termed the "mock reader." The choice of vocabulary, tone of address, use of imagery, selection of examples in the text are all gestures that indicate not just *who* is speaking, but to *whom.* Gibson felt that the "mock reader" was a role, or a part that the actual reader was invited to play, and that our response to a piece of literature depended upon our willingness to enter into this role (Tompkins, xi).

How does this concept of "mock reader" or assumed audience affect the interpretive performer? Since interpretation is a performance art, it is obvious that the performer-as-persona must be speaking to someone. This is as true for a third-person narrative storyteller as it is for a more easily defined first-person speaker. In oral reading, the attitude of a speaker toward both her or his subject, and her/his audience is made manifest by vocal quality and tone of voice as much as by the language employed.

Sarcasm, for example, is conveyed by a particular pattern of circumflex intonation and stress.

In fact, the whole notion of "locus," or the positioning of the narrative speaker relative to the work, can be conveyed largely through vocal and physical gesturing. For example, a persona in a confessional novel would *sound* different if her or his words are delivered to intimate friends or disapproving neighbors, days after the events described or decades later, in earnest sincerity, with nostalgia, with regret, or with cynical acceptance. Rhetoricians and communication theorists claim that a speaker's message is shaped by her/his awareness of audience.

I have constructed several exercises to help student performers concretize their perceptions of the assumed audience. One assignment, which strengthens the performer's awareness of the dialogic nature of performance, is to have students create a subtext in the present tense of the "dialogue" between their narrative persona and her or his listeners. The assumed audience, setting, and occasion that prompt the oral performance should be articulated by the performer. These subtexts are acted out and improvised, to stress the immediacy of the storytelling situation.

Although most prose literature is written in the past tense, performance always occurs in the present tense, in what actors call the "here and now." When the present tense, moment-by-moment experience of the persona telling her story to the listener is paraphrased, focus on the text recedes, since the relationship between persona and assumed listener/reader is one of the foundations of reader-response theory. Jane Tompkins (1980) states that:

> *The concept of the mock reader allows the critic to dramatize the social attitudes implicit in a text by reconstructing the kinds of understandings and complicities narrators and mock readers arrive at over the heads of the characters and quite apart from the manifest content of the prose. (xi)*

Authors, through their narrative personas, routinely make implicit assumptions about the gender, identification, and values of their assumed readers. Innumerable texts are written with a subtext that the narrative persona, even in third-person narration, is a man speaking to men. What happens when the actual listener, (whether silent reader or audience) is a woman? As Jonathan Culler (1982) and Elaine Showalter (1971) have asserted, "The hypothesis of a female reader changes our apprehension of a given text, awakening us to the significance of its sexual codes" (Culler, 50). Oral interpretation necessarily makes these sexual codes manifest.

At the outset of this paper I alleged that oral performance of literature is, in itself, a metacritical act. Let us consider all the critical choices involved in an interpretative reading of excerpts from two classics, Hemingway's *A Farewell to Arms* (1929) and Shelley's *Frankenstein* (1818). The performer, who may be male or female, will attempt to embody the narrative persona. The performer may wish to portray this speaker, although clearly male-identified, as either male or female. The speaker addresses his or her story to an assumed audience. Although the words and tone of the text may assume that the commonality of male experience is shared between speaker and listeners, the performer may choose to direct these words as if he/she were speaking solely to men, solely to women, or to both. Further, the actual audience to the performance will be composed of men, women, or a mixed sex group, each member of whom will respond to the tensions created by the disparities between how they are addressed and whom they know themselves to be.

Finally, we know that the performer-as-persona was first introduced to the text as a silent reader whose own creative construction of persona has been shaped by her/his closeness to or distance from the values and experience of the text's implied reader. Hence, every conscious choice of the performer is a manifestation of the significance of the sexual codes and other implicit values in the text.

Let us first consider a reading from Hemingway's *A Farewell to Arms*. The novel is told from the point of view of Frederic Henry, the first person narrator. Although considered a "classic" tale of love and war, Hemingway's novel is told from a decidedly masculine vantage point. From the reader's first introduction to Frederic Henry and Catherine Barkley's relationship, the narrative voice as written is clearly that of a man speaking to other men.

> *I didn't care what I was getting into. This was better than going every evening to the house for officers where the girls climbed all over you and put your cap on backwards as a sign of affection between their trips upstairs with brother officers. I know I didn't love Catherine Barkley nor had any idea of loving her. This was a game, like bridge, in which you said things instead of playing cards. (30)*

As the "you" in the above quote demonstrates, the speaker (whether with bravado or defensiveness) is presenting his experience with the explicit assumption that his listeners are male and potentially complicit in similar experiences with women.

Nowhere is the sense of the narrator as a man speaking to men more clear than at the novel's conclusion with Catherine's tragic death in childbirth. Even this tragedy is presented as Henry's loss. Hemingway devotes page after page of details of the meals Henry eats while Catherine is in the hospital in labor, but only one sentence to her actual death.

What happens when excerpts from this text are performed? If the reader is male, the gender-specific nature of the text may not be apparent, although female audience members may be called upon to "listen" as men and identify with Henry rather than with Barkley's plight.

Thus, the female spectator will not be included fully in the dialogic nature of the interpretative performance. Since she is not the assumed audience to whom the text was written, the female spectator is not included in the address as it is performed. At best, she is cast into the role of a distanced voyeur, left wondering at the professed universality of a dialogue that is constructed to exclude the possibility of her participation.

However, should the interpreter be female, the gender-specific nature of the text is immediately evidenced. For the female performer to interpret *A Farewell to Arms,* she must literally, as well as figuratively, assume a male persona. Thus, the text's posture, which forces all readers to "read as a man," is made manifest.

In performing excerpts from Mary Shelley's *Frankenstein,* a similar critical process is involved; however, the results differ significantly. The story of Frankenstein is told alternately from the vantage point of three different first-person narrators. The novel is presented in the form of letters sent by English explorer Robert Walton to his married sister, Margaret. Within this frame, the reader is told Dr. Victor Frankenstein's first person account of his creation. Finally, Frankenstein recounts the monster's first-person description of his own tale. Each of these characters is male.

In the novel as written, as well as in the extensive popular culture tradition that this novel has inspired, the doctor/creator and the monster are always depicted as male. What happens when a woman performs the text?

Dr. Frankenstein's description of the monster's creation has additional resonance when we hear a female reader explain:

A new species would bless me as its creator and source; many happy and excellent natures would owe their being to me. No father could claim the gratitude of his child so completely as I should deserve theirs. (39)

Critic Ellen Moers asserts in her text *Literary Women* (1976) that Shelley's *Frankenstein* can be viewed as a birth myth. This birth imagery is clearly suggested when viewing the text as interpreted by a female performer. Also highlighted is the fictive female reader, Margaret, the sister to whom Walton is presumably writing. Thus, in this case as well, a text is further enlightened for performer and audience through cross-gender performance. Playing against gender may both point out the limitations in a text and illuminate its hidden strengths.

According to Elizabeth Freund (1987), reader-response theory "refocuses attention on the reader instead of the text as the source of literary meaning..." (10). Just as every repeat performance an actor gives is in some measure different from the previous performance, every time a reader re-reads a text, the meaning of the text is somewhat changed. If, according to a variety of contemporary theoretical interpretations, meaning lies within the reader/listener/audience rather than within the signs and symbols of the text, what better way to enact this construction of meaning than through the oral performance of literature? Freund claims that:

> *The trend to liberate the reader from his [sic] enforced anonymity and silence, to enable him [sic] to recover an identity or the authority of a voice, is bedeviled by all the concomitant hazards, schisms, anxieties and jargons of liberation movements. (6)*

And well it should be—for the interpretation of art, like the creation of art, is a political act.

REFERENCES

Case, Sue-Ellen. 1988. *Feminism and Theatre.* New York: Methuen.

Culler, Jonathan. 1982. *On Deconstruction: Theory and Criticism After Structuralism.* Ithaca, NY: Cornell University Press.

Fetterly, Judith. 1978. *The Resisting Reader; A Feminist Approach to American Fiction.* Bloomington, IN: Indiana University Press.

Freund, Elizabeth. 1987. *The Return of the Reader.* New York: Methuen.

Gibson, Walker. 1950. "Authors, Speakers, Readers and Mock Readers," *College English* 11 (February): 65–69.

Greene, Gayle and Coppelia Kahn, eds. 1985. *Making a Difference: Feminist Literary Criticism.* London and New York: Methuen.

Hemingway, Ernest. 1929. *A Farewell to Arms.* New York: Charles Scribner's Sons.

Holly, Marcia. 1975. "Consciousness and Authenticity: Toward a Feminist Aesthetic," in *Feminist Literary Criticism: Explorations in Theory,* edited by Josephine Donovan, Lexington, Kentucky: University Press of Kentucky.

Iser, Wolfgang. 1974. *The Implied Reader: Patterns in Communication in Prose Fiction from Benyan to Beckett.* Baltimore, MD: Johns Hopkins University Press.

Long, Beverly Whitaker, and Mary Frances Hopkins. 1982. *Performing Literature.* New York: Prentice-Hall.

Moers, Ellen. 1976. *Literary Women.* Garden City, NY: Doubleday.

Moi, Toril. 1985. *Sexual/Textual Politics: Feminist Literary Theory.* London and New York: Methuen.

Prince, Gerald. 1973. "Introduction to the Study of the Narratee." *Poetique* 14:177–96.

Shelley, Mary. 1818. *Frankenstein.* New York: Bantam Classic Edition, 1981.

Showalter, Elaine. 1971. "Women and the Literary Curriculum." *College English* 32:855–62.

Tompkins, Jane, ed. 1980. *Reader-Response Criticism: From Formalism to Post Structuralism.* Baltimore, MD: Johns Hopkins University Press.

Willis, Susan. 1985. "Black Women Writers: Taking a Critical Perspective." In *Making a Difference: Feminist Literary Criticism,* edited by Gayle Greene and Coppelia Kahn. London and New York: Methuen.

Yordon, Judy E. 1982. *Roles in Interpretation.* Dubuque, IA: Wm. C. Brown.

CHAPTER 4

Rhetoric and Women: The Private and the Public Spheres

Lesley Di Mare
California State University, Los Angeles

In the past twenty years a considerable amount of research in the fields of history, psychology, philosophy, and literary criticism has focused on the treatment of women in Western culture and how that treatment has circumvented economic and political parity between the sexes. Although this lack of parity can be attributed generally to a patriarchal tradition in Western thought, a greater understanding of how the rhetorical tradition contributed to this lack of parity is necessary. The aim of this essay, then, is (1) to determine the ways in which the rhetorical tradition has contributed to conceptualizations of women that have led to their secondary status in contemporary society, and (2) to examine ways in which the rhetorical tradition can be utilized and altered to valorize the experiences and thought processes of women as well as men.

It is apparent that the rhetorical tradition, as it operated historically within the public sphere, carried great implications for society overall. Unfortunately, however, that tradition was used as a mechanism by the dominant culture to promote the concept that women were capable only of biological functions and, therefore, of only one role—that of childbearer and caretaker. This function and role required females to remain in the home (private sphere) with, ostensibly, no opportunity to acquire what were considered acceptable rhetorical skills, or worse yet, to develop rhetorical skills representative of women's approaches to discourse in the public realm—a dilemma highlighted in the following discussion.

THE RHETORICAL TRADITION AND WOMEN

What, we might ask, do women have to do with rhetoric? The answer—in countless Renaissance conduct books and treatises—is that they should have nothing whatsoever to do with it, that rhetoric is one thing that women should not be taught, even in the view of male authors who would leave other branches of study open to them. Leonardo Bruni, for example, in De Studies et Litteris, *a widely disseminated humanist text, though he recommends the opening of the study of the liberal arts to both sexes, adds a prohibition against the introduction of young girls specifically to rhetoric, which "lies absolutely outside the province of women."* [1]

Patricia Parker attributes this prohibition to the nature of rhetoric, which she describes as "specifically public speaking, the humanist training of young men to argue persuasively in public." [2] According to Parker, women were historically denied the right to rhetoric because it took them out of their proper province and disassociated them from their traditional role in the private sphere of the home.

Parker's observations are not unfounded. Aristotle, for example, imposed upon women the label of caretaker and nurturer by virtue of the fact that their purpose in life was to bear children and take care of the household. [3] Although Plutarch advocated instruction for women in mathematics, philosophy, and astronomy, he did so only inasmuch as such study developed moral virtue and not for the purpose of teaching women to reason or to apply that ability in any context outside the home. [4] In his essay "Philosophical Rudiments Concerning Government and Society," Thomas Hobbes, who rejected paternalism, argued nevertheless that by nature "women, not men, have power over children"—an argument that did little to encourage the notion that women had a place in the public sphere. [5]

In his work *The Renaissance Notion of Woman*, Ian Maclean discusses Martin Luther's view of women as "different rather than defective," inasmuch as Luther "refers playfully in his *Tischreden* to the scholastic belief that the different shape of men and women is accountable to the latter's imperfect formation," and "that it is not because of insufficient generative heat and body temperature that women have wide hips and narrow shoulders, but rather a sign that they have little wisdom and should stay in the home." [6] The preceding discussion supports the fact that for centuries women have been defined and conceptualized as individuals who are capable of performing only one function and role in society—that of childbearer and caretaker—a conception that still exists in contemporary society, and one that has been addressed by both feminists and researchers.

For example, in her treatise *The Human Condition*, Hannah Arendt argues that historically, *all* human activity has been relegated a proper location and that certain activities were considered appropriate for public display, whereas others were not. Arendt points out that neither women nor slaves were displayed publicly but rather were "hidden away not only because they were somebody else's property but because their life was "laborious, *devoted to bodily functions,"* and it is *"...the women who with their bodies guarantee the physical survival of the species"*[7] [emphasis my own].

In her book *Women in Western Thought,* Susan Moller Okin maintains that contemporary women are defined in terms of their biological function and that because "...the family and its needs define her [woman's] function, the socialization and regulation prescribed for her must ensure that her 'nature' is formed and preserved in accordance with this role."[8] Juanita Williams' treatise *Psychology of Women* points out that because the female sexual anatomy serves both sexual and reproductive functions, society perceives women as necessary to bear children but otherwise excludes them from the affairs of men.[9]

IMPLICATIONS

Although other disciplines (history, philosophy, art, film, and so on) have been used by the patriarchy to create the perception that women function best biologically, none has been used so effectively as the discipline of rhetoric. In effect, the rhetorical tradition has acted as a tool of the dominant cultural position to promote the notion that women are capable of only one function—a biological one. Such a conception of women has led society to believe that women cannot operate effectively in the public realm. As such, women have been prohibited from contributing to the evolution of Western society's political structure as a whole. Consequently, contemporary women are caught in a vicious circle wherein history creates destiny. Historically, women were perceived as capable of performing only biological functions and therefore were prohibited from doing anything rhetorical (public). Currently women are perceived as having limited rhetorical skills such that they are also perceived as being ineffective when engaging in rhetorical processes and, consequently, find it difficult to succeed in the public sphere. Ultimately, this situation contributes to a lack of economic and political parity between the sexes, and women's secondary status in society becomes a self-perpetuating one.

A second concern relates to women's ability to maintain their biological function and, at the same time, develop and assume a rhetorical role appropriate for their needs and experiences. The issue, then, is not whether women should shed their biological function, but rather *whether or not they*

*can assume any other role as long as society views them mainly in terms
of their biological functions.*

Indeed, current research indicates that women, in their attempts to
assume more than a biological role and to move from the private to the public sphere, encounter difficulties. In her book *Quiet Desperation,* Janice
Halper points out that "many men don't know how to interact with women
in a way that isn't sexual."[10] A study conducted by Fortune 500 supports this
observation.[11] This sexual interaction can be attributed to society's conception of women as serving only biological functions—functions which are
essentially sexual in nature and which encourage men to interact with
them in a style and with a language inappropriate in the public sphere. Such
interaction in the workplace causes frustration for both women and men.
Women are prevented from effectively assuming dual roles, and men tend
to communicate in a style which is both offensive and unproductive, and
which may lead to accusations of sexual harassment and discrimination.[12]

Although it is disheartening to realize that the rhetorical tradition that
is so much a part of the fabric of Western society has been used to such ends,
it is encouraging to note, as George E. Yoos comments, that rhetorical
processes should take their shape and form from the activities and the
inquiries of groups acting in the name of rhetoric. According to Yoos, we
should never allow our concept of rhetoric to define our community.[13]
Essentially Yoos's point is that rhetoric serves as the condition for the possibility of the emergence of any situation that the community desires. So, inasmuch as rhetoric has stood as the condition for the emergence of a patriarchy, it can also stand as the condition for the emergence of a dialectical
reciprocity between men and women that would undermine patriarchy.

Rhetoric itself, then, must be used by people to rupture the traditionally
held and naturalized ideas about the rhetorical tradition. For example,
Aristotle's original statement that rhetoric is the search for all the available
means of persuasion in a given situation should be the impetus for society
to reconstruct perceptions concerning accepted forms of rhetorical processes, as well as who might utilize those processes and in what contexts.
New forms of persuasion must blend with the old so that the rhetorical tradition comes to reflect both masculine and feminine processes.[14] Most
important, the conditions created by processes that constitute the "rhetorical tradition" must be considered both constructed and malleable.

This approach may be attacked by some feminists who argue that any
integration into and acceptance of the rhetorical tradition is an identification
with the patriarchal culture and, therefore, is unacceptable. In response to
this position, I extend Judith Barry and Sandy Flitterman-Lewis' argument
that lack of integration within the wider social sphere is a utopian vision that
presents obstacles and causes society to lose sight of solutions that are work-
able in practice.

CONCLUSION

This essay has illustrated that society overall and communication scholars in particular must now utilize the rhetorical tradition to reconstruct the perceptions we maintain of women and men in this society. It is utopian and destructive to dismiss the rhetorical tradition because of its association with the patriarchy; such a dismissal advocates a form of self-contained subcultural resistance that does not work in a dialectical relation with the dominant male culture. Instead, communication scholars must make every attempt to present women and men as effective users of rhetorical processes in both the private and public spheres.

NOTES

1.   Patricia Parker, "Literary Fat Ladies and the Generation of the Text," *Literary Fat Ladies: Rhetoric, Gender, Property* (New York: Methuen, 1987), 104.

2.   Parker, 104.

3.   Aristotle, "De Generatione Animalium," trans. by Arthur Platt Oxford at the Clarendon Press. First Edition 1912. London E.C. 4: Oxford Press The Amen House, 1949. Trans. into English under the editorship of J.A. Smith, M.A. and W.D. Ross, M.A.

4.   As discussed in R. Agonito, *History of Ideas on Women* (New York: Paragon Books, 1977) 86.

5.   Thomas Hobbes, "Philosophical Rudiments Concerning Government and Society," in Sir W. Molesworth, *The English Works of Thomas Hobbes,* vol. 2, chapters 8 and 9. (London: John Bohn, 1841).

6.   See Martin Luther, *Werke: Kritische Gesamtausgagbe* (Weimar, 1883-), XLII, 51–2; and *Tischreden,* No. 55 (Weimar, 1912–21), I, 19; as described in Maclean, *The Renaissance Notion of Woman,* 10.

7.   Hannah Arendt, "The Public and Private Realm," in *The Human Condition* (Chicago: University of Chicago Press, 1958), 72.

8.   Susan Moller Okin, *Women in Western Thought,* (Princeton, NJ: Princeton University Press, 1979), 70.

9.   Juanita H. Williams, *Psychology of Women* (New York: W.W. Norton and Company, 1977).

10.   Janice Halper, *Quiet Desperation* (New York: Warner Books, 1988).

11.   "*Working Woman* Survey Results: Sexual Harassment in the Fortune 500," *Working Woman,* December 1988, 72.

12.   *Working Woman,* 72.

13.   George E. Yoos, "Ich gelobe meine Treue dem Banner," *Rhetoric Society Quarterly,* Vol. XX No. 1, Winter 1990.

14.   See "Textual Strategies: The Politics of Art-Making," Judith Barry and Sandy Flitterman-Lewis, in *Feminist Art Criticism,* edited by Arlene Raven, Cassandra L. Langer, and Joanna Frueh (Stony Brook, NY: State University of New York Press, 1988), 87–97, for a discussion of integrating the feminine and masculine as a form of political ideology.

Unit II
Learning Gender

This unit further considers the topic for Section I: the way gender is constructed. Gender is seen as a social construction, accomplished by complex processes. The three articles in this unit illustrate the complexity of acquiring and enacting gender by approaching the topic from three different perspectives. The chapter by Steven Hartwell, Roger Pace, and Renata Hutak looks at gender as a psychological construct, a result of interaction within the legal system. Margaret Hawkins and Thomas Nakayama argue that gender is influenced by social learning, particularly the messages sent through advertising. Finally, Margaret Crowdes posits that gender is an experiential issue that finds its expression in language. Thus, all three of these chapters argue that gender is learned. However, they explore different methods of learning.

More specifically, Hartwell and his colleagues concur with Carol Gilligan's work on gender formation. They argue that in negotiation situations, women and men differ in ways consistent with Gilligan's framework. Further, women's preferred negotiation style, collaboration, is not inferior to men's preferred negotiation style, competition. Hartwell et al. note that avoidance is a different issue than collaboration or competition, one which is related to social learning, and thus, more changeable than the relatively stable styles developed by women and men. Hawkins and Nakayama approach the question of how we learn gender through an analysis of 1920s advertisements. They argue that many of the advertising appeals of the 1920s are still current, and still convey the same gender messages. The concluding article in Unit II, by Crowdes, suggests that women can gain control over gender definitions, finding empowerment through changes in experience, language, and physical action. Crowdes focuses on the experiences of Kathryn, a woman training in karate who transforms her gender identity through her training.

CHAPTER 5

Women Negotiating: Assertiveness and Relatedness

Steven Hartwell, Roger C. Pace, and Renata Hutak
University of San Diego

INTRODUCTION

Do gender differences influence women to negotiate differently than men? If so, do these differences place women at a disadvantage in competitive negotiations? This article initiates an empirical investigation of these questions.

Although scholars disagree about the nature of gender differences,[1] there is broad agreement among scholars that women exhibit a greater concern than men for the maintenance of personal relationships. Some scholars trace this greater concern to the difference in identity formation between girls and boys.[2] Girls develop their identities, according to this theory, by perceiving themselves as the same as or interrelated with their mothers as primary caretakers. Boys, in contrast, develop their identities as separate from their mothers, a process that leads to a greater sense of self-identified separateness. This early process of self-identification carries over into adulthood, creating in males an enhanced sense of separateness that promotes their greater competitive behavior.[3] Whatever the source of this gender difference, if this quality of relatedness is defined as the sympathetic handling of people in which personal values are perceived as more important than logical consistency, then women consistently describe themselves as possessing more of this quality than men.[4]

Carol Gilligan has asserted that women's morality is posited on relationships among people.[5] Based on Gilligan's work, at least one legal scholar has proposed that women lawyers, in bringing their emphasis on relationships to their legal work, may shift the traditional mode of legal negotiating away from a competitive win/lose model toward a more collaborative one.[6] Other scholars insist that women are inherently no more caring or nurturant than men.[7] One review of the literature reports that the relatedness-basis of feminine morality posited by Gilligan is not gender specific, but context-specific.[8] Men and women have equal access to a relatedness/cooperative or a competitive/rights based morality, but women more often find themselves in contexts for which a relatedness/cooperative approach is more appropriate.[9] Other scholars believe that the entire argument hides the reality that in a male dominated world, gender differences or similarities have been defined by men for purposes of maintaining male domination.[10] Still other scholars argue that the structure of scientific inquiry tends to emphasize differences, such as differences in gender, so that science has created and maintains an exaggerated model of gender differences.[11]

We decided to examine one aspect of this ongoing debate. The present study reports our initial attempt to examine the influence of relatedness among women on their success in competitive negotiating. To measure this quality of relatedness, we administered to our subjects the Myers-Briggs Type Indicator (MBTI), a forced-choice, pencil-and-paper, 90-item instrument. Among its four scales, the MBTI provides a "thinking/feeling" scale that differentiates subjects who respond using impersonal logic and analysis ("thinkers") from those who respond by applying values and considering personal relationships ("feelers").[12] We were particularly interested in the interrelationship between this quality of relatedness and law school socialization. We wanted to know whether the competitive atmosphere of law school socialized women into being less concerned about relationships.[13] To measure this quality of competitiveness, we administered the Thomas-Kilmann Management of Difference Exercise (MODE), a forced-choice, pencil-and-paper, 30-item instrument that asks the subjects to choose among competitive, accommodating, and avoidance strategies.[14] We then compared the subjects' MBTI and MODE scores with their success in negotiating.

METHOD

The MBTI and the MODE were administered to 34 undergraduate (UG) students (14 males and 20 females) and 34 law school (LS) students (22 males and 12 females). The undergraduate students were enrolled in a communication course. The law students were enrolled in a legal negotiations course. Students in both courses were exposed to a variety of interpersonal skills and strategies in learning to interview and negotiate.

All the students in both courses were asked to participate in a simulated landlord-tenant negotiation as a part of their regular classwork. Students within each course were randomly paired and assigned a time and place to negotiate.[15] The student negotiators were asked to make a good faith attempt to negotiate a lease on behalf of their "client" within the one-half hour allotted them. The negotiation raised both competitive and collaborative issues. The students were advised that they would suffer no penalty for failing to complete the negotiation. All of the negotiations were audiotaped. Following the negotiation, the students were asked to complete a form detailing their impressions of the negotiation and what agreement they had reached, if any. Additionally, the LS students participated in eight other scored negotiations over the semester as part of their regular course work. In these other negotiations, the LS students were paired randomly into dyads.

RESULTS

T-test analyses were made of the scores of undergraduate and law school women on the MBTI thinking/feeling scale and the MODE competition/avoidance/accommodation scales. Although the LS women scored slightly higher than the UG women on the MBTI "thinking" scale and lower on the "feeling" scale, the differences were not significant.[16] In contrast, the difference in scores between LS and UG women on the MODE scales of competition and accommodation was significant ($p < .01$), the LS women scoring as significantly more competitive and significantly less accommodating.[17] None of the differences in means between UG and LS men was significant.[18]

Negotiation "success" was measured using two indices. The results of the audiotaped landlord-tenant negotiation, in which all the students participated, were tabulated by assigning values to each of the important monetary features of the lease. The total cumulated semester score for the LS students was tabulated, providing a second index for these students.

A Pearson product moment coefficient was calculated between the two indices of success with avoidance and competition. With both indices, success negatively correlated with avoidance. With the cumulated semester score, the correlation was significant (LS semester cumulative scores, $r = -.30$, $p < .05$); in the landlord-tenant negotiation, the correlation between avoidance and success with landlords was $r = -.30$, and approached significance, $p = .06$; with tenants, $r = -.20$, $p = .15$). There was no significant correlation between competition and success (LS semester cumulative scores, r = .09, p = .32; landlords, r = .01, p =.49; tenants, r = .12, p = .27).

No significant correlation was found between feeling and success with either of the two indices (law student semester cumulative scores, r = .01, p = .49; landlords, r = .30, p = .06; tenants, r = .07, p = .36).

DISCUSSION

Our hypothesis that the effectiveness of women's negotiating correlates negatively with avoidance but does not correlate negatively with relatedness is posited on several factors. First, we posit that relatedness and avoidance are qualitatively different aspects of personality. Relatedness is a stable element of personality that is relatively resistant to socialization. When faced with a conflict, a person who scores high on the relatedness scale (that is, MBTI "feeling") prefers to engage in cooperative or collaborative, as opposed to competitive, behavior.[19] In contrast, those who score high on the "thinking" scale, when faced with a conflict prefer to engage in competitive behavior.[20]

Avoidance, as we intend here, measures the degree to which an individual is neither competitive nor cooperative. An avoider simply does not address the conflict. We surmise that women, more than men, are socialized into avoiding conflict. As women (and men) are socialized into more assertive behavior, they move away from avoidance toward either competitive or collaborative negotiation conduct. As they become more assertive, "thinkers" move toward competition and "relatedness feelers" move toward collaboration.

People can learn to become more assertive so that they do not employ avoidance conduct when faced with conflict.[21] The law school women were significantly more assertive (that is, their competition scores were higher and their accommodation and avoidance scores were lower) than the undergraduate women. We cannot say conclusively that the higher levels of assertiveness among law school women resulted from their law school socialization. It may be that only the more assertive undergraduate women, for example, choose to go to law school. However, we surmise that law school socialization serves to make women, as a group, more assertive. First, as noted, the law school women scored significantly higher on assertiveness than undergraduate women and on a par with law school men. Second, law school men showed no such movement toward assertiveness. The avoidance scores of law school men were in fact slightly higher than that of undergraduate men. Hence, if "avoidance" did function as a self-selection factor in choosing to attend law school, it functioned only with women and not with men. Third, the socialization of women toward assertive conduct through their attendance at law school comports with the literature reporting on how women experience law school.[22]

Based on our study and our reading of the literature, we offer the following hypothesis. Women do, as a group, prefer to negotiate in significantly different ways from men. Women as "feelers" are more concerned about issues of relatedness than men. This concern leads women toward more collaborative and less competitive models of negotiation than men. The concern for relatedness, whether found in women or men, is a relatively stable element of one's personality and not subject to change through such socialization processes as law school.[23] "Feeling" women (and men) are not significantly disadvantaged in competitive negotiations with "thinking" men. Women, however, are more likely than men to be avoiders until and unless they are trained formally or socialized by an appropriate environment into becoming more assertive.

The popular belief that women are less able than men to negotiate competitively is based on a confusion between competition and assertiveness. An assertive negotiator may be either competitive or collaborative. Assertive people negotiate more successfully than unassertive (avoiding) people, irrespective of whether their assertive conduct takes the form of competition or collaboration.

A finding that assertive, relatedness-collaborative women negotiate as successfully as assertive, competitive men may carry important moral implications. If, as Gilligan asserts, relatedness forms a preferred moral basis among women for settling conflict, then our findings suggest that a woman need not compromise her moral base of relatedness in order to negotiate successfully. She can maintain her moral perspective and also satisfy her need for professional competence.[24]

NOTES

1.   Juanita H. Williams, *Psychology of Women: Behavior in a Biosocial Context,* 3d ed., (New York: Norton, 1987).

2.   Nancy Chodorow, *The Reproduction of Mothering: Psychoanalysis and the Sociology of Gender,* (Berkeley, CA: University of California Press, 1978).

3.   Elizabeth Janeway, *Man's World, Women's Place,* (New York: Morrow, 1971), 48–57.

4.   Isabel Briggs Myers, *Gifts Differing,* (Palo Alto, CA: Consulting Psychologists Press, Inc., 1980), 65–67.

5. Carol Gilligan, *In a Different Voice: Psychological Theory and Women's Development,* (Cambridge, MA: Harvard University Press, 1982). Gilligan's assertion that women employ a different form of moral reasoning than men is contested by Lawrence J. Walker, "Sex Differences in the Development of Moral Reasoning: A Critical Review," 55 *Child Development* 667 (1984).

6. Carrie Menkel-Meadow, "Portia in a Different Voice: Speculations on a Woman's Lawyering Process," *Berkeley Women's Law Journal,* 39, 39 (1985).

7. John M. Broughton, "Women's Rationality and Men's Virtue: A Critique of Gender Dualism in Gilligan's Theory of Moral Development," 50 *Social Research* 597 (1983).

8. Lawrence J. Walker, Brian de Vries, and Shelley D. Trevethan, "Moral Stages and Moral Orientations in Real-Life and Hypothetical Dilemmas," 58 *Child Development* 842, (1987).

9. For example, the subjects in Carol Gilligan's study in *In a Different Voice* (note 5, *supra*) were women who had faced the personal decision of an abortion. Women uniquely face this moral dilemma for which a morality based on relationships may be more appropriate than a morality based on rights. Because of the roles women tend to play within the society, women may find themselves more often than men facing moral dilemmas that deal with interpersonal relationships for which a relationship-based morality is more appropriate.

10. Catherine MacKinnon, *Feminism Unmodified: Discourses on Life and Law,* (Cambridge, MA: Harvard University Press, 1987).

11. Rachel T. Hare-Mustin and Jeanne Maracek, "The Meaning of Difference: Gender Theory, Postmodernism, and Psychology," 43 *American Psychologist* 455 (1988).

12. Isabel Briggs Myers, *Manual: The Myers-Briggs Type Indicator,* Princeton, NJ: Educational Testing Service [distributed by Consulting Psychologists Press, Palo Alto, CA]. (1962).

13. The competitiveness of law school itself has been commented on often. See, for example, Roger C. Cramton, "The Ordinary Religion of the Law School Classroom," 29 *Journal Legal Education* 247 (1978); "Beyond the Ordinary Religion," 37 *Journal Legal Education* 509 (1987).

14. K.W. Thomas and R.H. Kilmann, The Thomas-Kilmann Management of Difference Exercise, (Tuxedo, NY: Xicon, 1974). The MODE includes two other scales, compromise and collaboration.

15. The students were assigned to negotiate by means of one of three different media: face-to-face, telephonic or interactive video. This independent variable had no significant effect on any of the variables reported herein. F probabilities for the reported variables ran between .54 and .80; F ratios between .0930 and .6203.

16. Thinking (women): the UG mean was 7.67, SD=5.12; the LS mean= 11.15, SD 7.76. Feeling (women): the UG mean was 12.24, SD 4.43; the LS mean was 9.85, SD 5.71.

17.   Competition (women): the UG mean was 4.1, SD 2.38; the LS mean was 6.77, SD 2.92, p<.01. Accommodation (women): the UG mean was 6.50, SD 2.65; the LS mean was 3.92, SD 2.02, p<.01.

18. Women (UG and LS together) scored significantly higher than men on the "feeling" scale. The mean for women was 11.32, SD 4.97 and for men, 9.06, SD 4.61, p<.05. Women scored significantly lower than men on the "thinking" scale. The mean for women was 9.00, SD 6.39, and for men 12.03, SD 7.04, p<.05.

19.   The Thomas-Kilmann Conflict Mode Instrument distinguishes "accommodating" behavior, which is cooperative and avoiding, from "collaborative" behavior, which is cooperative and assertive. This subtle but useful distinction is not always made in the literature.

20.   Among all students, combining both undergraduate and law, the Pearson product moment between thinking and competition was r=.2721, p<.05; between feeling and collaboration (that is, an assertive-cooperative style), r=.2093, p<.05; between feeling and accommodation (that is, a non-assertive-cooperative style), r=.3259, p<.01. As one might anticipate, thinking negatively correlated with accommodation, r=−.3259, p<.01, and feeling negatively correlated with competition, r=−.3329, p<.01. These findings closely replicate the finding of Joan Mills, Daniel Robey, and Larry Smith, "Conflict-Handling and Personality Dimensions of Project-Management Personnel," 57 *Psychological Reports* 1135 (1985). Subjects in the Mills study were 199 project management personnel, the majority of whom were "technical" types, e.g., engineers, architects, and data processors.

21.   Ronald J. Delamater and J. Regis McNamara, "The Social Impact of Assertiveness: Research Findings and Clinical Implications," 10 *Behavior Modification,* 139 (1986).

22.   "PROJECT Gender, Legal Education and the Legal Profession: An Empirical Study of Stanford Law Students and Graduates," 40 *Stanford Law Review,* 1209, 1218-22 (1988). Much of the material in the Introduction to this paper was drawn from the PROJECT article.

23.   We take no position on the nature-nurture debate about why women exhibit more concern for feelings than men. A recent review of the literature reports that various cognitive differences between the genders in the United States among school-age children (e.g., verbal, spatial, and quantitative abilities) have noticeably declined over the past 30 years or so. Alan Feingold, "Cognitive Gender Differences Are Disappearing," 43 *American Psychologist* 95 (1988).

24.   Again, we include here men as well as women whose preference leans toward relatedness and collaboration.

CHAPTER 6

Discourse on Women's Bodies: Advertising in the 1920s

Margaret A. Hawkins
California State University, San Bernardino

Thomas K. Nakayama
Arizona State University

In 1921 Atlantic City hosted a women's swimsuit "beauty" competition, an event that crowned this nation's first "Miss America." This was yet another attempt to institutionalize standards of beauty for white women. Set against a period of political conservatism in the face of the early labor and women's movements, the 1920s represents a time of incredible change in the lives of all U.S. women (Banner; Ewen). The employment of women during World War I heightened an awareness of women as an economic force, particularly for the middle classes. John Held, Jr. of *The New Yorker* (Banner 154) drew the "flapper" who became the vision of the new woman. The flapper, not as virginal as Mary Pickford's "sweetheart," yet much more adolescent in comparison to Theda Bara's vamp, took on the surface impression of the liberated woman. Yet who was she really? And what did this image represent?

To many advertisers, this new woman represented rebellion and free-dom, whereas many feminists viewed her appearance as a backlash reaction to the work of women's activism (Banner 153). Women's suffrage resulted in the loss of a central cause for social feminist reformers. At the same time, the middle class renewed its recognition of women's sexuality. Together, these facts led to striking contradictions in the gender politics of the period. These issues are concurrent with the larger context of political repres-sion in the 1920s: the Oriental Exclusion Act of 1924, the tremendous rise and influence of the Ku Klux Klan, and so on. The 1920s also saw the rise of the influence of advertising as an industry and ideological force, with women centered as the focal point of consumerism.

It is within this unique historical configuration that we situate our reading of 1920s advertisements. Advertising in the 1920s is symptomatic of larger, more sustained cultural beliefs, attitudes, values, and behaviors in American society. As a cultural forum, advertising is one battleground upon which the much larger war of cultural constructions of gender is waged. In order to understand gender relations in the 1920s, we read ads from the period against Carl Naether's *Advertising to Women,* a 1928 book that approaches advertising both prescriptively and descriptively. In this text, Naether offers a comprehensive view of women's nature and advertising approaches geared toward this "distinct class of buyers" (v). Although Naether offers a 1920s perspective on the production of advertising copy, we use Naether's text to inform our reading of the advertisements of the period. Although we are contemporary readers of these advertisements, we believe that this reflexive move underscores a tension that opens up interesting observations on gender relations in the 1920s.

In his historical study of advertising, Stephen Fox notes that "the most enduring effect of twenties advertising on 'the habits and modes of life' involved the discovery of the human body" (97). The "discovery" of the female body, we suggest, involved more than a recognition that it emitted smells, was subject to halitosis, and contained yellow teeth. More insidiously, advertisers focused on displaying and idealizing an impossible female body type: the body of a prepubescent female. Understood as a cultural struggle within patriarchy at the time, this idealized female body is, as we see it, a crucial weapon in disempowering women by idealizing the body of a girl.

MALE DISCOURSE IN DRAG

Naether argues that women are incapable of writing advertising copy. He writes that women's discourse lacks "in definite degree the vital selling punch to impress itself deeply on the gentle reader's mind and promptly lead her straying thoughts into the straight and narrow path of final—buying—action" (18). Suggesting that women lack linearity in their thinking, Naether argues that advertising copy should be written by men, despite his observation that "a woman understands the needs of her own sex much better than does a man" (17). Although the relationship between writing styles and gender is interesting at face value, we need to examine the implications of this relationship in more detail.

The process for creating advertising copy is essentially the creation of male discourse, i.e., assertive, purposeful, persuasive discourse. Thus, Naether advocates beginning the process of writing advertising copy with men, but utilizing women to "feminize" the advertisements (19). This feminizing process, what we might call "audience adaptation" today, masks several assumptions about "women's nature" that we would not make today.

First, Naether buys into a "pedestal view" of women. He writes: "Most of us, even when conversing with them [women], studiously maintain an attitude of patience, refinement, and respect" (25). Advertising copy, accordingly, should reflect "a certain amount of deference and dignity" (25). Although this particular perspective on women is historically specific to white women, cultural constructions of racial difference are ignored by Naether. His use of the term "woman" or "women" is nevertheless specific to white women.

Second, women, in Naether's view, lack objectivity. We presume, conversely, that men, for Naether, are objective. According to Naether, the self-centered, narrow vision of woman is such that "even the woman in business finds it difficult to contemplate objectively those very matters which business decrees should be viewed in a light wholly impersonal" (31). This particular characteristic of women makes it difficult for them to write advertising copy. But conversely, advertisements should be directed to this self-centered characteristic of women.

Third, women are essentially emotional creatures in Naether's view. Since women refuse to reason when making purchases, it is to the advertiser's advantage to appeal to women's emotions rather than offering them logical reasons for purchasing particular commodities. Naether writes: "My opinion in the matter is that *very few women like to reason* much in connection with the purchase of goods" (148). Yet, it is important that the advertiser not make this appeal too directly, since "The average woman stoutly objects to being told that her feelings rush in often to clinch her decisions for her" (150). So Naether is insisting on viewing women as basically emotional beings despite the resistance of women to this label. His insistence on emotions substantiates the approaches he advocates toward advertising to women.

Fourth, Naether feels that women are incapable of producing advertising discourse. Within Naether's view of the advertising process, which he defines as male-centered, power and social control are to be wielded by men. The advertiser's power is seemingly unlimited, in Naether's view:

> *The advertiser...has it within his power not only to affect temporarily, but to mold permanently, the thought and attitude of a particular buying public. (234)*

The advertiser has this power since his goal in advertising is to dupe the reader completely. He writes:

> *The reader is to swallow the statement whole, to accept it unqualifiedly, for, if she does not, the seller's message has missed its point and considerable costly space has been wasted. (235)*

Within this vision of advertising, the power of men selling commodities to women becomes more influential in constructing gender relations in the 1920s. Thus Naether sees 1920s advertising as male discourse directed at women in a one-way communication framework. We have chosen, then, to describe advertising copy as "male discourse in drag" in order to underscore our distance from Naether's understanding of the advertising process. Not only do we question how he is making the distinction between male and female discourse, we also find the assumptions upon which this distinction is based to be untenable. The concept of drag allows us to emphasize male mocking of the feminine.

FOUR APPEALS IN CONSTRUCTING THE FEMALE BODY

The importance of maintaining a healthy body does not appear to be an acceptable end in and of itself for the woman of the 1920s. Naether tells us that the appeal toward health "is seldom made on its own strength, sellers of the commodities just mentioned finding it most effective when it is closely linked to the strong desire which women manifest for beauty, style, and comfort" (205). Of these three auxiliary appeals, beauty and style are the most important, and ultimately, Naether sides with beauty as the strongest appeal. After all, the majority of "toilet aids...are for exterior application" and therefore "they are at best nothing but artificial means with few, if any, health-giving powers" (205).

Ironically, the one area where the appeal to health seems to be the strongest is the marketing of corsets. Naether appears to support the use of corsets for health reasons because many "unhealthful practices in to-day's mode of living leave their mark upon the feminine figure, if they are not counteracted in some way" (208). Although it is not clear why modern life does not leave its mark upon the masculine figure, it is plain that Naether sees the corset as counteracting the influences of culture. In other words, the wearing of a cultural garment, the corset, is necessary to become more "natural."

But corsets are the exception. In general, Naether finds the appeals to health unconvincing because women prefer to "*simulate health* through artificial make-up and cover-up" (214). This seemingly unique characteristic of women is important in that it lays the foundation for making appeals to beauty and style.

Naether believes that women are interested in decorating their bodies to create a particular look; they are not interested in working toward health. Our interest here is in exploring one facet of that "look," the emphasis on the prepubescent figure in the female.

In Naether's view, style is central to the existence of most women (221). Women's desire to adhere to fashion motivates them to disregard other aspects of clothing in favor of style. For example, Naether notes that "outer garments, such as gowns, wraps, coats, frocks, and dresses, are worn mainly for one reason—to be seen" (223). Here the emphasis is on conspicuous display of clothing style, even if such clothes are ultimately detrimental to health. Health, we have already seen, is a secondary appeal to buying. The basic motivation behind the urge to be stylish is, as Naether observes, the wishes of men: "It has been said that woman will venture in her manner of dress to whatever extremes man directly or indirectly wishes her to go" (225). Unfortunately, Naether does not make it clear how women know what men desire. Advertising appears to be one of the primary communication media through which women understand men's desires.

For women, beauty is an important tool or weapon with which they are able to manipulate male interest in them. This is the central appeal of those advertisements that are directed towards enhancing women's beauty, which is "effective in subjugating and dominating the affections of men" (244). Through beauty, then, women's commodified bodies become more desirable to men. Women gain power through manipulation, according to Naether.

As noted earlier, Naether makes no effort to recognize explicitly that he is focusing on advertising to white women; however, his definitions of beauty appear to be centered on white women:

> *Well nigh every woman's wish to possess eyes that, softly shaded by long beautiful lashes, radiate brilliancy; a complexion that is smooth and velvety, showing rosy health through cheeks and lips; hands that are well shaped and white and soft; and whatever else she considers needful to make her physical self pleasing to the point of magnetism is largely a desire to fascinate the other sex. (251)*

If "every woman" wants hands that are "white and soft," these are reflections of desires of (white) men. Although it is not made clear if women of color want to make themselves appealing to white men, it is clear that the basis for these desires is the attraction of men.

Although Naether notes that "the beauty appeal is, as we have seen, fundamentally a sex appeal" (25), but he does not advocate further emphasis on this aspect of our lives since "the American woman is sex-conscious enough without the advertiser endeavoring to make her more so" (260). Yet, Naether also observes that it is a "natural desire" for women to want "to display physical charms peculiar to her sex" (260). This display, however, is expressed "unobtrusively, modestly, finely, if, indeed, at all" by "modern, civilized woman" (260). As we read Naether, this ideal woman is, of course, white and bourgeois.

READING ADVERTISEMENTS

Having discovered the body in the 1920s, advertisers quickly focused on aspects of the female body. From feet to hair, women were told that they had a number of problems or potential problems that others would notice. Issues of health were certainly not foregrounded. In a 1925 ad for Blue-jay plaster, women were told that: "There'll come a moment when your feet must be seen!" And any "disfiguring blemishes" must be removed since "all eyes will be upon you, will appraise your stockingless legs and feet."

Yet, overall the advertisers focused on creating a slimmer, smoother female body that did not have large breasts or large hips. This particular idealization is one that even hosiery manufacturers tried to tap into. The Holeproof Hosiery Company claimed, in 1925, that its hosiery had "a fit that's trimmer."

Women were told "why fat is being fought" by Marmola prescription tablets: "Largely because of short skirts...Look about you—note how slenderness prevails." Clearly, the focus is on slenderness for the *female* body. Marmola claims to aid in losing weight, but as Naether argued, women were more interested in a surface presentation as opposed to making significant changes in their health. Fortunately for women in the 1920s, wraparound corsets came to the rescue! In their advertisements, Redfern claimed that with their corsets, "there is no suggestion of 'hips'." This idealization of a hipless, slim body is grounded in an appeal to style and fashion, and constructs an ideal that the adult female body cannot become without significant purchasing of commodities. The absolute importance of fashion, however, is blatantly revealed when Redfern claims that its corset "eliminates the difference between the real and the ideal, between your own figure and the silhouette of fashion." Thus, the 1920s woman is told that if her "figure is of the 'average type'," she will need the corset. Warner's "invisible corset" makes similar claims: "It produces flat, smooth backs, close-fitting thighs, and assures success for the new type of closely draped gowns." The basis of these appeals is style, not health. Neither of these ad campaigns focused on any health benefits to be derived from wearing the corset.

Other representations of the female body in advertising reinforced the idealization of the hipless, breastless female. In drawings, women's bodies were stretched to achieve this "look," as Roland Marchand explains:

> *Never did advertising artists distort and reshape men's bodies as they did when they transformed women into Art Deco figurines. Women in the tableaux, as symbols of modernity, sometimes added more than a foot to their everyday heights and stretched their elongated eyes, fingers, legs, arms, and necks to grotesque proportions. The proportions of some women in the tableaux suggested a height of over nine feet. (181–182)*

These women, as Marchand points out, were women of high social status; they were not domestics or women of lower status. These gigantic, slender women are featured in advertisements for products as diverse as the Hupmobile Eight and Eno, an effervescent saline.

Aside from simply being a body type that was used to give status to a particular product, advertisers perceived the desire to be thin, primarily among women, as a useful advertising appeal. Lucky Strike cigarettes, for example, launched a large campaign to market their cigarettes to this desire:

> *Every woman who fears overweight finds keen interest in new-day and common-sense ways to keep a slender, fashionable figure. Overweight must be avoided. "Better to light a* Lucky *whenever you crave fattening sweets."*

The Lucky Strike campaign combined appeals to beauty and health as a further emphasis on "a slender, fashionable figure."

Women during the 1920s were also told that they should shave their underarms and legs, further reinforcing the fetishizing of the girl's body while denying the woman's. After all, there was now "an easy way to remove superfluous hair from the underarms and limbs:" Evans's Depilatory Outfit. Similar products were not advertised to men.

Without hips, breasts, and superfluous hair, the "stylish" woman of the 1920s still had to rework her nonsuperfluous hair, especially since that hair could reveal her age. The issue here is only marginally one of grey hair; women were told that dark hair was also a sign of aging. In advertisements for Marchand's Golden Hair Wash, blonde hair is directly correlated with youth: "Glorious golden hair [is] glorious only as long as it retains that charming youthful brightness," youthfulness, of course, which can be restored by using this particular commodity. After all, "Marchand's Golden Hair Wash is specially prepared to bring back the golden tint of girlhood." These advertisements directly relate having the hair of girlhood with the power to manipulate men:

> *Beautiful, colorful hair! It is Nature's crown—a gift to the daughters of Eve that they might have a subtle power that has urged men to love and protect their homes or to create or vanquish empires. And always the lure of beautiful colorful hair has helped to weld happiness and to hasten romance.*

Easily recognizable here is Naether's argument that women desire to empower themselves through beauty for manipulation purposes. However, this manipulation is through the embodiment of a relatively powerless figure, the preadolescent girl.

Should grey hair become an issue, La Creole hair treatment was readily available. After all, the advertisements claim, "You should not let your hair grow old." This product claims to "bring back hair that has grown gray, gray-streaked or faded to its youthful color and beauty." To put to rest white readers' concerns of racial "contamination," the advertising copy reads: "Creole beauty still marks the race, a proof of pure European descent." Obviously, this product does not challenge Naether's constructed female consumer.

We should also point out that the dominant style for much of the 1920s was "bobbed hair." Writing against bobbed hair in 1925, Chandler Owen argued that this hair style enables "women to appear to be what they ain't—also let them sell, to an extent, apparent youth for real youth" (140). Although Owen dislikes the style, we can clearly see the youthful appearance it gives: women are further imitating the looks of young girls. Advertisers, of course, did not overlook the opportunities this style opened up for them—Listerine, for example, tried to market its product to women:

> *The current vogue of wearing the hair bobbed has revealed to many women that they have dandruff. In the past, folks thought of dandruff only as something that spoiled the appearance of a man's blue serge suit.*

Listerine, of course, claimed to solve that problem without discoloring the hair or staining fabrics.

Women's skin, too, was not ignored in the recreation of the stylish 1920s female body. Ingram's Milkweed Cream told women:

> *A smile adds immeasurably to your charm but it does sometimes leave lines. Of course, you must smile...but you need not have lines and wrinkles that mar the beauty of your face...that make you old...before your time!*

Again, the emphasis is on youth. After all, "Beauty here is all-important." This cream, however, was not only for wrinkles: it worked on "your throat, nose and chin;" women were to ask themselves: "Does your neck match your face?" Ingram's, of course, solved all these problems. Woodbury's Facial soap also tapped into the same market by promising that "you can keep it [skin] smooth, clear, flawless, long after youth is passed." Playing off the motto, "A skin you love to touch," Woodbury's emphasized the rejuvenation powers of this soap, but directly targeted the soap for "girls and women." Hinds Cream claimed to offer "the charm of youth." Even Fleischmann's Yeast, which was not marketed specifically for beautifying skin, tapped into this particular desire. A testimonial by one of the women who ate the yeast again emphasizes the importance of the schoolgirl: "The effect was marvelous. In three weeks my pimples were drying up. In two months I was cured—my color was like that of a schoolgirl." The pattern here is clear: It was important for females to have youthful skin. We found no such ads that were similar for men. In a two-page advertisement for Listerine, men are told that Listerine "stops the smarting" after shaving, while women are told that

Listerine will make them "look—and feel—younger."

The development of the flapper in the 1920s coincides with the development of this female body type. The flapper in Murad cigarette ads has a slender, almost anorexic, body, and tiny, pointed feet. With bobbed hair and flat chest, she looks (and acts) like a girl:

> *When you tell your fiance that you have a sick headache and can't go out, and later on at a dance he finds you in the arms of his rival, don't explain. . .*Offer Him a MURAD.

The flapper also appears in ads for Timken Roller Bearings. Again, we see the short hair, slim bodies, tiny feet, and almost girlish game playing. Her ridiculous body proportions, and trivializing body positions (standing on one foot, clinging to a father figure) further emphasize the dependency and childishness of the flapper.

Finally, we should note that other advertisements from this period further emphasized the girlish nature of women, from the woman in the Kelly-Springfield tire ad who exclaims: "Oh, dear, I'm so afraid of the Avenue when it's wet. Drive carefully, won't you William?" to the woman in the American Chain Company ad who is "skid shocked"—frightened because her car skidded when she braked. This insistence on the weakness of women is seemingly a part of the constitution of her body. Her nerves are weak. It is for women, not men, that one should buy Hoo-Dye Shock Absorbers:

> *Countless thousands of women are today losing half the pleasure and benefit of motoring that might be theirs. Countless thousands are suffering needlessly from shock, strain and nervous apprehension—expending many times the energy of the man at the wheel. These thousands literally bounce about on the rear seat, due to the roughness of the roads and uncontrolled spring action.*

The weakness of women leaves them equated with children whose body type they imitate anyway. Smith & Wesson attempt to appeal to men arguing that women and children need to be protected. Ex-Lax focuses on appealing to women and children. Although it is for children, it "brings roses back to the cheeks" of women. Ex-Lax tells women: "You'll like Ex-Lax, as much as children do."

Placing women in the same discursive category as children and addressing them as children represents one of the extensions of idealizing the girl's body. Women begin to look like children and men are told to look at them as children. This particular view of women stands in stark contrast to the political advances made by women in the 1920s. Because these advertisements and Naether's discussion clearly focus on white women, it is the negotiation of gender relations among whites that is at stake here. Against the backdrop of the historical period, such advertising appeals seem odd, but it is important to remember that advertising discourse is male discourse. As such, its appeals and representations need to be viewed as the voice of patriarchy. Although this may not have been the outward intention of Naether or the advertisers, the restriction of writing advertising copy to a particular group (men) and developing a system around gender differences reinforces a patriarchal system. In these advertisements, we have seen the relatively vague and flexible notions of style and beauty defined toward the development of a preadolescent body type: hipless, breastless, slender, light haired, with shaved underarms and legs and youthful skin. These are tied to style (short skirts and bobbed hair) and related to the power of women to attract men. Against the backdrop of the political advances made by women, advertising has to be seen as a reactionary force during this period.

CONCLUSIONS

In his study of advertising, Daniel Pope marks a strong break between advertising in the 1920s and contemporary ads when he writes:

A few slogans and themes have persisted, but in general the advertisements of 1920 would be as out of place in today's newspaper as would the head-lines and news stories from that year. (284)

Although Pope senses a definite difference in advertising appeals, this break does not seem as clear to us. Many of the same appeals to clear skin, white teeth, avoiding grey hair, and the like do not seem farfetched from television and magazine advertisements we see daily. Our historical moment differs from that of the 1920s, but it remains to be seen if advertising still performs the reactionary function for white females that it did in the 1920s. Our evidence suggests that this may be the case. This is certainly an area that requires further research.

We see a parallel in the co-optation of the language and images of a women's/feminist movement during the 1920s and the 1990s as well as an institutionalizing of the ideal body. Today we see a trend in idealizing young girls' bodies by making them more like adult women's bodies through the use of commodities (make-up, plastic nails, etc.), which maintains an almost pedophilic obsession with youth and young female bodies. Perhaps such representations and obsessions need to be understood as reactions to women's/feminist movements, but this inquiry is beyond the scope of this paper.

Most adult females find it impossible to embody the 1920s ideal woman. The emphasis on thinness shows a dwindling of strength as a visible aspect of women. The focus on white upper- and middle-class women is probably a reaction to the most threatening group of women to the white, male-centered society. Poor women, women of color, and other disenfranchised groups did not have the capital or the intimate relationships with white men that empowered the white women of the bourgeoisie. Thus, we see the 1920s "new woman" as a trivialized, nonthreatening woman who was created in reaction to the strides made by women. As Pumphrey states: "Her childishness becomes our maturity. Her distance transforms our sexuality. Her passivity becomes our authority." (202)

REFERENCES

Banner, Lois W. 1984. *Women in Modern America: A Brief History.* Orlando, FL: Harcourt Brace Jovanovich.

Ewen, Stuart. 1976. *Captains of Consciousness: Advertising and the Social Roots of the Consumer Culture.* New York: McGraw-Hill.

Fox, Stephen. 1984. *The Mirror Makers: A History of American Advertising and Its Creators.* New York: William Morrow.

Marchand, Roland. 1985. *Advertising the American Dream: Making Way for Modernity, 1920–1940.* Berkeley, CA: University of California Press.

Naether, Carl. 1928. *Advertising to Women.* New York: Prentice-Hall.

Owen, Chandler. 1925. "Bobbed Hair." *The Messenger* 7 (March):139–40.

Pope, Daniel. 1983. *The Making of Modern Advertising.* New York: Basic Books.

Pumphrey, Martin. 1987. "The Flapper, the Housewife and the Making of Modernity." *Cultural Studies* 1 (May):179–94.

CHAPTER 7

Mind, Body, and Language: When a Woman Notices Her Humanity

Margret S. Crowdes
National University, San Diego

Social controls of women's bodies and minds, and the ways in which androcentric definitions of femininity, sexuality, and power constrain women's development and possibilities, are pivotal points in feminist scholarship. Therefore, women's challenges of and efforts to regain control over definitions and uses of their minds and bodies are central concerns in analyses of power asymmetries and social change. A necessary strength of feminism in this regard is the realization that effective feminist activity—i.e., empowerment—must be a lived-out experience that characterizes "ordinary" as well as "scholarly" thought, language, and practice.

Polaristic debates over the definition of the relationship between language and reality, academic and movement concerns with language, and related perspectives on power and change have sometimes sabotaged the sharp clarity that characterizes feminist analyses (Cameron, 1985:69; Jenkins and Kramarae, 1981). For instance, some Marxist-feminist analyses of power and change diminish woman's individual power, making her appear personally powerless and dependent in relation to "larger social constraints and forces" believed to determine her consciousness. Yet, critics of determinist analyses have often overstressed the power of the individual, underestimating the complexities and power of patriarchy in ordinary experience, thought, and language behavior. Feminist scholars have not been immune to these disputes and their impact on research design and methods (Cameron, 1985).

Studies of women's talk across a variety of speech contexts have substantially amplified the viability of merging macro-micro analyses of

sociopolitical forces and processes. Some have revealed the combined
forces of institutionalized and interactional power, illustrating linguistic reg-
ulatory components of the oppression of women (Fisher, 1983; Todd,
1983; in cross-sex informal discourse: Fishman, 1983; West and Zimmerman,
1985; Sattel, 1983, for examples). Other studies highlight women's richly creative and powerful conversational styles and substantive discourse (Buker,
1987; Jenkins, 1982; Kalcik, 1975; Jenkins and Kramarae, 1981). Two essential truths about language and communication are revealed in these and
other studies: (1) Although language as "...a human faculty and communication channel may belong to everyone,...*the* language, the institution,
the apparatus of ritual...can be controlled by a small elite," and (2) analysis
of women's conversations reveals a portrait of women empowered, "not one
of silent or inarticulate women who struggle to express their experience and
feelings" (Cameron, 1985).

My purpose here is to contribute to interdisciplinary feminist dialogue
committed to going beyond determinist-essentialist, macro-micro antago-
nism in analyses of power and change. I assume the perspective that a feminist theory of the role of language and communication in social change cannot stop at exposure of the oppression of women as speakers, but must
concurrently illustrate a praxical "prospect of struggle and liberation." The
picture is more hopeful, as one analyst says;

> *when we concentrate on metalinguistic and discursive processes linked
> to women's identity and role in particular societies. These processes can
> be challenged much more easily and effectively than* langue, *meaning,
> alienation, and other such abstractions. (Cameron, 1985:161)*

The necessarily praxical foundation of emancipatory transformation requires
supercession of dualistic notions about language, mind, change and humanity rooted in the patriarchal worldview and social structure. For a woman this
has a special significance and urgency, insofar as her knowledge of herself
as a sovereign human being and the patriarchal language and image of her
as "woman" condition a dualistic opposition in the roots of her own identity. This opposition can be observed in ordinary language use; the power
of that contradiction in a woman's conceptualization of her personal power
impacts the substance of, and the degree to which she realizes freedom from,
the contradiction. This, in turn, shapes her action in the world.

With this philosophical point in mind, I wish in the following section
to briefly examine a sequence from one woman's story about some personal
and social results of her choice to practice a martial art. My intent is to practice a feminist way of interpreting an interplay between transformation and
constraint: I see this interplay in a conceptual relationship between the
speaker's personal articulations of development of body confidence and
empowerment, and androcentric language habits.

METHODOLOGICALLY SPEAKING

Interdisciplinary studies of discourse illustrate the powerful fact that speaking is a form of personal thought *and* sociocultural action which, combined, constitute total experience. Discourse analysis of one woman's work in making sense of and explaining personal changes can contribute to an illustration of dynamic interaction between forces of power and empowerment in the composition of her experiences of personal change.

The "explanatory structure" and "creation of coherence" (Linde, 1987) in narrative, and the relationship between the point of a story and sociocultural presuppositions (Polanyi, 1979) are pivotal methodological categories of interpretation in my analysis. First, speaking is an action through which personal experiences and sociocultural knowledge are linked. The discourse analyst's task is "to understand what people are doing when they speak" without assuming some absolute standard against which the speaker succeeds or fails (Linde, 1979:31). Second, in order to perceive the speaker's "creation of coherence" in her story, the analyst must assume that speakers choose the parts they have chosen "because they are the most relevant to the question and answer being constructed...and the only ones necessary to establish the conclusion" (Linde, 1979:31). The tacit and manifest explanatory system functioning in the discourse is "the system of assumptions about the world which the speaker uses to make events and evaluations coherent" (Linde, 1985:6); relationships between explanatory concepts give important clues about the simultaneous impacts of personal experience and sociocultural presuppositions. Finally, speakers have to make a point worth making; what the point *can* be is significantly related to sociocultural constraints on "attitudes, beliefs, and crucially important key concepts about the way things are or ought to be, and most especially about the way people are, what they need, and how they should behave" (Polanyi, 1985:212). Points are made obvious by clusterings of evaluative devices (stressors, intensifiers, repetitions) around certain utterances and not others (Polanyi, 1979). With these three ideas in mind, I will examine the following account of personal changes, resulting from the practice of karate, which took place in one woman's mind and body, and I will examine the language she has chosen to describe and explain the impact these changes have made in her relationship to the world.

Katherine is a white, professionally employed woman living in a Southern California city. At the time of this narration she was 28 years old and was working as a computer programmer. She had been training in karate for three years. I asked Katherine if she thought training in karate had made any difference in her life. She emphatically declared that it had. She explained:

> *For me, being the 28 that I am, I thought I would be long gone already, you know, there's not going to be a prayer for me body-wise. At the age of 18 my body was going downhill. And I no longer believe that now, in fact, I am so* excited *to have a body as I do right now. The thing is, my gosh, I can* use *it. I can do physical labor that* doubles *what most women I know can in a pretty rigorous sport. And yet I have not given up* one *ounce of my femininity, and I can't* imagine *a more exciting experience in terms of my body right now. I am a woman and a human being and I have just really reached a level of pride in terms of my body. . .how that shows, I can walk in on a business meeting and wear a full skirt and the whole bit and stand erect because I have very good posture and I have a very good outlook on myself and I'm not going to hide behind my bangs or hide behind a chair or anything. I can stand really proud, and uh, that's a really good feeling. I can also get in the grubbiest clothes and turn soil because I physically have the strength to. It just touches every aspect of how I relate to the world.* [roman text indicates speaker emphasis]

Katherine routinely practices an activity that requires an integrative and dynamic balance between mind and body, technique and spirit. It requires self-possession. This integration or balance contrasts significantly to our "normal" fragmented and hierarchical ways of understanding and interacting. Katherine's practice of this mind-body relationship initiated changes in her understanding and definition of herself and enhanced her development of personal power and self-determination; the logic of her explanation of this essentially human process manifests significant gender-specific discourse patterns in the androcentric sociocultural context of contemporary Western society.

FUNCTIONS OF CONTRADICTION IN EXPERIENCE AND DISCOURSE: PRINCIPLES OF COHERENCE AND CONSTRAINT, ACTS OF TRANSFORMATION

The explanatory system is a crucial aspect of the *evaluative structure,* which "conveys information about what the events mean to the speaker, [and] how they are to be understood by the addressees" (Linde, 1985:6). A key point in this sequence of Katherine's account is that karate practice induced dramatic and significant changes in her body and personal identity, which changes fundamentally impacted how she related to herself and the world. Katherine uses certain conceptual juxtapositions in order to build and communicate the development of these relationships. Three juxtapositions in particular strike me as significant: (1) body pride and ability to do hard physical activity/femininity; (2) woman/human being; (3) body before/body after.

The central and emotionally active presence of contradiction in her experience and discourse has special significance vis-a-vis a feminist perspective on gender, language, and personal/social change. Her explanation is organized by both contradiction of *and* collusion with dominant androcentric sociocultural presuppositions. A conceptual tension is reflexively established as Katherine positively counters a sociocultural presupposition about women, (e.g., self-determining women are less feminine, and self-determining women are a proper measure of neither womankind nor of humankind) while simultaneously relying on the language structure in which these presuppositions are syntactically, lexically, and semantically constructive.

A comparative point further illustrates this logic. If in the course of ordinary dialogue, a man included the assertion, "I am a man and a human being" as a central point of an explanation, it would probably strike the listener as strange and redundant; there is no need for a man to assert his humanity because "common sense" tells us that man and human are continuous with the same being (however, a man's assertion of his humanity is a reasonable utterance, for different reasons, for men historically dehumanized by racist practices). A relationship between semantics and syntax (Grice, 1975) and a gender-specific implication of this relationship can be illustrated with this example: the statements "I see a dog and it's a mammal," and "I am a man and a human being" are redundant conjunctions. Linguistically, the statements "I am a woman and a human being" and "I am a man and a human being" are both conjunctions; but they are not equivalent: her statement is a contradictory conjunction and his is a redundant one, each referencing fundamentally different ontological experiences. Because movement toward self-determination is a human process in which women's possibilities and conceptual projections have been diminished, whereas men's experiences and conceptualizations have been privileged and normalized, Katherine's choice of explanatory concepts in her story of personal empowerment must involve reformation of both her gender and human identity in order to communicate the full implications of her changes.

Katherine references and corrects two contradictory presuppositions with one utterance: "I am a woman and a human being." This assertion negates the negation (feminine is not self-determining, self-determining woman is not human), and avoids an either-or choice between two indispensable dimensions of her sentient being, which are similarly indispensable to her explanation of personal empowerment. The language she uses to communicate functions simultaneously as constraint and empowerment.

Experience and Discourse:
A Nexus of Personal-Social Change

Katherine says her practice has initiated changes that touch "every aspect of how [she] relates to the world." To the degree that she has changed her way of using her mind and body, and to the degree that her concepts of "woman" and "human" and subsequent social actions have changed, then change that runs deeper than private or cosmetic lexical alterations has taken place. At the same time, those progressions toward self-determination are contradictory. Katherine's speech typifies some of the conceptual-linguistic work that women do, that women in fact *have* to do, as they encounter qualitatively new experiences of mind and body, which initiate redefinitions of the entire system of relationships through which they construct their personal identities, and through which they assert the power of those redefinitions in everyday life. When women thus begin to break the confines of "socially imposed shame" about their bodies, a shame that has functioned to keep "people submissive to societal authority by weakening in them some inner core of individual authority...[thereby crippling]...human pride" (Dinnerstein, 1976:73–74), then a measure of qualitative change is surely taking place.

In this sense, within the parameters of her ethnicity, class, and daily conditions, Katherine contributes to the work of feminist praxis; her bodily (martial arts practice) and speech actions display the logical loop of reinforcement between experience, language, and physical action vis-a-vis empowerment. One observer of the relationship between words and practice has observed, "True practice is done not [only] with words but with the entire body."

> *What you have been taught by listening to others' words you will forget very quickly; what you have learned with your whole body you will remember for the rest of your life. (Funakoshi, 1976:106)*

Although contrived still by lingering prejudice and by contradictions, speech behavior is praxically constituent of feminist change to the degree to which personal empowerment is consciously lived.

REFERENCES

Alcoff, Linda. 1987. "Justifying Feminist Social Science," *Hypatia: A Journal of Feminist Philosophy* 2, 3:107–27.

Buker, Eloise A. 1987. *Storytelling Power: Personal Narratives and Political Analysis.* Redding, CA: Hawthorne Press.

Cameron, Deborah. 1985. *Feminism and Linguistic Theory.* New York: St. Martin's Press.

Dinnerstein, Dorothy. 1976. *The Mermaid and the Minotaur: The Sexual Arrangement and Human Malaise.* New York: Harper and Row.

Fisher, S. 1983. "Institutional Authority and the Structure of Discourse," in *Discourse Processes,* Apr.–June, 7, 2:201–5.

Fishman, Pamela. 1983. "Interaction: The Work Women Do," in *Language, Gender, and Society,* edited by Thorne, Kramarae and Henley. Rowley, MA: Newbury House.

Funakoshi, Gichin. 1976. *Karate Do My Way of Life.* Tokyo, Japan: Kodansha Intl. Ltd.

Grice, H.P. 1975. "Logic and Conversation," in *Syntax and Semantics,* vol. 3, edited by P. Cole and J. Morgan, 41–58. New York: Academic Press.

Grimshaw, Jean. 1986. *Philosophy and Feminist Thinking.* Minneapolis, MN: University of Minnesota Press.

Hawkesworth, Mary. 1989. "Knowers, Knowing, Know: Feminist Theory and Claims of Truth," *Signs: Journal of Women in Culture and Society,* 14, 3:533–57.

Jenkins, Mercilee, and Cheris Kramarae. 1981. "A Thief in the House: Women and Language," in *Men's Studies Modified,* edited by Dale Spender. Oxford, England: Pergamon Press.

Jenkins, Mercilee. 1982. "Stories Women Tell: An Ethnographic Study of Personal Experience Narratives in a Women's Rap Group" (unpublished paper).

Kalcik, Susan. 1975. "...Like Ann's Gynecologist or the Time I Was Almost Raped:" *Journal of American Folklore,* 88, 3–11.

Kramarae, Cheris. 1981. *Women and Men Speaking.* Rowley, MA: Newbury House.

Linde, Charlotte. 1979. "The Creation of Coherence in Life Stories" (unpublished paper).

———. 1985. "Private Stories in Public Discourse: Narrative Analysis in the Social Sciences," *Narrative Analysis: An Interdisciplinary Dialogue,* edited by U. Quasthoff. Amsterdam: Elsevier.

———. 1987. "Explanatory Systems in Oral Life Stories," in *Cultural Models in Language and Thought,* edited by D. Holland and N. Quinn. Cambridge, MA: Cambridge University Press.

Polanyi, Livia. 1979. "So What's The Point?" *Semiotica,* 25(3/4):207–30.

———. 1985. *Telling the American Story.* Norwood, NJ: Ablex.

Sattel, J.W. 1983. "Men, Inexpressiveness, and Power," in *Language, Gender and Society,* edited by Thorne, Kramarae and Henley. Rowley, MA: Newbury House.

Thorne, Barrie, Cheris Kramarae, and Nancy Henley. 1983. *Language, Gender and Society.* Rowley, MA: Newbury House.

Todd, A.D. 1983. "The Prescription of Contraception: Negotiations Between Doctors and Patients," *Discourse Processes,* Apr.–June, 7, 2:171–200.

West, Candace, and Don H. Zimmerman. 1985. "Gender, Language, and Discourse," in *Handbook of Discourse Analysis,* vol. 4, edited by Van Dijk. 103–24.

Unit III
Expressing Gender

In the preceding section, the authors explored several of the ways in which humans learn the gender specific behaviors expected of them in Western culture. Although these expectations may be the same for all women and all men, enactment varies from person to person. Womanliness and manliness take on dimensions through expression, showing how people adapt gender specific behavior to fit the situation in which they find themselves.

Each chapter in this unit focuses on a slightly different "playing field" of gender expression. Fay considers female poets who write like men, seeing the poets as dissidents who rely upon a male muse. Also concerned with responses to art, but this time to critics' responses, Lockridge shows how gender crosses sex lines. She argues that some male critics' characteristic perspectives on art reflect a feminine principle, whereas others' emerge from a male principle. Using a small group of women as her focus, Yanni traces the evolution of the metaphor of "conversation" within this group, seeing that metaphor as uniquely womanly. Hoar looks at the way in which power and gender interact in communication, suggesting that women should work to mainstream women's ways of talking. Finally, Jaasma analyzes the different ways women and men view and use interaction on new ideas within the business world. This section shows that communication styles of women and men differ significantly within and across sex lines.

CHAPTER 8

Rhythm, Gender, and Poetic Language

Elizabeth Fay
University of Massachusetts, Boston

The nature of the problem I wish to discuss is that of genre, rhythm, and gender in relation to poetry. I propose to focus on semiotic poetics and the rhythms of language, by examining a methodology capable of describing the complex interrelations of sexual politics and poetic voice, utterance, and ideology. This method as I will elaborate it is a feminist dialogics.

The discourse of barrier crossing, genre expectations, and gendered valuations of metre and style raised in discussions such as this one discloses the problematic position of the woman poet in relation to audience. When feminist dialogics was first put forth as a feminist revision of dialogic theory in several recent articles and conference sessions, I thought a satisfying way to read through and into women's texts had arrived.[1] But instead, I found that feminists using dialogic theory were often merely applying the concepts of Mikhail Bakhtin's theories concerning utterance, discourse, and the intersection of languages to women's texts without retooling Bakhtin's gender-blind critical base. I want to posit a feminist dialogics that instead would counter gender assumptions and gaps in Bakhtin's system with Julia Kristeva's semiotic understanding of where language in its different modes arises, and what impels textual linguistic crises.[2]

Feminist dialogics in current critical thought refers to a dialogism of conflicting discourses, and a deconstructionist reading of texts whereby the slippage is not into disjunction but into another, alienated class language. Within the social register these different discourses do not recognize nor receive each other; each assigns different meanings to words, speaks to different ideological ends, and conflicts with users of different semantic lexicons.

This way of reading texts discloses the sexism of the socialist agenda present in Bakhtinian dialogism, which implicitly determines gender as bind-ing as class, and gendered languages as sex-controlled. I am a woman, therefore I do not speak the language of men and my language is in conflict with and miscomprehended by a male audience. The difficulty of this theory is that feminists need to recognize gender as a floating social construct *not* bonded to the biological genes that construct our bodies.

To avoid negotiating the patriarchal implications of a sex determined class system in which speakers cannot cross discourse lines, feminist dialogic theory needs to consider the impact of social and psychological, as well as linguistic formation processes on the individuated speaking subject. "Individuation" refers to separation and autonomy, and bespeaks the cutting off of the self from the institutional powers of family, school, and social groups which control childhood, but also the insertion of self into these and other social institutions by whose rules we agree to abide. Our social contract then, creates another loss of individuation and returns us to a form of infant status within the larger group identities to which we belong. To formulate gender as two restrictive groups ignores the choices we make to simultaneously join various other groups related to race, class, culture, education, and vocation.[3] To clarify meaning, I will refer to male and female as the biological sex, and men and women as those individuals who agree to the behavioral rules society has associated with the sexes. When I speak of a poet or thinker who resists the societal norms of their sex, I refer to their nonfixed self-positioning on a gender continuum.

By viewing gender as a choice or imposition of social identity, something as refusable as class, education or profession, we step beyond the ideological blindspot of a patriarchal prisonhouse of language. We can then foreground the critical traditions of poetics, and utilize this resulting awareness to reread the artistic as well as the social text. This moves us one plane beyond the focus on moments of resistance occurring in the social space of language conflict, allowing us to attend to the traditions of poetry and poetic theory within the framework of a different kind of feminist dialogics.

Two strains of poetic convention have been maintained throughout our literary heritage: The first is recognized in the highly symbolic, culturally encoded, and rule-bound poetic forms of the elevated or high style; the second is known by its impassioned tone, unregulated metre, and organic form. The first is immediately recognizable in the highly intellectual and restrained quality of Pope's verse; the second in the unrestrained and seemingly unregulated quality of the Romantic irregular ode. The gender inflections of regular versus irregular odes, for instance, or of epics that record the public space of shared cultural history versus the private space of internal leaps into the transcendent, is that of culturally encoded "masculine" rationality versus "feminine" irrationality.[4] Because both these forms partake of the high or elevated style, they have been dominated by men poets voicing masculine, even patriarchal concerns. Although the two strains are gender identified, they are both practiced almost entirely by male poets; the gender associations are inscribed via patriarchal myth, so that the regulated forms of public poetic utterance are overseen by Apollo's dictates of light and reason, whereas the irregular, even irrational flights of transcendent poetry are spiritually closest to sibylline babblings.[5] Even the female muse who inspires the poet does so through irrational, nonverbal impulses, not through intellectual argument.

Thus far we have accounted for gender and poetic utterance without ever broaching the problematic status of women and/or dissident poets within this central literary and mythic tradition. What happens when a woman poet uses logical symbolic forms for both domestic—that is, female—concerns, and also for transcendent, or public—that is, male—concerns? Concurrently, what happens when a woman poet accepts the feminine conceptual framework of irrational, even sibylline musings? And, just to complicate matters, what happens when a woman poet outwardly accepts this identification yet structures her babblings according to traditional prosody and metres? These questions will put to the test the following theoretic underpinnings for the feminist dialogics I am proposing, and I will examine them through the work and standard critical reception of Christina Rossetti and Sylvia Plath.

Briefly, the feminist dialogics I am proposing focuses more on the theory of Julia Kristeva than Mikhail Bakhtin, principally because as the first European translator of his sociolinguistic theory, she was early influenced by his concept of the utterance, and the play of this influence on her theoretical redressing of semiotics provides us with the thought structure by which to rethink dialogics. Crucial is Bakhtin's understanding of the speaker as immersed in an ongoing dialogue that constitutes the languages and range of specialized speech systems that speaker uses. Where Bakhtin's theory gapes for Kristeva is in his nondifferentiation between parents and society as providers of the language flow, and in his inclusion of artistic language with other specialized social dialects. For Kristeva, language itself is not the unified word colliding between class differences as it is for Bakhtin, but a split entity imparted to the infant first nonlingually by the mother, and then later by the father as the child begins the process of language acquisition.

That first mother-oriented step into communication is the entrance into the semiotic, where meaning derives from rhythm. This may be bodily rhythms or music, but it is not words. Its adult correlation is the sibylline mutterings and riddles of the transported poet, and Kristeva theorizes that this "poetic language," as she calls such babblings and wordplay (familiar to us in Joyce's *Finnegan's Wake*) has its origin in the mother-child bonds of birth and infancy. The second step into language is the entrance into the symbolic, and it is represented by the unassailable oedipal father who himself represents society and societal dictates. It is this language which we speak every day and which I am speaking now; it is this way of meaning by which we comprehend logically, and through which we philosophize. The symbolic bounds us, and we work through its rules to accomplish meaning; poets who write in the rational high style of public discourse use the symbolic to transcend the everyday and use mathematical metres and highly repetitive patterns to achieve this transcendence. The semiotic, however, with its uncontainable rhythms, pulsations, and erratic music, occasionally irrupts volcano-like into symbolic discourse. This is the muse, the sybil, the mother whose energies are equally divine but close to madness and chaos; these are dangerous energies that transport, but whose mysticisms do not always allow the poet ιο speak meaningfully. These rhythms are also the source of revolution, divergence, and dissent because they come from the seat of difference itself.[6] The battle in the individual psyche that spurs dissent "is never over," as Kristeva remarks, "and the poet shall continue indefinitely to measure himself against the mother, against his mirror image," which results in an "aggressive and musicated discourse of a knowledge that attacks phallic power" (*Desire in Language,* 193).

Where Kristevan theory proves problematic for a feminist perspective is in her insistence on origins, for the mother's difference as madness translates into defining the poet as biologically male, and indeed, Kristeva's mother-child model is based on the male child, whereas woman remains muse and nursemaid. Kristeva is not easily criticized, however, for her notion that the sex of the writer is unimportant because we all have both male and female orientations. This point would seem to refer to gender theory and nullify her theoretic base of biological sex determining a child's relation to society. But it is exactly in the realm of social roles, societal expectations, social history, and literary history that Kristevan theory falls short for the feminist critic.

Where do women poets, perhaps not of the contemporary period, but certainly within recent literary history, who socially attempt to fulfill their predestined roles but who artistically defy them, fit in this schema? It would seem they are mad, particularly if they dissent not only in writing but in life as well. But if they are feminine writers, that is, if they accept their role as supporter and defender of the patriarchy by agreeing to live by and espouse its rules, they may not be mad, but aren't they then unimportant, trivial, feminine? If the purpose of the feminine is to seduce and reproduce the male, why is she writing at all, and if she writes to support the patriarchy, who is her audience except dissident females or young girls not yet fully indoctrinated—that is, unimportant readers? The feminine writer, however popular within her own period, does not survive literary history.[7] It is the dissident who survives, the woman whose gender identification is at least literarily masculine. That is, she defies—an impulse that according to

Kristeva originates in the mother, but is symbolically practiced against the oedipal father by the son. Interestingly, when we question who are the muses for the woman writer who trespasses in the masculine realm of transcendence and symbolic discourse, we must ask, "Can the mother be muse to herself?" When the answer is "probably not," what we find is that the muses are male.

If we look at Christina Rossetti and Sylvia Plath, two poets writing in England but marginalized first by their sex and second by their cultural backgrounds (Rossetti's father was Italian, Plath was American), we find that despite their strong insistence on leading feminine lives, their poetry addresses female concerns via masculine literary tradition. It is the poetry and not the lives that are radicalized, it is the poems which are secretive or angry, which predict the future or mythicize the present, which transcend, or conversely, play with the symbolic, rhythm, and tradition. For both poets, the muse is male, and for both it is this voice of inspiration to which their utterances are directed. Failing to consider the gendered foregrounding of the signifying dialogic moment in these two women's lyrics allows critics to underread the overdetermined inflection of the poetic word in these texts.

The difference in Rossetti's feminized male muse who aids her transcendence by offering her meditative calm instead of unspeakable transport, and Plath's patriarchal muse-target who spurs her anger and her achievement reveals their individual response to gender ideology. It also accounts for critical treatment of Rossetti's work as unimportant and, reflective of her decision to retire from the social world, boring. In the Pre-Raphaelite world of the female muse—of the beautiful, voluptuous, seductive, and tantalizing Lizzie Sidells, Jane Morrises, and Fanny Cornforths—there is little place for Christina Rossetti's Christ, no matter how feminized. Perhaps we can now understand Cecil Y. Lang's famous comment that any working definition of Pre-Raphaelitism "excludes nearly all the poetry of Christina Rossetti (Queen of the Pre-Raphaelites, so called)."[8] The male muse also makes comprehensible critical tendencies to label Sylvia Plath as mad, jealous, uncontrollable. For a poem entitled "Death & Co.," Plath's BBC commentary makes allusions to Blake and the psychological aspects of death, whereas her husband Ted Hughes's biographical note overwrites Plath's explanation of the poem: "The *actual* occasion [for the poem] was a visit by two well-meaning men who invited TH to live abroad at a tempting salary, and who she therefore resented" (*Collected Poems*, 294n).

If we return for a minute to Bakhtinian dialogic theory, it is the addressee who directs the word's reception. For both these women writers, the male muse is the immediate audience, the poem's addressee. Rossetti's love and Plath's hate are imminently tied to the literary tradition of the troubadour's love song, and of the poet singing his private words to an absent mistress.

It is worth considering not only Rossetti's well-known narratives in which men are either absent or consigned to peripheral status (as, for instance, in "Goblin Market," where except for the would-be rapist beast-men, the narrative takes place entirely among women), but also her muse-invoking devotional poems and meditations. In "A Better Resurrection" (Crump, 68), the speaker prays in one refrain after another, "O Jesus, quicken me," "O Jesus, rise in me," "O Jesus, drink of me." The speaker's transformation from living death to containment and vessel of the Christ reveals between the rhythmic reassertions of devastating emptiness and tedium the same imagery as male poets have traditionally used to speak of divine inspiration and muse-inspired poetic language. But where the male poet uses his inspiration to speak to other men, or as Wordsworth declares, "Prophets of Nature, we to them will speak...and we will teach them how" (*Prelude.* xiv. 444, 447) Rossetti addresses a different audience. She uses her poetry to feed Christ with her words and love, not because only he will listen, but because in the end he is the only one qualified to listen, the only one who *can* drink of her.

The most memorable of Plath's male-muse poems remains "Daddy," although "The Beekeeper's Daughter," "Lady Lazarus," and "Lesbos" are also trenchant examples. "You do not do, you do not do" ("Daddy," 222), the speaker intones, reversing the traditional muse-to-poet trajectory, and although the speaker acknowledges the difficulty of writing within patriarchy ("Every woman adores a Fascist," she notes), by the end of the poem both she and the community have killed off this muse whose only gift has been to "bit[e] my pretty red heart in two" (ll. 48, 56). The speaker is at once adult woman and little girl, at once adoring and hating, acceding and resisting. It is out of this conflict with and final discarding of the patriarch and the roles he imposes on her that the woman poet can irrupt into speech, reversing the cultural symbolic mode and intoning sibylline rhythms that call us back to childhood and the nonsensical yet often politically radical nursery rhymes learned from our mothers. Interestingly, when the male muse is absent, as in "Lesbos" where two embittered women share their hate, the speaker says "Now I am silent, hate/Up to my neck,/Thick, thick./I do not speak" (ll. 64–66). Irruption is prevented by feminine role playing in the social institution of patriarchal womanhood. Even the subversive hatred these speakers feel can only encode their revulsion in the repetitious but non-rhythmic mutterings of self-enforcing silence.

Beyond the dissidence the male muse allows the woman poet, what historical valuations are put on a woman like Christina Rossetti who outwardly accepts her gender role while poetically traversing male transcendent ground? Her resisting voice is not seen as revolt but as undemanding difference, and *her* transport is critically less important than endless scholarly speculations on her love life, and the possible real life names behind her poetic figures. The trivialization of the serious woman poet of the nineteenth century should hardly surprise us, but to find the same treatment of a woman poet in the mid-twentieth century is less easily swallowed. In the poem "Daddy," Plath is heavily criticized for identifying her speaker with the Holocaust victims, as if the philosophical, moral, and ethical issue of geno-cide is tainted by her touch, and is beyond her imaginative ken. Likewise, the strictly regulated metre of her poetry is dismissed in favor of a reading that focuses on her multiple suicide attempts and nervous breakdowns, thus emphasizing the irrational and unregulated aspects of her work.

Let me conclude by asking: Is Plath, like the Sybil, condemned to mis-readings by those who come to hear riddles, expecting not to understand? Is Rossetti's devotional work to be always viewed as tiresome plaints by a lovelorn romantic? If these women had not bound their lives with the tra-ditional feminine roles of daughter and sister, wife and mother, would their sex have so determined the reading of their gender resistant poetry? The dialogic interaction between female speaker-poet and her male muse articulates a gender conflict which feminist dialogics is peculiarly well situated to analyze and which traditional criticism is peculiarly well situated to ignore.

NOTES

1.   See Wayne C. Booth's early interest in the interaction between feminist criticism and Bakhtinian dialogics in "Freedom of Interpretation: Bakhtin and the Challenge of Feminist Criticism," *Critical Inquiry* 9 (1982): 45–76. More recently, Laurie Finke has written thoughtfully on the need for a feminist dialogics: "The Rhetoric of Marginality: Why I Do Feminist Theory," *Tulsa Studies in Women's Literature* 5 (1986): 251–72. The 1987 meeting of the MLA in San Francisco devoted several sessions to Bakhtin, including a special session entitled "Toward a Theory of Feminist Dialogics" chaired by Dale M. Bauer and Janet McKinstry, with papers by Kristina Straub, Diane Price Herndl, Jeanne Campbell Reesman, and Peter Hitchcock.

For interesting parallels, see Alice Jardine's "The Speaking Subject: The Positivities of Alienation," in *Gynesis: Configurations of Woman and Modernity* (Ithaca: Cornell University Press, 1985), 105–17; and Teresa de Lauretis's "The Technology of Gender," in *Technologies of Gender* (Bloomington: Indiana University Press, 1987), 1–30.

2.   Kristeva's *Revolution in Poetic Language,* trans. Margaret Waller (New York: Columbia University Press, 1984), figures most importantly for the founda-tions of my analysis; however, her recuperation and appropriation of Bakhtin's work in "Word, Dialogue, and Novel" and "The Bounded Text" (both in *Desire*

in Language, ed. Leon S. Roudiez (New York: Columbia University Press, 1980, 64–91 and 36–63), and "The Ruin of a Poetics," in *Russian Formalism: A Collection of Articles and Texts in Translation,* eds. Stephen Baum and John E. Bowlt (New York: Barnes and Noble Books, 1973; 102–19), all of which reflect her encounter with Bakhtin after the work on *Revolution,* are the significant essays to work with.

      3.   Pierre Bourdieu's sociological analysis of the social field produces a markedly sophisticated reading of the construction of class subjectivity under capitalist society. Bourdieu does not, however, view gender as more than one among several factors in the general account: *Distinction: A Social Critique of the Judgement of Taste,* trans. Richard Nice (Cambridge: Harvard University Press, 1984), and "Symbolic Power," trans. Richard Nice, in *Critique of Anthropology* 4 (Summer 1979), 77–85. The classic analysis of the construction of subjectivity in relation to ideology, despite current critiques of its underlying non-gendered essentialism, remains Louis Althusser's "Ideology and Ideological State Apparatuses," in *Lenin and Philosophy,* trans. Ben Brester (New York: Monthly Review Press, 1971; 127–86). Foucault's *The History of Sexuality* (vol 1; trans. Robert Hurley. New York: Vintage/Random House, 1980) remains seminal to any current thought on the socialization of gender; Foucault's work has recently undergone feminist analysis, as in *Feminism and Foucault,* eds. Irene Diamond and Lee Quinby (Boston: Northeastern University Press, 1988).

      For feminist analyses of the social construction of gender, see Sherry B. Ortner and Harriet Whitehead, *Sexual Meanings: The Cultural Construction of Gender and Sexuality* (Cambridge: Cambridge University Press, 1981); Judith Newton and Deborah Rosenfelt, eds., *Feminist Criticism and Social Change* (New York: Methuen, 1985); Joan Kelly, *Women, History, and Theory* (Chicago: University of Chicago Press, 1984); Gayle Rubin, "The Traffic in Women: Notes Toward a Political Economy of Sex," in *Toward an Anthropology of Women,* ed. Rayna Reiter (New York: Monthly Review Press, 1975), 157–210.

      4.   Simone de Beauvoir's analysis of feminine "immanence" and masculine "transcendence" in *The Second Sex* is the landmark text for any discussion of gendered discourse (trans. and ed. H.M. Parshley, New York: Alfred A. Knopf, 1953); see also Helene Cixous and Catherine Clement's *La Jeune Nee* (Paris: Union d'Editions, 1975) as an example of the psychoanalytic treatment of gendering in language. Margaret Homans' *Women Writers and Poetic Identity* (Princeton, NJ: Princeton University Press, 1980) is one of the earliest works to explore the gender-genre connection in the poetic field.

      5.   For a Kristevan description of these two Western poetic strains, see "The Novel as Polylogue" in *Desire in Language,* 192–93.

      6.   The basic text for this discussion is Kristeva's *Revolution in Poetic Language,* the first third of her doctoral dissertation. It was written as a semiotic analysis of discourse, and is more influenced by Roland Barthes, her thesis director, while her subsequent work shows her increasing interest in Freudian and Lacanian psychoanalytic theories of language.

7.   It is an interesting project, for example, to see how many women wrote poetry during the Romantic period for which we have only its six canonized men poets. Susan Levin has recently unearthed poems by Dorothy Wordsworth in the Dove Cottage Library, published in *Dorothy Wordsworth and Romanticism,* New Brunswick, NJ: Rutgers, The State University Press, 1987), but work is in progress on more celebrated writers as well; see Marlon B. Ross's *The Contours of Masculine Desire: Romanticism and the Rise of Women's Poetry* (New York: Oxford University Press, 1989). The Women Writers Project is responsible for furthering this interest, and the Romantic editor, Stuart Curran, estimates that more than 500 women poets published during what we have been conceiving of as a male-dominant literary period.

8.   *The Pre-Raphaelites and Their Circle,* ed. Cecil Y. Lang (Chicago: University of Chicago Press, 1975), xxvii.

REFERENCES

Bakhtin, M.M. 1981. *The Dialogic Imagination: Four Essays,* translated by Caryl Emerson and Michael Holquist; edited by Michael Holquist. Austin, TX: University of Texas Press.

———. 1986. *Speech Genres and Other Late Essays,* translated by Vern W. McGee; edited by Caryl Emerson and Michael Holquist. Austin, TX: University of Texas Press.

Kristeva, Julia. 1980. *Desire in Language: A Semiotic Approach to Literature and Art,* edited by Leon S. Roudiez. New York: Columbia University Press.

———. 1984. *Revolution in Poetic Language,* translated by Margaret Waller. New York: Columbia University Press.

———. 1986. *The Kristeva Reader,* edited by Toril Moi. New York: Columbia University Press.

Lang, Cecil B. 1975. *The PreRaphaelites and Their Circle.* Chicago, IL: University of Chicago Press.

McGann, Jerome J. 1980. "Re-Evaluating Christina Rossetti." *Victorian Studies* 23. Reprinted as "Christina Rossetti's Poems: A New Edition and a Revaluation," in *The Beauty of Inflections: Literary Investigations in Historical Method and Theory.* Oxford: Clarendon Press, 1988. Pp. 207-31.

———. 1983. "The Religious Poetry of Christine Rossetti." *Critical Inquiry* 10. Reprinted in *The Beauty of Inflections.* Oxford: Clarendon Press, 1988. Pp. 232–52.

Newman, Charles, ed. 1970. *The Art of Sylvia Plath: A Symposium.* Bloomington, IN: Indiana University Press.

Perloff, Marjorie. 1979. "Sylvia Plath's 'Sivvy' Poems: A Portrait of the Poet as Daughter." In *Sylvia Plath: New Views on the Poetry,* edited by Gary Lane. Baltimore, DE: Johns Hopkins University Press.

Plath, Sylvia. 1981. *The Collected Poems,* edited by Ted Hughes. New York: Harper and Row.

Rosenblatt, Jon. 1979. *Sylvia Plath: The Poetry of Initiation.* Chapel Hill, NC: University of North Carolina Press.

Rosenblum, Dolores. 1979. "Christina Rossetti: The Inward Pose," in *Shakespeare's Sisters,* edited by Sandra Gilbert and Susan Gubar. Bloomington, IN: Indiana University Press. Pp. 82-98.

Rossetti, Christina. 1979. *The Complete Poems of Christina Rossetti,* edited by Rebecca Crump. Baton Rouge, LA: Louisiana University Press.

———. 1904. *The Poetical Works of Christina Georgina Rossetti,* edited by William Michael Rossetti. London: Macmillan.

Stevenson, Anne. 1989. *Bitter Fame: A Life of Sylvia Plath.* Boston, MA: Houghton Mifflin.

Vološinov, V.N. 1976. "Discourse in Life and Discourse in Art (Concerning Sociological Poetics)," in *Freudianism: A Marxist Critique,* translated by I.R. Titunik, edited by I.R. Titunik and Neal R. Bruss. New York: Academic Press. Pp. 93–116.

Wordsworth, William. 1988. *Poetical Works,* edited by Thomas Hutchinson, rev. E. De Selincourt. Oxford: Oxford University Press.

CHAPTER 9

Six Readers Reading
Six Photographs

Rebecca Bryant Lockridge
University of Southern Maine

Understanding how perceivers make visual messages meaningful is a problem for scholars. For example, even when photographic critics read the same image, they often give widely divergent interpretations. In recent interviews, A.D. Coleman (1986) and Allan Sekula (1986) discussed a photograph by Walker Evans. Coleman talked about the "sad quality" of the image, saying it pictured a "lived-in environment." Alternately, Coleman focused on the relationship between the objects pictured in the image and the life activities that might take place there.

> *...that sense of people constructing rituals and ritual spaces and special places out of the most meager and barren of means. A couple of small cheap vases here and so forth seems to construct almost an altar, in effect....the fireplace is not in use...There's a table in front of the fireplace at this point, so let's assume it's summer. Or warm weather. And the fireplace I suppose would be the center of family activity in winter. [It] remains the center because it's become this kind of little altarpiece...*

On the other hand, while Sekula also mentioned the objects in the image—"a fireplace, a wooden mantel, shoes on the mantel, calendar, photos and the hand print in the paint, a child's hand print"—he placed the same photograph in a genre category. For him the image represented

Note: The critics interviewed were nominated by randomly selected members of the Society for Photographic Education, who were asked to nominate critics whose opinions they found particularly useful for understanding the messages transmitted by photographs.

something of a fantasy of a kind of yeoman sensibility that is spare, and pure and clean, despite adversity, and yet at the same time it's a photograph which is an extraordinarily detailed inventory of a segment of material culture.

Sekula also identified the Evans photo as a "*model* for some kind of descriptive practice, if one can win that model away from a sort of aestheticist direction which has been taken."

The following discussion demonstrates how value-laden constructs (which I define as belonging to either the feminine or the masculine principles) are embedded in the readings of the six photographic critics who participated in a study of six photographs. These gendered principles "guided" both the oral and written explanations critics gave about the meaning of photographs.

The mythological motifs of the feminine and masculine principles are symbolic principles of opposites long used to define human place in societies throughout the world. Based on assumed "essentialist characteristics" (that is, what is assumed "natural" to men and women), masculine and feminine principles go beyond the levels of sex (biologically determined) and gender (socially determined) behavior in that they are value patterns inherent in both visual and verbal symbols across time and cultures.

Carl Jung's definition of these principles as Logos versus Eros is well known. Jung framed the masculine principle in terms of Logos, "the word, hence rationality, logic, intellect, achievement, and the feminine principle (anima) as Eros (originally Psyche's lover, hence relatedness)" (Samuels, 1985, 210). He identified the feminine and masculine principles as archetypes of the collective unconscious, embedded in the structure of the human psyche and expressed symbolically. For Jung the human psyche consisted of a complex of opposites held in dynamic tension. Archetypes were "inherited thought patterns," sometimes described as "structured intuition" (Samuels, 1985, 29) or a priori perceptive tendencies used to order experience with the world; the masculine and feminine principles were the most crucial of these. In 1944, Jung wrote, "This primordial pair of opposites symbolizes every conceivable pair of opposites that may occur: hot and cold, light and dark, north and south, dry and damp, good and bad, conscious and unconscious" (Jung, 1974, 226). Like all archetypes, the masculine and feminine principles had positive and negative poles of "experience and emotions"—which must be balanced for psychological health (Samuels, 1985, 30). Although the energy generated between the positive and negative poles of these principles shaped *all* women and men, for Jung the feminine principle was more "natural" to women, the masculine to men.

THE STUDY

Based on findings of a previous study (Lockridge, 1983) that indicated the fruitfulness of such an approach, photographic critics were asked to read six photographs which the researcher had predetermined to be representative examples of the masculine and feminine principle in visual form. The collected discourse was examined for the presence of patterns of response that could be characterized as masculine-principled or feminine-principled.

This study was based on the assumption that neither observation nor language can be value free, thus all interpretive observations embody some perspective that assumes some value system. As Swanson (1977) puts it, whether critics are engaged in scientific inquiry or in rhetorical criticism, they all "work with the experience of objects rather than with objects themselves, unfiltered by experience" (212).

Based on Jung, the research question was, "Does a preference for either the feminine or the masculine principle structure the experience of a photographic critic in relation to a visual 'text' (photograph) under scrutiny?" All six critics who agreed to participate were male. The collected discourse was content analyzed for constructs consisting of a single word or an idiomatic phase. (For a thorough discussion of methodological procedures see Lockridge, 1989).

Space constraints allow for only a brief discussion of procedures and findings. Following is an explanation of how criteria for the masculine and feminine principle were established (for content analysis purposes), how the MP and FP photographs were selected, and how the masculine and feminine and androgynous (MP/FP) principles guided the interpretations Coleman, Sekula, and four other critics made of the Walker Evans photograph "Floyd Burroughs's Bedroom, Hale County, Alabama, 1936" (See Figure 1, page 106).

Derivation of Masculine/Feminine Principle for Content Analysis

Criteria for establishing the masculine principle and feminine principle as tools for discourse analysis were derived by two means. First, several sources outlining characteristics of these principles were consulted. These characteristics were synthesized with those from additional sources which might make no reference to the MP and FP as such, but which nevertheless described similar dichotomous characteristics. For example, Robert Ornstein (1972) identifies a "duality in human consciousness long recognized in other cultures" that acknowledges the complementary presence of "intellect" and "intuitive" poles (64). Ornstein argues that all conceptualizing, including that of the scientist, combines these two dualistic modes. Although he refers to the Chinese yang-yin symbol (opposites existing in dynamic, harmonious relationship) and its "day-night" metaphor with "male and female poles," his table of polar concepts ("Two Modes of Consciousness") does not label these as MP or FP dichotomies (67).

Second, operating under the epistemological assumption that similar value "ideas" exist in words and pictures alike, the MP/FP characteristics identified in the verbal sources were translated into visual symbols based on a determination of correspondence between the two modes.

Verbal

Verbal sources used to establish criteria for the MP/FP dichotomies included dualities appearing in mythic, psychoanalytic, feminist, social scientific, artistic, and scientific books and journal articles by Jung (1944), Neumann (1954, 1974), Singer (1977), Freud (1933), de Beauvoir (1953), Bachofen (1861), Appignanesi (1973) and others. These both relate to and differ from Jungian notions of Logos and Eros. For example, whereas Jung identified Logos (MP) as active and Eros (FP) as passive, in this study these were aligned with Eastern philosophy (Hindu and Buddhist tantra) with the masculine designated as static because it is "essentially cognitive; wisdom, realization, beatitude and spiritual illumination." The feminine becomes dynamic—the principle of "movement, energy and activity" (Singer, 1977, 177).

Helene Deutsch (1944), a follower of Freud, also modified Freud's and Jung's notions of "feminine passivity" to "activity directed inward," thus feminizing the interiorization of sensibility which she opposed to masculinized attention to concerns of the exterior world (1973, 190). Deutsch's construction resembles other Jungian comments:

> *To feminine consciousness Jung grants the realm of "infinite nuances of personal relationships which usually escape the man entirely." But to the man he grants the "wide fields of commerce, politics, technology, science, and the whole realm of the applied masculine mind." (Samuels, 1985, 219)*

Moreover, post-Jungian Erich Neumann (1954) construes the masculine "consciousness" as embodying the development of culture, the rules and values of civilization that provide order to human existence, and the evolution of the individual and the ego. Feminine "consciousness" embodies life and nature; an orientation toward the tragedies of human life (birth/death), chaos, and mystery; and submission to the whole versus the alienated individual separate from the collective. Neumann's notions place "civilization," "order," and "isolation" at the masculine-principled pole of the MP/FP construct and feminine-principled "nature," "chaos," and "connection" at the other. In addition, many scholars (among them Simone de Beauvoir, 1953) speak of the masculine as a cultural "norm" and the feminine as the "other."

Furthermore, we might frame Jung's polarities of spirit (MP)/matter (FP) as religion (MP)/magic (FP). In *The Great Mother*, Neumann (1955, 1974) notes that although "the feminine is by nature unable to cast off materiality," due to birth-giving and nurturing, which extend to earth fertility and sexuality, there is "a patriarchal consciousness that says [to quote Bachofen (1948)] 'The victory of the male lies in the spiritual principle'" (1974, 57). This construction places masculinized divine incarnations (religion) in opposition to feminized materiality construed as "magic authority" (Wehr, 1987, 107). As Neumann explains it, "magic, which was originally governed by the Feminine, began no doubt as 'food magic' and developed by way of fertility magic into sexual or 'love magic'" (1974, 172). [See Table 1 for summary.]

Many scholars are wary of offering "fixed" characteristics of the MP and FP. Even scholars interested in these principles as Jung characterized them accuse him of sexist bias, in aligning women with personal relationships/nature and men with civilization and the "applied mind," claiming these have helped solidify stereotypic misconceptions of women as emotional and men as logical—contributing to the devaluing of women (e.g., Lauter and Rupprecht, 1985).

Moreover, many writings about the masculine and feminine principles tend to move loosely back and forth between characterizing a contrasexual cognitive system and identifying gender behavior traits associated with real men and women (e.g., Lauter and Rupprecht, 1985; Nicholson, 1989). Jung has been criticized for his lack of clarity in this regard (Singer, 1977; Samuels, 1985; Wehr, 1987).

Although these are intriguing issues, my purpose is not to question the correctness of the polarized conceptions offered here as representative of the MP and FP, to present the ones listed as "fixed," nor to associate the MP with personality characteristics of real men nor the FP with real women. Rather, I offer these superordinate constructs and their conversion into visual form as tentative suggestions. I intend only to demonstrate how these dichotomous principles may be used to structure experience expressed through oral, written, and visual forms and how adherence to one pole or the other may influence our interpretations of the world.

The conceptual position I take agrees with the transtemporal, transcultural, and transsexual positions held by post-Jungians Samuels and Singer. Samuels and Singer urge scholars to transcend both Jung's possible patriarchal bias and sex-linked notions of social/cultural constructions of

Table 1. **Common Dichotomous Divisions of the Masculine and Feminine**

Source	Masculine	Feminine
I Ching * (T'ai chi)	*The Creative:* heaven, Yang.	*The Receptive:* earth, Yin.
Medieval Alchemists **	*Sol:* sun, gold, symbol for light, strength, energy, power.	*Luna:* moon, dark, receptive source of vitality and refuge in times of difficulty or need.
Tantra ** (Hindu & Buddhist)	*Static principle:* cognitive wisdom, realization, beauty and spiritual illumination.	*Dynamic principle:* connotative, movement, energy, activity.
NUMEROUS SOURCES	*Patriarchal ideology:* celestial god, ruling principle heaven-ward, axis mundi, dominion over nature.	*Matriarchal ideology:* earth goddess, ruling principle earth bound, circular (snake with tail in mouth), at one with nature.
	Light, day, sun.	Dark, night, moon.
	Spirit.	Matter.
	Rational.	Emotional.
	Clarity.	Mystery.
	Scientific.	Mystic.
	Order.	Chaos.
	Intellectual.	Intuitive.
	Objective, power and violence, dominant, outward- or world-oriented.	Subjective, emphasis on sexuality, subordinate, psychic or inner-oriented.
	Norm.	Other.
	Patriarchy: sees polarities in human nature, males dominant and more valuable.	*Matriarchy:* sees totality and unity of human nature.
PSYCHOANALYTIC: S. Freud & others ("Femininity" in *New Introductory Lectures on Psychoanalysis,* Vol. 22)	Emphasis on civilization.	Emphasis on life and nature.

Table 1. *continued*

Source	Masculine	Feminine
C. Jung	Total psyche (self), masculine apart from maleness; animus = masculine consciousness in women.	Feminine apart from femaleness; anima = feminine consciousness in men.
	Logos.	Eros.
E. Neumann* *(The Origins and History of Consciousness)*	Consciousness and intellect.	Consciousness and intuition. Creative element, principle of energy and change.
J. Singer** *(Androgyny)*	Individual approach.	Cooperative approach.
Feminist.		
S. de Beauvoir*	Transcendent ego-consciousness: I, self; will.	Immanent, other
S. Firestone* *(The Dialectic of Sex)*	Materialistic, scientific, technological mode.	Humanistic, aesthetic, idealistic mode.
S. Griffin *(Woman and Nature)*	Patriarchy requires separation of mind from emotion, body from soul.	Women, matter, nature, earth.
Social Scientific:		
K. Marx *(Economic and Philosophic Manuscripts)*	Production: objectified individuality. Object of labor: duplication of man in world of own creation.	
	Capitalism: atomization, alienation.	*Socialism:* communal bonds.
J. Campbell *(Myths to Live By)*	Defines male role through "male societies."	Defines female role through life, nature orientation.
Blackburn***	Intellectual.	Sensuous.
Oppenheimer***	Time, history.	Timelessness, eternity.
Artistic:		
L. Appignanesi *(Femininity and the Creative Imagination)*	Concerned with modes of production and exchange; outer, "objective" world.	Mystification, interiorization, introspection, mediation; inward, "subjective" life.

*NOTE: Sources which identify their dichotomous categories as masculine- or feminine-principled.

**SOURCE: J. Singer, *Androgyny* (Garden City, New York: Doubleday, 1977).

***SOURCE: Robert Ornstein, *The Psychology of Consciousness* (San Francisco: W. H. Freeman and Company, 1972): 67.

"feminine" and "masculine" behavior and focus instead on Jung's *aim* of valuing the Feminine equally with the Masculine, because "then we may have a
tool, even a methodology, for understanding our cultural vicissitudes"
(Samuels, 1985, 229). In Singer's (1977) view, because the FP and MP
exist in the human psyche, individuals have a *choice* about what FP/MP value
pattern will structure their experience (unlike biological sex or socially determined appropriate gender behavior). Thus the psyche of either a man or a
woman can function *more* completely within the parameters of *either*
principle. For Singer, an individual who makes sense of events by applying
both principles with similar frequency is functioning under the *principle of
androgyny* (21).

Visual

The Masculine/Feminine Principle and Pictorial Components.   Briefly,
the assigning of MP or FP characteristics to the subject matter and structural
forms comprising a photograph was made as follows:
    Subject matter. For example, given the frequent aligning of the mas-
culine pole with culture/civilization, the researcher categorized static
human-made objects of civilization (cars, buildings, monuments, etcetera)
in a photograph as MP. Similarly, the words used by critics to name such "still-
life" objects were classified MP. So too, the researcher assumed that images
of courthouses or schools, or signs announcing "Stop" and "Go" referred to
the laws, rules, and conventions of culture, as did words such as "respectability," "status," or "social reform." (MP).
    Based on frequent aligning of the feminine pole with personal rela-
tionships/nature, the researcher classified photographs of humans engaged
in life activities (dancing, talking, eating, etcetera) as FP, depending, for example, on whether a person was pictured alone (MP isolation) or in a group
of two or more people (FP connection) (Singer, 1977; Neumann, 1954).
Similarly, photos picturing (and words naming) activities such as "sociability,"
"sexuality," "energy," "change," "nursing" were characterized as FP, along with
natural things (snow, trees, rocks).
    Structural forms. Based on the value idea that the MP is symbolized
by the sun, day, and spirit and the FP by the moon, night, and matter (as in
the "light of the spirit" versus the "dark of earth or matter"), *light*, even-toned
pictorial tonalities (conveying the open light of day) were aligned with the
MP. *Dark* tonalities (conveying the shadowy, mysterious night) and high-con-
trast tonalities (which unify light and dark and activate the visual field of an
image) were aligned with the FP. Masculine-principled light is also associated
with "intelligence" and "consciousness," feminine-principled dark with
"intuitive" "unconsciousness."

Pictorial *space* that encloses the pictured subject via dark tones or the enclosing *geometric forms* of the triangle and circle connotes FP "intimacy" and "connection," as in the mandala or the Urobos (Neumann, 1955, 1974). In MP space, forms are "separated" or "isolated" from each other. This sense of separation is sometimes aided by even-toned lighting, and sometimes by horizontal and/or vertical lines that tend to move the viewer's eye out of the pictorial field of the image (conveying interest in the world outside the pictorial frame).

Pictorial components that contribute to a sense of *balance* are considered MP because balance connotes "order, harmony, and clarity." These include horizontal and vertical straight lines, simple shapes, and symmetrical relationships between forms suggesting that "time" has been stopped, organized, and stabilized so as to reduce *movement* or change and to reduce human tension. The FP opposite would convey "complexity," through curved lines, complex relationships between positive and negative space, asymmetrical balance, and motion to suggest the sense of chaos, struggle, accident, discord, change, and the irrationality of human life.

In all visual works there is a *dynamic* interplay between subject matter and formal aspects that have *tension*-heightening or tension-reducing tendencies. More tension exists in the interaction of opposites, less in complementaries. Examples of tension-producing subject matter are scenes of people living in unhealthy, "abnormal" conditions or the juxtaposition of young and old or beautiful and ugly. Formal elements that tend to cause tension are camera angles other than the "normal" eye-level camera angle (high, low, birdseye, oblique); opposing tonalities of light and dark; and complex relationships between positive and negative space.

Facial expressions (smile, frown, tears) suggest the emotional, subjective, traits of the FP, whereas passive facial expressions convey MP objective detachment. A direct stare is considered masculine-principled since it conveys a "conscious" confrontation with the world outside the photograph. A deflected gaze is FP, conveying, instead, attention to the "interior sensibilities" of the pictured subject, either to something pictured in the image, or of submission to feelings.

Photographs Read

The set of six photographs chosen by the researcher to represent the masculine and feminine principles were not especially well known black-and-white photographs from published texts. These ranked higher on four semantic differential scales, for their adherence to the FP and MP, than did other photographs in the researcher's collection of FP and MP images.

The four scales were based on pictorial categories typical of aesthetic analysis. Two of these scales ranked visual elements observable in the image—(1) *Contents* (*what* is pictured; i.e., subject matter) and (2) *Pictorial Components* (structural forms) of a photograph. Two scales ranked verbal interpretations of the visual message conveyed by the relationship of contents and pictorial components—(1) *Affective Qualities* (characteristics attributed to the image by the viewer) such as "clarity," "intelligent," "alienating" (MP) and "complex," "mysterious," "comforting" (FP) and (2) *Themes* (*idea* or point of view in the image). MP examples—rules of civilization; technology; FP examples—personal relationships; imperfections of human life; nature.

Semantic differential scores from one to five were assigned for the elements identified in each of the four main categories. Average ratings were assigned for each and across all four categories as well. The following three photographs were selected to represent the feminine principle (average scores included): "Okefenokee Swamp, Georgia, 1937," Margaret Bourke-White (4.75); "Wuthering Heights, 1945," Bill Brandt (4.85); and "From the Flashlight Series, Andover, Connecticut, 1978," Siegfried Halus (4.75). For the masculine principle: "Hale County, Alabama, 1936," Walker Evans (1.17); "Train Crossing the Desert Near Kelso, California, 1980," William Garnett (1.05); and "Central Park, 1980," Tod Papageorge (1.05).

Analysis of Data into Content Categories

Based on findings from a previous study (Lockridge, 1983) the researcher expected that the six critics could be characterized as preferring the MP, the FP, or the androgynous (MP/FP) principle for their explanatory value (versus constructs neutral to these principles). Although the coding classification scheme was flexible enough to allow value patterns other than the MP and FP to emerge, the researcher's expectations were verified on the basis of analysis of (1) frequencies and ratios of a total of 12,578 single-word or idiomatic phrase constructs coded by the researcher and a co-coder and (2) analysis of the relationship between superordinate and subordinate constructs critics used to structure their readings. Seven superordinate, dichotomous FP and MP construct categories emerged from the data, along with six neutral categories. The FP categories were Nature, Dark, Non-Mind, Magic, Connection, Chaos, and Other. The MP categories were Civilization, Light, Mind, Religion, Isolation, Order, and Norm. Table 2 lists examples of superordinate and subordinate constructs used by the critics.

Based on value patterns found in the discourse, the critics were designated "fixed" on one of the principles if they consistently preferred constructs of that principle to express their experience with a photograph, regardless of whether it was an MP or an FP photo. Coleman (FP) and Sekula

Table 2. **Examples of Masculine-Principled, Feminine-Principled and Neutral Constructs Found in the Discourse of Critic-Participants**

Masculine-Principled Constructs	Feminine-Principled Constructs
Civilization	*Nature*
City	Landscape
Rules of civilization	Life processes
(status, respectability,	People
responsibility)	Irresponsibility
Things of civilization	Things of nature
(books, clothes, camera)	(clouds, rain, flowers)
Culture	Energy and change
Society	Sociability
Successful	Sexual
Light	*Dark*
Illumination	Shadows
Flash	Darkness
Clear	Murky
Sun	Moon
Mind	*Non-Mind*
Conscious	Unconscious
Intelligent	Sentimental
Idea	Confusion
Certain	Poignant
Study	Suggestive
Established	Sad-quality
	Sensibility
Religion	*Magic*
Priest-like	Mystical powers
Sacred (established ritual)	Unpredictable events
Ideal	Mysterious
Ceremonial	Illusion
Altar	People constructed rituals
	Wall Sings
Isolation	*Connection*
Aloneness	Relatedness
Private	Public
Detachment	Intimacy
Divergent	Together
Discontinuous	Associated
Opposition	United

Table 2.   *continued*

Masculine-Principled Constructs	Feminine-Principled Constructs
Order	*Chaos*
Lack of tension	Tension
Pure	Grimy
Constraint	Trouble
Critical	Craziness
Clean	Adversity
Obvious	Confused
Norm	*Other*
Standard	Difference
Always	Occasionally
Ordinary	Extraordinary
Typical	Exception
Familiar	Strange
Average	Alien

Neutral Constructs

Semiotics	*Photography*
Signs	Image
Icons	Composition
Symbolic	Picture
Trope	Frame
Rhetorically	Illustrate
Indexical	Transcription
	Captions
	Heading
Values	*Pictorial Components*
Wonderful	Accent
Eloquent	Mark
Gorgeous	Tone
Remarkable	Shape
Beautiful	Form
Egregious	Direction (up, down, back, foreground)
Measurements	*Power*
Small	Power of the image
Large	Power of people
Full	Power of camera

(MP) were identified as fixed critics. Max Kozloff and Andy Grundberg were found to be androgynous-fixed in that they frequently used both MP and FP constructs; however, Kozloff verbalized his experience with the photos most often with FP constructs, whereas Grundberg relied most often on MP constructs.

If the critic preferred one of the principles in general for its explanatory value, but gave FP readings when the photograph was FP and MP readings when the photograph was MP (thereby demonstrating a response to the principle pictured in the photograph), he was characterized as a fluid critic. Bill Jay's readings were androgynous-fluid FP, Allan Trachtenberg's androgynous-fluid MP. Analysis of the discourse collected when all critics read the same photograph showed these value-laden patterns.

Reading of Walker Evans Photograph "Hale County, Alabama, 1936"

Although we might assume that all six critics would attribute MP pictorial traits to the MP Evans image, and MP interpretations as to what the photo was "about" (theme) it seems *most* likely that they would have noticed the same pictured "facts" (subject matter and formal structure). (See Figure 1). That is, it would seem that all critics would mention the fireplace, vases, shoes, and other MP objects of civilization and comment on the MP even-toned lighting, eye-level camera angle, and cross-shaped geometric forms. Instead, the data verified the researcher's expectation that although a given critic mentioned *some* of the pictorial elements of the MP principle, in general a critic "saw" more contents, identified more pictorial components, ascribed more affective qualities, and interpreted more themes "consubstantial" (Burke, 1950, 1969, 62) with his preferred construction system— MP, FP, or MP/FP. For example, Coleman (fixed FP) mentioned many Nature items and construed MP items in relation to FP notions. Sekula (fixed MP), on the other hand, both "saw" and construed aspects of the Evans photograph in relation to the superordinate construct Civilization (MP).

Contents/Pictorial Components. Analysis of the "fact" of the fireplace pictured in the Evans photograph illustrates this finding. All critics except Sekula paid particular attention to the fireplace when explaining the image to the researcher. For Sekula (1986) the fireplace was part of a "visual list" since the image was an "extraordinarily detailed inventory of a segment of material culture" (Civilization). Androgynous MP critics Grundberg (fixed) and Trachtenberg (fluid) made similar readings. Grundberg (1986) referred to the "vernacular architecture of this fireplace with this table in front of it" (a

Figure 1.   Walker Evans, "Fireplace and Objects in a Bedroom of Floyd
Burroughs's Home, Hale County, Alabama, Summer 1936." *Let Us Now
Praise Famous Men.* 1941. Plate 8. 1960. Plate 9. Farm Security
Administration Collection in the Library of Congress, Washington, D.C.

material object indigenous to a place—Civilization). Trachtenberg (1986) described the fireplace as "altar-like, particularly with the table covered with some sort of white cloth" (a metaphor of Religion [MP] conveyed through human-made objects of Civilization).

In contrast, Coleman (fixed FP) also said the fireplace was "an altar, in effect" (Religion), but construed it in relation to FP Connection/Nature as a "center of family activity in winter" (Coleman, 1986). Androgynous FP critics Kozloff (fixed) and Jay (fluid) read the fireplace using both MP and FP constructs. Kozloff (1986) called it a "miniature shrine (Religion)—[part of] a setting of inanimate objects (Civilization) as relevatory of a style of life" (Nature). Jay (1986) thought the decorations on top of the mantle were "the mark of the human—of the man who lived here [who] wanted some decoration so he made these scallops on the mantlepiece—but of different sizes." ("The hand of man" is a metaphor for material culture [Civilization] construed by Jay in terms of human activity—Nature). In addition, Jay's emphasis on the dissimilar scallops invokes the construct Other—that which is not the norm.

In sum, all six critics reported on the fireplace in relation to Religion and/or Civilization (MP), with the MP critics relying solely on these categories and the FP critics adding comments subsumed by the FP categories Connection, Nature, and Other.

As for the "facts" of structural forms, there was some variation from the MP/FP pattern identified above. Only Coleman, Grundberg, and Trachtenberg mentioned any forms in the photo. They used MP and FP constructs equally to examine how Evans's asymmetrical (FP) framing of the photograph affected the visual message of the otherwise symmetrical (MP) image.

Affective Qualities. Although the attribution of characteristics to the photo followed the typical MP/FP patterns, only Coleman, Sekula, and Trachtenberg mentioned these characteristics. Coleman (fixed FP) thought the Evans photo had a "sad quality" with some "emotionally positive notes" (FP feeling/Non-mind) (Coleman, 1986). Sekula (fixed MP) said the image evoked a "yeoman sensibility that was spare and pure and clean, despite adversity" (Sekula, 1986). "Sensibility" (Non-mind) was construed in relation to a social type ("yeoman"/Civilization). So too, FP "adversity" (Chaos) was read by Sekula in relation to "spare," "pure," "clean" qualities of MP harmony or Order. Trachtenberg (androgynous-fluid MP) remarked "There's something sacred—some way in which that wall sings" (Religion/Magic) (Trachtenberg, 1986).

Theme. Yet it was the themes (ideas) the critics interpreted that most clearly demonstrated their preference for the FP or MP. The three FP critics read Evans's photo as a comment on the nuances of life (Nature), the three MP as a commentary on aspects of culture (Civilization). As in the readings of subject matter and affective qualities, the Nature/Civilization superordinates were applied variously, depending on whether the critic was fixed or fluid.

For Coleman (fixed FP), Evans had made a statement about "people constructing rituals...out of the most meager and barren of means," (Nature/Magic, Adversity/Chaos) (Coleman, 1986). Sekula's reading, on the other hand, was subsumed by the constructs Civilization and Order, since he identified the image as a *type* of visual statement, a model with implied rules and procedures:

> *It's a photograph which is an extraordinarily detailed inventory of a seg-*
> *ment of* material culture—*seems to me it constitutes a* model *for some kind*
> *of* descriptive practice, *if one can win that* model *away from a sort of* aes-
> theticist direction *which has been taken (Sekula, 1986)*. [emphasis mine]

Both androgynous critics, Kozloff (fixed FP) and Grundberg (fixed MP), organized their readings by applying the superordinates Civilization, Nature, and Chaos. Kozloff emphasized Chaos/mystery and Grundberg Civilization/photographic technology. Like Sekula (fixed MP), Kozloff (androgynous-fixed FP) referred to the Evans image as an "inventory of these various objects" (Civilization). Kozloff (1986), however, construed it as a "rebus" (as in mystery, or puzzle—invoking FP Chaos) "used to describe or to project something about the lives of the people who live there" (Nature/human life). Grundberg (1986) (androgynous-fixed MP), also thought the photograph was "deceptive" (FP Chaos), remarking that although one *could* read the theme as a "report about another culture" (Civilization), it was really about "mainstream culture, bourgeois culture inhabiting this place through the photographic process" (Civilization/technology).

As expected, androgynous-fluid critics Jay (FP) and Trachtenberg (MP) were more responsive to the MP in the photograph. For Jay (androgynous-fluid FP) (1986), the Evans photo provided visual "information" (MP Mind) about "who lived there (Nature), for how long in that culture" (MP time/Civilization). He also spoke of the human activity (FP) of reading images in relation to photographic technology (MP)—"the camera...gives you an opportunity to take a journey with the eyes across the whole surface [of the photo]." Trachtenberg (androgynous-fluid MP) (1986) focused on Civilization, pointing out that the hand dipped in plaster, along with the other artifacts of material culture in this "wonderful, brilliant (MP Light) picture...takes us far back toward something called origin and finds there the 'hand of man'; that is, it finds there culture" (Civilization).

To summarize, whether characterized as fixed or fluid, when the MP critics read the Evans photograph they typically experienced it via the MP superordinate construct Civilization, in addition to MP Religion, Order, and

Light. From the contrast value pole of the FP, the superordinate construct Nature typically seemed to shape the experience of the FP critics, although they also construed the Evans photo in relation to MP Civilization and Religion and FP Connection, Chaos and Other.

DISCUSSION

The value patterns that emerged from verbal responses to the researcher's standard set of photos demonstrated that the six critics were not reading an a priori reality inherent in the photographs. Instead, in George Kelly's (1955, 1963) terms the construction systems of either the MP or the FP acted as "templates" to abstract meaning. Moreover, this MP/FP preference was discovered to be consistent in readings conducted in all stages of this study, occurring when (1) each critic was asked to *choose* ten or more photographs he "felt positive" about; in (2) each critics' *writings* about those ten or more photographs made prior to the interview session, as well as (3) the *oral* explanation provided during interviews reported on here.

This finding leads to the data-based conclusion that no difference existed between facts and values expressed by critics; both observations of "facts" (subject matter and structural forms) and interpretations concerning image qualities and themes reflected each critic's preferred construction system.

Do other ways exist to describe this information? Because explanations of patterns and relationships among descriptive information are always linked to the data interpretation method used, organizing the data in this study into FP/MP constructs is only one of many categories of interpretations that could be employed to understand the readings. For example, it could be argued that Coleman is a modernist critic interested in examining his feelings about an image and the feeling tone in it, whereas Sekula approaches photographic images from a socio/historical perspective. Coleman (1986) did say it was important to "surrender yourself to the work" (a condition of the so-called aesthetic experience) rather than to "respond ideologically," whereas Sekula (1986) identified himself as a "Marxist historian" interested in the functional use of photography in the social realm. One therefore might expect Coleman to identify more Non-Mind (feeling) constructs in photographs, Sekula more Civilization (political). However, Coleman (1986) also claimed a longstanding concern with "photographs as social artifacts," insisting that "art is a political process, among its other functions"; he produced criticism to "deal with the work of the photograph" rather than with his "own vision of the world." Yet as we have seen, Coleman's verbalized reactions to his experience of the researcher's FP and MP photographs were consistently feminine-principled.

Although the differences in theoretical approach Coleman and Sekula mentioned (1986) might explain some differences in the readings, I argue that framing these readings as aesthetic versus socio/historical, or modernist versus postmodernist cannot adequately explain the consistency of kinds of constructs selected. They do not explain, for example, why Coleman (1986) named many Nature items ("cacti," "low plants," or "shrubs") in the MP photo by William Garnett—which pictured a train crossing a desert— whereas Sekula (1986) mentioned none, but construed the train in that image as having "rationality" (Mind). Neither do they account for the polarized interpretations these two critics made of the FP Bourke-White photograph, which pictured a '30s depression-poor woman holding her child on her lap in front of an oval-framed image of an ancestor. Coleman (1986) noted the feeling sensation the Bourke-White photograph evoked (Non-Mind) and the continuum of the life-cycle represented by the three persons (Connection). Sekula (1986) labeled the mother a "social Madonna" (Civilization) and, although he acknowledged the continuity of a female line, he saw the mother as "played off against the respectability of the presumed ancestor" as in discontinuity (Isolation). Nor do they provide a reason for Coleman's (1986) "emotional" preference for photographs with "dark enclosed interiors" (Dark) and "deep space" and Sekula's (1986) equally strong contrary preference for "uninflected" photographs (those unchanged by the photographer with respect to lighting and point of view [Norm]). Labeling Coleman a "traditional" critic and placing him in an aetheticist/modernist category and labeling Sekula a "rhetorical" critic and classifying him as a social/historical/postmodernist does not account for the coherent FP and MP conceptual frameworks dominating their readings. Coleman used the FP superordinate constructs of Nature, Dark, Non-Mind, Magic, Connection, Chaos, and the Other to structure his readings; Sekula relied on the MP superordinate constructs of Civilization, Light, Mind, Religion, Isolation, Order, and the Norm.

It seems more useful to view the Coleman/Sekula readings as contrasting constructs clustering around two poles. The "relative values" located on each pole may be characterized as feminine-principled or masculine-principled and act as the "principles" of each individual construction system (described by Kelly, 1955, 1963).

CONCLUSION

Based on findings in this study and others I have conducted, I recommend the gendered concepts of the feminine principle, masculine principle and androgynous (MP/FP) principles as analytic tools. They give us a vocabulary for shaping an understanding of guiding principles in critical discourse. Although the precise characteristics of these principles and subsequent determination as to whether they are generally useful for explaining the responses of other critics to other photographs or of other kinds of rhetors to other discourse situations will require more study, the findings cited here suggest the value in such an approach.

Does this research point us in other directions? Although this study suggests that orientation toward one principle or the other is not sex-specific (all six critics were male), the discourse of female photographic critics should be analyzed as well. Or in a related question, we might ask if males in general prefer the MP and females the FP as construction systems for structuring experience.

The FP/MP may also prove useful for examining critical rhetorical strategies used to persuade audiences. One principle, for example, might be used negatively to devalue objects construed as belonging to the other. Some evidence exists that judgments about "good" and "bad" photographs are influenced by critical adherence to one pole or the other of the FP or MP dichotomy (Lockridge, 1983). Evidence also suggests that adherence to either FP or MP construction systems may help explain the current clash of competing theories in the field of photographic criticism, where "traditional" and "rhetorical" critics argue for the greater value of their preferred paradigms (Lockridge, 1989).

Or, given the power of language in the construction of reality, analysis of discourse and MP/FP patterns might provide insight into shifting cultural notions about what is and what ought to be. Whether discourse situations, sex/gender relationships, rhetorical strategies, or verbal or visual language is the object of critical analysis, the possible impact of an archetypal element in human experience should not be ignored.

REFERENCES

Appignanesi, Lisa. 1973. *Femininity and the Creative Imagination: A Study of Henry James, Robert Musil, and Marcel Proust.* New York: Vision Press Limited.

Bachofen, Johann Jakob. 1861. *Das Mutterrecht.* Stuttgart, Germany: Krais and Hoffman.

———. 1948. *Das Mutterrecht.* Basel, Germany: B. Schwabe.

———. 1967. *Myth, Religion, and Mother Right: Selected Writings of J.J. Bachofen.* Trans. Ralph Manheim. Bolligen Series LXXXIV. Princeton, NJ: Princeton University Press.

Burke, Kenneth. 1950. *A Rhetoric of Motives.* New York: Prentice Hall.

————. 1969. *A Rhetoric of Motives.* Berkeley, CA: University of California Press.

Coleman, Alan D. Taped interview. July 1986. (Critic, Chair of Photography at New York University).

de Beauvoir, Simone. 1953. *The Second Sex.* New York: Alfred A. Knopf.

Deutsch, Helene. 1944. *The Psychology of Women: Volume I—Girlhood.* New York: Grume and Stratton.

————. 1973. *The Psychology of Women: Volume I—Girlhood.* New York: Bantam Books.

Freud, Sigmund. 1933. *New Introductory Lectures in Psychoanalysis.* New York: W. W. Norton.

Grundberg, Andy. Taped interview. July 1986. (Photographic reviewer for *New York Times Magazine* and *Modern Photography*).

Jay, Bill. Taped interview. June 1986. (Critic and Associate Professor of Fine Arts at Arizona State University).

Jung, Carl. 1904. *Collected Works.* Edited by Sir Herbert Reed, Michael Fordham, and Gerhard Adler; trans. R.F.C. Hull. Bollingen Series 20. Princeton, NJ: Princeton University Press.

————. 1944. *Psychologie und Alchemie.* In *Collected Works,* edited by Sir Herbert Reed, Michael Fordham, and Gerhard Adler; trans. by R.F.C. Hull. Bollingen Series 20. Princeton, NJ: Princeton University Press.

————. 1974. *Dreams.* Trans. R.F.C. Hull. Bollingen Series. Princeton, NJ: Princeton University Press.

Kelly, George. 1955. *The Psychology of Personal Constructs.* New York: W.W. Norton and Company.

————. 1963. *A Theory of Personality: The Psychology of Personal Constructs.* New York: W. W. Norton and Company.

Kozloff, Max. Taped interview. July 1986. (Photographer, critic, former editor of *Artforum*).

Lauter, Estella, and Carol Schreier Rupprecht. 1985. *Feminist Archetypal Theory: Interdisciplinary Re-Visions of Jungian Thought.* Knoxville, TN: University of Tennessee Press.

Lockridge, Rebecca Bryant. 1983. *Margaret Bourke-White and Walker Evans: The Aesthetics of Feminine- and Masculine-Principle.* Master's thesis, The Ohio State University.

————. 1989. *"Rhetorical Strategy" and "Meaning": A Constructivist Approach to the Feminine- and Masculine-Principled Judgments of Photographic Critics.* Ph.D. dissertation, The Ohio State University.

Neumann, Erich. 1954. *The Origins and History of Consciousness.* Trans. by R.F.C. Hull. Bollingen Series. Princeton, NJ: Princeton University Press.

————. 1955. *The Great Mother: An Analysis of the Archetype.* Trans. by Ralph Manheim. Bollingen Series. Princeton, NJ: Princeton University Press.

————. 1973. *The Origins and History of Consciousness.* Trans. by R.F.C. Hull. Bollingen Series. Princeton, NJ: Princeton University Press. Third printing.

————. 1974. *The Great Mother: An Analysis of the Archetype.* Trans. by Ralph Manheim. Bollingen Series. Princeton, NJ: Princeton University Press. Second edition, second printing.

Nicholson, Shirley. 1989. *The Goddess Re-Awakening: The Feminine Principle Today.* Wheaton, IL: Theosophical Publishing House.

Ornstein, Robert E. 1972. *The Psychology of Consciousness.* San Francisco: W.H. Freeman and Company.

Samuels, Andrew. 1985. *Jung and the Post-Jungians.* London: Routledge and Kegan Paul.

Sekula, Alan. Taped interview. August 1986. (Photographer, critic, Director of Photography Department at California Institute of the Arts).

Singer, June. 1977. *Androgyny: Toward a New Theory of Sexuality.* New York: Anchor Books.

Swanson, David L. 1977. "A Reflective View of the Epistemology of Critical Inquiry," *Communication Monographs,* 44, (August):207–19.

Trachtenberg, Allan. Taped interview. June 1986. (Chair of American Studies Department, Yale University).

Wehr, Demaris S. 1987. *Jung and Feminism: Liberating Archetypes.* Boston: Beacon Press.

PHOTOGRAPHS CITED

Bourke-White, Margaret. 1975. "Okefenokee Swamp, Georgia." 1937. In *You Have Seen Their Faces.* New York: Arno Press. p. 106.

Brandt, Bill. 1977. "Wuthering Heights." In *The Print.* 1945. New York: Time-Life Books, Inc. p 157.

Evans, Walker. 1941. "Fireplace and Objects in a Bedroom of Floyd Burroughs's Home, Hale County, Alabama, Summer 1936." In *Let Us Now Praise Famous Men.* Plate 8. 1960. Plate 9.

Garnett, William. 1981. "Train Crossing the Desert Near Kelso California." In *Aperture.* 1980. No. 85. p. 23.

Halus, Siegfried. 1979. "From The Flashlight Series, Andover, Connecticut, 1978." In *Aperture.* No. 82. p. 35.

Papegeorge, Tod. 1981. "Central Park, 1980." In *Aperture.* No. 85. p. 20.

CHAPTER 10

Speaking Metaphorically: A Cultural Enactment of Community Among Women

Denice A. Yanni
University of Massachusetts, Amherst

"Girl talk" was a socially acceptable term that trivialized the kind of talk that occurred when women gathered together. Only in recent scholarship has woman-to-woman communication been validated as a vital activity (Jones, 1980; Johnson and Aries, 1983; Stanback, 1985). My own study involves seven graduate women enrolled in a course on the nature of feminist leadership.

The purpose of this study is to examine the ways in which women communicate with each other when organized through a collaborative effort for a designated purpose. The nature of the topic, the size of the group, and their high level of motivation provided a rich foundation for the development and study of a woman's speech community. I was interested in exploring the characteristics of the communicative exchanges employed by the women and how they use speech as a cultural resource to symbolize "community." In order to respond to these issues, I chose an ethnographic method that addresses the relationship between communication and culture.

THEORETICAL FRAMEWORK

As a means of providing a heuristic framework for conceptualizing how the communicative interaction in a specific speech community can be framed as a cultural event, I referred to the theories of Hymes (1962),

Schneider (1975), Philipsen (1980), and Turner (1980). Hymes provides a foundation for an ethnography of communication by emphasizing those questions particular to in situ studies: "We must know what patterns are available in what contexts, and how, where, and when they come into play" (105). In this manner he establishes the criteria and context for a cultural claim.

Schneider states that the study of culture is "a study of social action as a *meaningful* system of action" (199). His basic assumption is that culture is both a systematic and meaningful expression which is observable since it is embodied in social action. He further identifies two dimensions of social action, the normative and the cultural. The normative refers to specific instructions for action, whereas the cultural responds to the belief system of a community. These concepts relate to a system of usage evidenced by constitutive and regulative rules.

Philipsen provides additional insight in his discussion of the forms and functions of cultural communication. He defines "ritual" as one of the "characteristic forms used to affirm and negotiate a sense of shared identity" (6). This corresponds to my intention to study the nature of community as it is spoken in a cultural context.

Rituals not only function as an expression of community; they also serve to mark changes that occur in the structuring of meaning. Turner quotes Van Gennep's insight that rituals usually "accompany transitions from one situation to another and from one cosmic or social world to another" (160). This capacity for transition implies that rituals may also operate on a meta-communicative level.

By examining the data in light of this theory base, I will demonstrate how speaking metaphorically is a communicative pattern systematically used by these women as a ritual enactment of community.

My study is not designed to make a cultural claim that *all* women speak metaphorically or are more adept at this kind of talk in contrast to other forms. In the tradition of the ethnography of communication, which contextualizes social meaning, my findings are specific to this speech community. Nichols (1980) clarifies the nature of such a distinction:

> *Women's experiences have much in common throughout the world to be sure. And it is possible that we may identify certain common patterns in women's lives and women's speech. But women are members first and foremost of their own small speech communities, and it is in the daily context of their lives as speaking members of a larger group that their language must be examined. (140)*

My intent is to present metaphorical speaking as a form of cultural communication fulfilling distinctive functions that are prominent for this community of women.

COLLECTION AND ANALYSIS OF DATA

Seven women, motivated by an interest in exploring the nature of feminist leadership, created a graduate course to address this topic. I attended the "Feminist Leadership" class from September through November 1987. It was held once a week for two and a half hours. I did not verbally participate, but smiled at jokes and visually acknowledged members when they spoke. During each session I tape-recorded the discussion. If I was unable to attend, another woman recorded the class for me.

The method I employed in listening to the tapes was an application of my theoretical framework in that I was attentive to the possibility of a systematic pattern that recurred as the women spoke to each other. Certainly not all significant communicative events within a speech community are manifested in coherent patterns or as expressions of commonality. Contradiction and diversity are equally illustrative. My purpose, though, was to explore how cultural coherence was spoken. Hence, I chose a methodological approach that enabled me to focus on a shared expression of community identity. By using this research technique, I observed concrete instances of a social phenomenon which was repeated throughout the data collected. The women used metaphors prolifically. I was struck not only with the regular usage but also with the dynamic interaction that occurred within the group once a metaphor was introduced into the discussion. Speaking metaphorically appeared to be a conduit for articulating the spirit of this community. In an effort to document this occurrence, I will present first an analysis of the form that speaking metaphorically takes as a communication event and then an interpretation of how speaking metaphorically functions for these women. I conclude with a discussion of the implications this study has for communication theory.

SPEAKING METAPHORICALLY
AS A COMMUNICATION EVENT

Speaking metaphorically is a communication event possessing an internal logic of progression. Whether this event was initiated purposefully or spontaneously, it includes the following three stages: presentation, description, and affirmation. I will describe these stages and illustrate them with an example from the data. My purpose in citing examples is not to focus on the particular metaphor used in a given situation; rather, it is to highlight the communicative pattern within the speech community that is marked by the use of metaphors. In order to better illustrate this pattern, I have chosen to follow the development of one metaphor, "conversation," through the various stages.

Presentation: A metaphor is introduced into the conversation by a member to fulfill one of two purposes: (1) to provide clarification, explication, or a personal response to an idea under discussion; or (2) to initiate the formulation of a new idea. The presentation of a metaphor frequently followed an analytical discussion where it served to illustrate a specific principle, as in the following case: For one of the class sessions, the group read a book on a particular theory and one woman volunteered to present an overview of it. After providing a rather detailed explanation replete with abstract principles she proceeded in the following manner:

> *"We need a different form to represent what we know and a conversation is one. Because in a conversation we're all putting out our piece. So, we're all having this group dialogue. Here we all are, together, doing something. But the conversation is never fixed."*

Here, "conversation" is the metaphor introduced in order to clarify the nature of knowledge as a processual event rather than a static codification.

In the second instance, when the group is "working at an idea," that is, trying to expand a concept beyond available meanings, a member will offer a metaphor to the group:

> *During a discussion about whether or not one could even conceive of the term "leadership" in a feminist context, one woman contributed: "Well, do I just cast leadership off and abandon it because of the notion of leadership that we have? That it's the single individual standing out above the rest and directing things? Versus the shifting center of leadership. Leadership as a state [of being]."*

In this context, the use of a metaphor serves to reformulate an idea. Leadership is recast in terms of positionality rather than personality. These examples indicate how members of the group introduced metaphors. Speaking metaphorically enabled them to move between discursive and descriptive speech to ensure understanding. It was also instrumental in generating conceptual innovations.

Description: Two forms of this stage exist: (1) singular description—an individual is solely responsible for developing the terms of the metaphor she introduces. She may do so naturally in her explanation, or the group may ask questions requiring further elaboration from her; and (2) collaborative description—members of the group participate in the descriptive activity. They do so by providing new images that substantiate the original metaphor or by introducing new metaphors that support the meaning of the original one.

Use of a metaphor involves employing descriptive language, which is either an individual or communal effort. Whereas the singular description is, literally, self-explanatory, it is interesting to note how the collaborative description occurs. Continuing the example given in the presentation stage, the introduction of the metaphor, "conversation," provides an example of both forms of collaborative activity. After the first woman finished her explanation of the metaphor she introduced, the following interaction occurred:

> *Second Woman:* "It's more fluid and not pinned down. Not tangible and not stopped in motion."
>
> *First Woman:* "I think jazz music is another one."
>
> *Third Woman:* "You mean improvisational."

A different metaphor, "jazz music," was introduced as having a parallel meaning to "conversation" and the description was then elaborated upon by another member. It seems as though a metaphor becomes a cultural artifact. Individuals do not claim ownership and are quite amenable to the potential development and subsequent use by other members.

Affirmation: The introduction and description of a metaphor is usually accepted and valued as a positive contribution to the discussion. I discovered no instance in which a metaphor was evaluated negatively or considered inappropriate. Members may challenge the relevancy of the imagery to the issue under discussion. But in that case, the challenge reverts to the descriptive stage and is again responded to singularly or collaboratively. The individual has the option to re-negotiate her metaphor in light of the current perspective, or another member may re-align the terms of a previously introduced metaphor. Both instances of renegotiation occurred in the following discussion: "Conversation" had been introduced as a new metaphor and seemed to displace a previous metaphor that the group had been working with, "a quilt." The discussion continued:

> *Second Woman:* "It's [a conversation] more fluid and not pinned down. Not tangible and not stopped in motion. When a quilt is finished, it's finished. And a conversation keeps going."
>
> *Third Woman:* "I was thinking the quilt has a commitment to the design. It's not that you can't change it. But that if you begin a pattern, if you begin something, the kind of expectations that are going to finish it are going to come out in the design."
>
> *Second Woman:* "A conversation can evolve and change."
>
> *First Woman:* (who introduced "conversation") "I think jazz music is another one."
>
> *Fourth Woman:* "You mean improvisational."

Fifth Woman: "But jazz has a basic pattern. I don't think it's the melody the jazz player plays with, but with certain patterns that have been practiced. Maybe the melody the jazz player plays with is like the topic of a conversation."

Second Woman: "I was going to say but conversations are like that, too, though. Because there are forms that we know and we're not as fluid with a conversation as we could imagine—the forms of talking, and topics, and all. Each of our understandings is from the chords we've practiced. And the melody is whatever the topic or theme."

All three metaphors have been re-negotiated to embrace a sense of directionality: the "quilt" has a "commitment to the design"; the "conversation" has a topic; and "jazz music" has a melody line. What seems most important in this activity is that speaking metaphorically serves as a cohesive strategy, rather than positioning individuals in opposition to each other. The expansiveness of this form of speaking allows the women to continually expand the boundaries of community membership so that all communication is an inclusive activity.

Although further research is required before making conclusions, my hypothesis is that since this is a particular category of "descriptive speaking" rather than "discursive speaking," it is not evaluated by criteria concerning how well it constructs an argument, but how well it presents an insight. This calls for a different response, which may be fulfilled in the descriptive stage. Additional data are required to test this explanation.

FUNCTIONS OF SPEAKING METAPHORICALLY

After studying the instances of this form of talk, I believe it functions as a cultural resource and as a metacommunicative device for this community of women. As a cultural resource it serves to initiate an interactive process. Although introduced by a single member, its purpose is to engage the entire community. Each individual, then, is pivotal to the development and expression of the speech community. She *must* speak in order to establish the foundation of a cultural identity based on participation and valuing of the individual.

On a metacommunicative level, speaking metaphorically makes a shift in the kind of talk that occurs. The data indicate there is a transition from discursive speaking to descriptive speaking. In addition, a secondary function related to context is the unique capabilities this form possesses for responding to the content of the course, feminist leadership. It is particularly adept for formulating emergent ideas, as was required for considering a topic about which there are minimal resources.

Cultural Resource

Speaking metaphorically is a model for conducting social life. A member receives an immediate response from the community. This response may be one of approval, pleasure, encouragement for, and/or participation in developing the imagery, as indicated in the following example:

> *First Woman:* "I'd like to go back to this 'leadership as a state.' Something in what you were both saying made me think of somehow leadership for women is women inviting something to happen."
>
> *Other Women:* "m-m-m-m-mmm."
>
> *First Woman:* "I don't know where that's going so I'd like to listen more."
>
> *Second Woman:* "Do you have an idea of what you mean by that?"
>
> *First Woman:* "I just wrote down, 'someone inviting,' as you were talking and I wonder if you'd go back to your concept [referring to the woman who introduced the metaphor] 'leadership as a state.' You meant it as a process?"
>
> *Third Woman:* "As a state of being. And I, yeah, as a process because it's a state of being that's continually changing, and it moves between the persons that are part of...the group...It's not within the person."

The women are continually prompting each other with sounds of interest and delight or questions. The emphasis of this communication event is on the experience of a shared identity. In this way, speaking metaphorically is comparable to the "call-response" strategy studied in relation to black communities (Daniel and Smitherman, 1976). Although a historical tradition and specific religious and social structure is constitutive of the black experience, its function is similar in the interactions among these women. The metaphor serves as the "call" eliciting a "response" from the group. Daniel and Smitherman describe this "interactive system":

> *Call-response...embodies communality rather than individuality. Emphasis is on group cohesiveness and cooperation...the existence of the "call" which is issued by a single individual in the Group, underscores the importance of individual roles within the Group. The individual is challenged to do what he can...By taking advantage of process, movement, and emotional, intuitive, and spiritual guidance, the individual can exercise his sense of Self by virtue of his unique contribution to the Group. (34)*

Speaking metaphorically is a frame for the communal enactment of a shared identity. To know how and when to introduce a metaphor is to have access "to implicit understandings shared by members of the speech community, i.e., it is to have access to the culture" (Philipsen, 1975). What is commonly shared by these women is a desire to engage each other, to present a challenge for generating new meanings in a nonjudgmental environment and to be recognized for their accomplishment. Each individual understands that, in introducing a metaphor, she will be listened to attentively and valued for her contribution since she advances the general purpose of the group. By extension, members of the community know their role upon hearing a metaphor is to create the cognitive space necessary for working toward new ideas and affirming the individual woman as a valued member.

Metacommunicative Device

In addition to serving as a cultural resource, speaking metaphorically is a metacommunicative device that shifts the kind of talk occurring within the community. Speaking metaphorically enables the community to move from discursive, positional speech to descriptive, collaborative speech. The women consistently employed this technique to provide an open forum for nonevaluative speech and enable new meanings to be developed, new occasions for redefining concepts as well as the nature of community. This is in contrast to a more analytical talk requiring the systematic development of an argument. In analytical talk, a member takes a stand and presents it to the community as an individual accomplishment. In metaphorical talk, the individual stands within the community and initiates a process for mutual accomplishment. It is a question of positionality between the self and the community.

A study describing a framework of epistemological positions among women (Belenky et al., 1986) identified a form of talk called "real talk." Certain dimensions of "real talk" illustrate the metacommunicative function of speaking metaphorically:

> *Constructivists make a distinction between "really talking" and what they consider to be didactic talk in which the speaker's intention is to hold forth rather than to share ideas. In didactic talk, each participant may report experience, but there is no attempt among participants to join together to arrive at some new understanding. "Really talking" requires careful listening; it implies a mutually shared agreement that together you are creating the optimum setting so that half-baked or emergent ideas can grow..."Real talk" [is] a way of connecting to others. (144–45)*

It is primarily a cooperative venture culminating in group solidarity and new expressions of knowledge.

A secondary function further relates this form of speaking to the specific content of the course. Although some studies have been done on women and leadership, it is difficult to find material on the nature of *fem-*

inist leadership. Consequently, the women had to draw from a variety of sources on management, leadership, and organizational development in order to provide a foundation from which they might postulate new concepts. Speaking metaphorically is especially suited to promoting the "emergent idea," for endorsing speculation in a supportive environment.

For these reasons, speaking metaphorically is a unique device for enacting community, introducing occasions for cooperative exploration, and promoting the formulation of content-specific knowledge.

It is apparent that since speaking metaphorically has varied functions, there are different guidelines for when and why this form of talk is used. As indicated in my conceptual framework, Schneider refers to these varied functions as the normative and cultural aspects of social action which correspond to regulative and constitutive rules, respectively. I have derived the following rules as ones that relate to the nature and function of speaking metaphorically.

The following rules are normative in that they provide specific instructions for how individuals should act in this speech community. That is, they fulfill a regulative function:

1. Speaking metaphorically is appropriate for certain functions within the group and inappropriate for others.

Although speaking metaphorically conveyed new ideas and responses, it was not efficient for task-oriented activities. It was not used for agenda-setting or determining what readings to prepare for the following week.

2. Speaking metaphorically is to be received as a positive contribution to the discussion. No negative evaluation is allowed.

Whenever an individual introduces a metaphor, all community resources are galvanized to respond in a positive manner. This may be done by an affirmative remark or by elaborating on the metaphor to develop the most acceptable terms of description.

By exploring the cultural dimension of speaking metaphorically, we can illuminate the underlying belief system of this community. These constitutive rules refer to the cultural aspect of enacting meaning and respond to substantive issues concerning the identity of the community:

1. Speaking metaphorically is an expression of shared identity.

When individuals introduce a metaphor they are displaying a desire and capability for engaging the group in a collaborative activity. Since the assumption is that this form of speaking is immediately valued, individuals receive an instantaneous acceptance and acknowledgment of their value as community members.

2.   Speaking metaphorically provides an opportunity for creating meaning, initiated by the individual and affirmed by the community.

This form of talk is not only a cultural resource for enacting community, but a cultural tool for creating meaning. Each member has the potential for adding new meanings, new perspectives to the culture. They all occupy a privileged position. Consequently, the system of meaning is not fixed but constantly expanded upon.

These rules provide additional information for examining how speaking metaphorically is enacted and what it means.

CONCLUSION

This study focuses on the occurrence of a communicative event in a speech community of women. Rather than studying the individual metaphors, I focused on metaphors as a patterned activity of speech. Regardless of the information negotiated by particular metaphors, the use of this speech pattern itself indicates the manner in which a specific speech community constructs meaning. By examining the nature and function of speaking metaphorically, I have established that it is a native category of speech operating as a key symbol that accesses a community's meaning system. These women "spoke" shared identity. That is, they conveyed a sense of individual worth, provided an environment conducive to the development of new concepts, and created an inclusive community by engaging in metaphorical speech.

In addition, this study supports research indicating the experience of "real talk" among women. The women who formulated the course on feminist leadership initiated this form of talk through speaking metaphorically. Additional research with women's groups could further validate "real talk" as a category of speech and contribute to explaining how it takes shape, when it is used, and in what capacity it functions within different groups.

REFERENCES

Belenky, Mary Field, et al. 1986. *Women's Ways of Knowing: The Development of Self, Voice, and Mind.* New York: Basic Books, Inc.
Daniel, J.L., and G. Smitherman. 1976. "'How I Got Over': Communication Dynamics in the Black Community." *Quarterly Journal of Speech,* 62, 26–39.

Hymes, Dell. 1962. "The Ethnography of Speaking." In *Anthropology and Human Behavior*, edited by T. Gladwin and W.C. Stuntwart. Washington, D.C.: Anthropology Society of Washington.

Johnson, Fern, and Elizabeth Aries. 1983. "The Talk of Women Friends." In *Women's Studies International Forum, 6*, 353–61.

Jones, D. 1980. "Gossip: Notes in Women's Oral Culture." In *Women's Studies International Quarterly, 3*, 193–98.

Nichols, Patricia C. 1980. "Women in Their Speech Communities." In *Women and Language in Literature and Society*, edited by Sally McConnell-Ginet, Ruth Borker, and Nelly Furman. New York: Praeger.

Philipsen, Gerry. 1975. "Speaking 'Like a Man' in Teamsterville: Cultural Patterns of Role Enactment in an Urban Neighborhood." In *Quarterly Journal of Speech, 61*, 13–22.

———. 1980. "The Prospect of Cultural Communication." Unpublished manuscript, University of Washington.

Schneider, David M. 1976. "Notes Toward a Theory of Culture." In *Meaning in Anthropology*, edited by K. Basso and H. A. Selby. Albuquerque, NM: University of New Mexico Press.

Stanback, Marsha H. 1985. "Language and Black Woman's Place: Evidence from the Black Middle Class." In *For Alma Mater: Theory and Practice in Feminist Scholarship*, edited by Paula A. Treichler, Cheris Kramarae, and Beth Stafford. Urbana, IL: University of Illinois Press.

Turner, Victor. 1980. "Social Dramas and Stories About Them." In *Critical Inquiry, 7*, 141–68.

CHAPTER 11

Genderlect, Powerlect, and Politeness

Nancy Hoar
Western New England College

"You are what you communicate."
"People judge you by what you say and what you do."
"Your actions tell people how you want to be treated."

Aphorisms such as these encapsulate our attitudes about the importance of communicative effectiveness in our lives. The ways in which our communicative behaviors reveal who we are have been explored in a growing body of literature, and one of the most exciting subsets of this literature examines the influence of gender upon communication.

Genderlect is speech that contains features that mark it as stereotypically masculine or feminine. To be sure, genderlect does imply more intrasex homogeneity than actually exists (Kramarae, 1981, 92; Thorne, Kramarae, and Henley, 1983, 14); even so, the term *genderlect* is a useful label to refer to the set of features that mark stereotypical masculine and feminine speech. Moreover, the term is useful in referring to *expected* as well as observed behavior because "we know more about which gender-based message cues people are expected to use than about how often a given individual actually uses any of these cues in a given setting" (Bate, 1988, 56); and expectations and stereotypes are, of course, powerful filters in our perceptions of others. The term *genderlect* need not be limited to speech, however; it can be extended to include nonverbal communication that is stereotypically masculine or feminine.

Although genderlect may seem to be a basic communication descriptor, it is actually a derived descriptor, for it is dependent upon *powerlect,* i.e., communication that contains features that indicate the relative status of its users. Genderlect is actually the expression of powerlect interpreted according to culturally based gender expectations. We will examine the work of several communication scholars to see why this is so. We will also see why gender and power are concomitant with a third factor—politeness.

The influence of gender upon communication has intrigued communication scholars for the past two decades. Robin Lakoff's "Language and Woman's Place" (1973a) was a spark that stimulated investigations by many other researchers. Lakoff's description, a product of observation and introspection, focused on the syntactic and lexical features that characterize feminine genderlect. The most salient features she found are questions in place of statements and requests, tag questions, and "fluffy" adjectives of approval or disapproval.

Lakoff's descriptions have been examined and reexamined by other scholars. Some studies have confirmed Lakoff's work (Bailey and Timm, 1976; Hartman, 1976, 1978), although others have not (Dubois and Crouch, 1975; Kuykendall, 1980; Metts and Bryan, 1984; Valian, 1977). Perhaps this lack of consistent confirmation or disconfirmation is due to situational variables that have not remained constant in these and other investigations (Brown, 1976; Brown and Levinson, 1980; Crosby and Nyquist, 1977; O'Barr, 1982).

Other communication scholars such as Cheris Kramarae have found additional lexical and semantic features of feminine language, particularly stereotypical feminine language (i.e. feminine genderlect). In an early study Kramarae explored stereotypes of feminine language by examining the captions of cartoons appearing in the *New Yorker* (1974). The most salient features of this stereotypical feminine genderlect she identified were "trivial" topics, apologies and self-deprecation, and hedges and vague qualifiers. She also found examples of the fluffy adjectives described by Lakoff.

Even though Kramarae's data reflect stereotypes of women's speech rather than speech women actually use, and even though these data are more than a decade old, these stereotypes are far from inactive. Every semester since 1982 I have constructed captions containing these features of feminine genderlect, as well as captions containing features of masculine genderlect and captions with "neutral" speech; and I have asked my undergraduate students to visualize the cartoon that might accompany these captions and to identify the speaker of the caption. Every semester my students, both male and female, identify masculine genderlect speakers as male and feminine genderlect speakers as female (or as "wimpy" males). Even these students of the 1980s and 1990s are unwittingly perpetuating the "muted group" (Kramarae, 1981) situation of women.

In addition to Lakoff's anecdotal study and Kramarae's study of stereotypical speech, there are other methods of studying gender-influenced communication. Candace West and Donald Zimmerman collected covertly recorded conversations between male-female dyads in a nonexperimental environment and analyzed them using Harvey Sachs' rules governing the organization of conversations, namely that one person is supposed to speak at a time (West and Zimmerman, 1983; Zimmerman and West, 1975). West and Zimmerman found that women followed these rules but men did not: the men began before the women had finished speaking and the women were forced to surrender (though not without protest) their conversational turns (also see Spender, 1980). Also, women not only had their "conversational space" violated, but they often paused longer before beginning to speak after men had finished their turns, thus avoiding encroaching upon men's "conversational space."

In addition, West and Zimmerman found that women had less control over the length and viability of their discourse, and less control over the topics of discourse. When men introduced ideas, women usually accepted and pursued these ideas. However, when women introduced ideas, men often ignored the women's ideas and pursued their own interests. In one segment of conversation a woman asked her male partner about his term paper and listened politely to his response. She then tried unsuccessfully four times to talk about her own term paper, and each time she was interrupted by his request for a cigarette or a match. Clearly, any leadership she may have shown in initiating the topic soon evaporated.

Perhaps even more disheartening than being interrupted or circumvented is being ignored. This, too, happened to women much more consistently than to men. In the conversations recorded by Pamela Fishman (1980, 1983) women were active participants, usually followers rather than leaders, whereas men acted as leaders or nonparticipants, but not as followers. Often women attempted to engage their male partners in a conversation but received only minimal response ("hmmm," "umm"). This resulted in female monologues punctuated by expectant but unfulfilled pauses. The women had to work harder to keep the conversation alive. Since one means of eliciting conversational participation is to ask questions, this tactic can result in the features observed by Lakoff: tag questions and questions in place of statements (Fishman, 1980). As we noted before, these features can make the speaker look weak and unassertive.

The genderlect features described by Lakoff, Kramarae, West and Zimmerman, and Fishman all point to speech that is characterized as weak, tentative, hesitant, and trivial. For example, a tag question mitigates the assertive force of the statement it follows, apologies and self-deprecation lower the speaker's importance, and a participant's inability to control the topic of discourse relegates that participant to the role of perpetual follower and precludes the role of leader. In short, feminine genderlect is the speech of someone whose status is low.

We see, then, that what is actually being communicated by "genderlect" is not so much masculinity or femininity but relative amounts of status and power. Women who hold powerful or high status positions are not likely to use features of low powerlect in practicing their professions. However, because many women tend to hold lower status positions, they are more likely to use speech containing features of low powerlect, and these have come to be identified as features of female genderlect (Graddol and Swann, 1989).

The interaction of status and gender can be seen in nonverbal communication as well. Because of their smaller larynxes (and because of cultural influences: Mattingly, 1966; Sachs, Lieberman and Erickson, 1973), women have higher pitched voices. Higher-pitched voices connote childhood rather than adulthood; and this connotation suggests lower status and power, for children are typically concerned with trivial matters, whereas adults are concerned with more serious matters; moreover, children are expected to defer to adults. Unsurprisingly, women who aspire to influential positions are often advised to cultivate lower-pitched voices, voices that communicate authority. These women are also advised to speak louder, to project their voices. For example, Graddol and Swann (1989, 38–39) describe Margaret Thatcher's voice training program, the goal of which was to lower her pitch. This contradicts the early socialization of many who were admonished as little girls to talk in a quiet, ladylike manner.

Because of their smaller physical size, women have smaller movements and take up less personal space. Albert Mehrabian (1981) postulated that implicit nonverbal communication conveys three fundamental messages: liking, interest, and status (or power). One of the external indicators of status is size. Bigger indicates more. A longer stride and larger gestures signify greater status. Needless to say, a larger person will naturally have a longer stride and larger gestures, even without socialization that reinforces and amplifies these differences. Women do, in fact, exhibit a smaller stride and smaller gestures than men do, and socially prescribed feminine posture (crossed legs and hands in lap) promotes contraction rather than expansion of personal space (Bate, 1988; Eakins and Eakins, 1978; Henley, 1973/1974, 1977; Pearson, 1985, 252).

Mehrabian asserted that a second external indicator of status is relaxation. He noted that powerful animals such as bears and lions are able to relax much of the time, whereas less powerful animals such as gazelles and rabbits must be alert much of the time. Mehrabian felt that the same is true of human beings. Higher status persons display more relaxed posture than do lower status persons, who display their attentiveness in posture and facial expression. Compared to the sitting, standing, and walking postures of men, women's postures are less relaxed, more attentive (Pearson, 1985, 252).

Attentiveness is communicated through eye contact and through smiling. Women give more eye contact and smile more than men do (Henley 1973/1974; Muirhead and Goldman, 1979; Silveira, 1972; Thayer and Schiff, 1974). Eakins and Eakins postulated that people use eye contact (not mutual gazing) to get feedback on the appropriateness of their own behavior. The greater the eye contact, the more the person is seeking evidence of approval. Only a lower status person needs to be so concerned about approval. Eakins and Eakins have also noted that listeners are more likely to look at speakers than speakers to look at listeners. Inasmuch as men seem to dominate mixed-sex conversations, it is not surprising that women do more listening and therefore give more eye contact.

Women smile more than men do (Dierks-Stewart, 1979; Frances, 1979; Silveira, 1972). Not only does smiling indicate pleasure and attentiveness, but Eakins and Eakins have suggested that smiling also indicates submission and approval seeking. Whether female smiling results from actual submissiveness and approval seeking or whether it is a socialized behavior, it conveys the message of lower status. Finally, Mehrabian noted that smiling is an indication of liking and interest. When a person's smiles are unreciprocated, when a person gives more attention than he or she receives, that person holds lower status.

This close relationship between gender and status has been investigated at length; the influence of a third factor, politeness, has not received as much attention (with the notable exception of Brown, 1976, 1980, and Brown and Levinson, 1978, 1980). But what is politeness? Brown and Levinson (1978) have described two fundamental politeness strategies: positive politeness strategies, which seek to affirm closeness and solidarity, and negative politeness strategies, which seek to show respect and to defer to the other's self-determination. Closely related to these strategies, and compatible with them, are Robin Lakoff's Rules of Politeness, later renamed Rules of Rapport (1973b, 1979):

1. Don't impose.
2. Give options.
3. Be friendly.

The first two (Don't impose, Give options) are negative politeness strategies, whereas the third (Be friendly) is a positive politeness strategy. If we were to interpret Lakoff's Rules of Politeness into specific behaviors, we would find several genderlect/powerlect features. We would find a set of instructions like this:

Don't Impose
a. Be sure to soften your assertions with hedges, qualifiers, and tag questions; better yet, phrase your assertions as questions.
b. Be sure to soften your requests by stating them as questions.
c. Mitigate the full force of your opinions and feelings by expressing them with weak expletives and vague adjectives of approval or disapproval (preferably approval).

d.   Follow your partner's choice of topic of discourse; do not try to promote your choice of topic (you may find that you will be ignored).

e.   Allow your partner ample time to talk, even if you must curtail the length of your own discourse; allow yourself to be interrupted, if need be.

f.   Do not evoke strong feelings that could be unpleasant for your addressee; stick to trivial topics.

g.   Keep your movements small and your posture constrained so that you will minimize your personal space and thereby grant more personal space to others.

h.   Likewise, cultivate a quiet voice in order not to intrude upon the auditory space of others.

i.   If you fail to observe any of the above suggestions, be sure to apologize and self-deprecate; better yet, apologize or self-deprecate from time to time anyway (you might have unknowingly offended).

Give Options

a.   Always state a request as a question; it gives your addressee more opportunity to decline.

b.   Allow your addressee to control the topic of discourse so that he or she can choose what to talk about.

c.   Allow yourself to be interrupted but do not interrupt your partner; this allows your partner to talk as much as he/she pleases.

Be Friendly

a.   Be attentive in posture and in facial expression to show that you care about your addressee.

b.   Give your addressee as much eye contact as you can; this shows your interest in your addressee and your desire to win his/her approval.

c.   Most important, smile! There is no better way to indicate your liking for your partner.

    If you have followed the above instructions, you have followed Lakoff's Rules of Politeness. You are a polite person.

    These Rules of Politeness and their implementation are socially determined. It is not difficult to imagine these instructions in a woman's magazine or in a how-to-be-popular book intended for women. It is more difficult to imagine these instructions appearing in a publication intended for a male audience.

    The implementation of these rules is also culturally determined. Different cultures place varying degrees of emphasis upon each of these three rules. For example, in mainstream America, women are expected to follow Rule 1 (Don't impose) more closely than men are, hence the greater number of weak powerlect features in female genderlect. In upper- and middle-class England, however, both men and women are expected to avoid imposing. As a result, upper- and middle-class English men have features of weak powerlect in their speech, such as adjectives that mainstream Americans would consider feminine adjectives (Lakoff, 1973a, 53). Some Americans would consider these men to be overly polite and less masculine than American men. Of course, upper- and middle-class English men and women would consider these men to be polite and masculine.

Conversely, some cultures place less importance on Rule 1 than Americans do. Israeli men and women, for example, value friendliness and forthrightness and do not give as much attention to imposing or not imposing. The speech of these men and women contains direct assertions and requests without hedges and other mitigators. To mainstream Americans, Israeli men may seem forthright, sometimes impolite; to mainstream Americans, Israeli women may seem not only impolite, but also unfeminine. Of course, these women are neither impolite nor unfeminine to fellow Israelis (see Tamar Katriel's exploration of the "Dugri" speech of native born Israelis, 1986).

In concluding our examination of gender, power, and politeness, we should consider the practical consequences of the interrelatedness of these three factors, specifically with regard to increasing the power of women—not the power to dominate, but the power to achieve. This is the kind of power described by Bate (1988, 39 and 40) and by Thorne, Kramarae, and Henley, "power as energy, effective interaction, or empowerment" (1983, 19). This was the kind of power exercised by female students in a graduate seminar who empowered each other by using collaborative strategies; they did not divide a fixed commodity (power), but instead they created more.

Our specific concern is the interaction between people who are (or should be) equals. These interactions should be characterized by a reciprocated level of politeness. Thorne, Kramarae, and Henley point out that polite, collaborative styles of communication are powerless only when they are not reciprocated (1983, 18 and 19). In the interaction between unequals women can avoid overly polite, overly deferential forms of communication. This does not mean, however, that women should adopt a "masculine" style of communication; many women would be uncomfortable doing this and could be perceived negatively by others (Costrich, Feinstein, and Kidder, 1975; Koester, 1982; Mills, 1985; Scott, 1980; Wiley and Eskilson, 1982). We should avoid dichotomizing what is really a complex situation: One need not become superior in order to avoid being inferior, and one need not be impolite in order to avoid being powerless.

A person who understands the verbal and nonverbal features of genderlect/powerlect can communicate more flexibly and more effectively.

For example, a woman who constantly is being interrupted by her addressee (who is interrupting not to affirm the woman's statements but to change the topic of discourse) need not become an interrupter, too. She can request that the interrupter stop interrupting or she can politely wait for the interrupter to finish, then ignore the attempted change of topic, and proceed with her ideas at the point of interruption, thereby maintaining her agenda of interests.

Finally, many feminist scholars have pointed out that women cannot change their status simply by changing their communicative style (Spender, 1980, 79) and that female genderlect should be considered an alternative, rather than an ineffective, communicative style (Kramarae, 1981, Spender, 1980, Tong, 1989). These views are very similar to those regarding the use of Black English Vernacular vis-a-vis Standard English. Both of these positions advocate a change in societal attitude.

I agree. However, when measured in the context of a life span, social change comes slowly. I believe that one must play the game that's being played, even while working to change the rules of the game. I believe this because those who can play the game are more likely to change the rules than are those who cannot or will not play.

In short, communicative style is not the only determiner of how women are perceived and treated, but it is a powerful influencer. Women should use communicative style as one important tool in achieving the social and professional status that they themselves want.

REFERENCES

Bailey, L.A. and L.A. Timm. 1976. "More on Women's—and Men's Expletives." *Anthropological Linguistics.* 18:438–49.

Bate, B. 1988. *Communication and the Sexes.* New York: Harper & Row.

Brown, P. 1976. Women and Politeness: A New Perspective on Language and Society. *Reviews in Anthropology,* May/June:240–49.

————. 1980. How and Why Women Are More Polite: Some Evidence from a Mayan Community. In *Women and Language in Literature and Society,* edited by S. McConnell-Ginet, R. Borker, and N. Furman, (111–36). New York: Praeger.

Brown, P., and S. Levinson. 1978. "Universals in Language Usage: Politeness Phenomena." In *Questions and Politeness: Strategies in Social Interaction,* edited by E. Goody, (56–289). Cambridge: Cambridge University Press.

Brown, P. and S. Levinson. 1980. "Social Structure, Groups, and Interaction." In *Social Markers in Speech,* edited by K.R. Scherer and H. Giles, (291–341). Cambridge: Cambridge University Press.

Costrich, N., J. Feinstein, and L. Kidder. 1975. "When Stereotypes Hurt: Three Studies of Penalties for Sex-Role Reversals." *Journal of Experimental Social Psychology* 11:520–30.

Crosby, F., and L. Nyquist. 1977. "The Female Register: An Empirical Study of Lakoff's Hypotheses." *Language in Society* 6:313–22.

Dierks-Stewart, K. 1979. "Sex Differences in Nonverbal Communication: An Alternative Perspective." In *Communication, Language, and Sex: Proceedings of the First Conference*, edited by C.K. Berryman and V.K. Edman, 112–21. Rowley, MA: Newbury House Publishers.

Dubois, B.L., and T. Crouch. 1975. "The Question of Tag Questions in Women's Speech: They Don't Really Use More of Them, Do They?" *Language in Society*, 4:289–94.

Eakins, B., and R. Eakins. 1978. *Sex Differences in Human Nonverbal Communication.* New York: Houghton Mifflin.

Fishman, P. 1980. "Conversational Insecurity." In *Language: Social Psychological Perspectives,* edited by H. Giles, W.P. Robinson, and P.M. Smith, 127–32. New York: Pergamon Press.

———. 1983. "Interaction: The Work Women Do." In *Language, Gender and Society,* edited by B. Thorne, C. Kramarae, and N. Henley, 89–101. Rowley, MA: Newbury House.

Frances, S.J. 1979. "Sex Differences in Nonverbal Behavior." *Sex Roles,* 5:519–35.

Graddol, D., and J. Swann. 1989. *Gender Voices.* Oxford: Basil Blackwell.

Hartman, M. 1976. "A Descriptive Study of Men and Women Born in Maine Around 1900 as it Reflects the Lakoff Hypothesis in Language and Woman's Place. In *The Sociology of the Languages of American Women,* edited by B.L. Dubois and I. Crouch, 81–90. San Antonio, TX: Trinity University.

———. 1978. "Sex Roles and Language." Paper presented to the 9th World Congress of Sociology, Uppsala, Sweden.

Henley, N. 1973/1974. "Power, Sex and Nonverbal Communication." *Berkeley Review of Sociology,* 18:1–26. Also in *Language and Sex: Difference and Dominance,* edited by B. Thorne and N. Henley, 185–203. Rowley, MA: Newbury House.

———. 1977. *Body Politics: Power, Sex and Nonverbal Communication.* Englewood Cliffs, NJ: Prentice-Hall.

Katriel, T. 1986. *Talking Straight: "Dugri" Speech in Israeli Sabra Culture.* New York: Cambridge University Press.

Koester, J. 1982. "The Machiavellian Princess: Rhetorical Dramas for Women Managers. *Communication Quarterly* 30(3):165–72.

Kramarae, C. 1974. "Women's Speech: Separate But Equal?" *Quarterly Journal of Speech,* 60:14–24.

———. 1981. *Women and Men Speaking: Frameworks for Analysis.* Rowley, MA: Newbury House.

Kuykendall, E. 1980. "Breaking the Double Binds." *Language and Style,* 81–93.

Lakoff, R. 1973a. "Language and Woman's Place." *Language in Society,* 2:45–80.

———. 1973b. "The Logic of Politeness, or Minding Your P's and Q's." Papers from the Ninth Regional Meeting of the Chicago Linguistic Society. University of Chicago.

———. 1979. "Stylistic {   r of Style." In *Language,*
Sex, and Gender,   ιter, and L.L. Adler, (53–78).
New York: Annal{   of Sciences.
Mattingly, I. 1966. "Spε   ιct Size." Paper given at
Acoustical Socie'
Mehrabian, A. 1981. *S̨*   *nmunication of Emotions and*
Attitudes, 2nd ι_   ι Press.
Metts, S., and G. Bryan. 1984. "Politeι̣ι̣ϲ̣ϲ̣.   versational Indicator of Sex
Roles." Presented at Central States Association Convention, Chicago.

Mills, J. 1985. "Body Language Speaks Louder than Words." *Horizons: University of Cincinnati Alumni Magazine,* February:8–12.

Muirhead, R.D., and M. Goldman. 1979. "Mutual Eye Contact as Affected by Seating Position, Sex, and Age." *The Journal of Social Psychology,* 109:201–06.

O'Barr, W. 1982. "Speech Styles in the Courtroom." Chapter 5 of *Linguistic Evidence: Language, Power, and Strategy in the Courtroom.* New York: Academic Press.

Pearson, J. 1985. *Gender and Communication.* Dubuque, IA: William C. Brown.

Sachs, J., P. Lieberman, and D. Erickson. 1973. "Anatomical and Cultural Determinants of Male and Female Speech." In *Language Attitudes: Current Trends and Prospects,* edited by R. Shuy and R. Fasold, 74–84. Washington, D.C.: Georgetown University Press.

Scott, K.P. 1980. "Perceptions of Communication Competence: What's Good for the Goose is Not Good for the Gander." *Women's Studies International Quarterly* 3:199–208.

Silveira, J. 1972. *Thoughts on Politics of Touch* (Volume 1). Eugene, OR: Women's Press.

Spender, D. 1980. *Man Made Language.* London: Routledge and Kegan Paul.

Thayer, S., and W. Schiff. 1974. "Observer Judgment and Social Interaction: Eye Contact and Relationship Inferences." *Journal of Personality and Social Exchange* 30:110–14.

Thorne, B., C. Kramarae, and N. Henley. 1983. *Language, Gender, and Society.* Rowley, MA: Newbury House.

Tong, R. 1989. *Feminist Thought: A Comprehensive Introduction.* Boulder, CO and San Francisco, CA: Westview Press.

Valian, V. 1977. "Linguistics and Feminism." In *Feminism and Philosophy,* edited by M. Vetterling-Braggin, F. A. Elliston, and J. English, 154–66. Totowa, NJ: Littlefield, Adams.

West, C., and D. Zimmerman, 1983. "Small Insults: A Study of Interruptions in Cross-Sex Conversations Between Unacquainted Persons." In *Language, Gender, and Society,* edited by B. Thorne, C. Kramarae and N. Henley, 103–17. Rowley, MA: Newbury House.

Wiley, M.G., and A. Eskilson. 1982. "Coping in the Corporation: Sex Role Constraints." *Journal of Applied Social Psychology* 12(1):1–11.

Zimmerman, D., and C. West. 1975. "Sex Roles, Interruptions, and Silences in Conversation. In *Language and Sex: Difference and Dominance,* edited by B. Thorne and N. Henley. Rowley, MA: Newbury House.

CHAPTER 12

A Comparison of Male-Female Interaction Norms Regarding New Ideas

Marjorie A. Jaasma
California State University, Stanislaus

In recent years a great deal of research has focused on the study of women in management because the number of women in management positions has been increasing. Their presence requires a rethinking of old assumptions. A review of the literature emphasizes both the similarities and the differences between males and females in management, but this paper focuses on several differences that have been identified.

One of these differences is that females have less self-confidence than males (Maccoby and Jacklin, 1974; McCarty, 1986). This is significant for management because self-confidence is a necessary characteristic of leadership and successful management (Rendel, 1977; White, De Sanctis, and Crino, 1981). Women indicate this lack of self-confidence by attributing personal failure to lack of ability (Crandall, 1969; Wood, 1975), by preferring male bosses to female ones (Robie, 1973), by rating women as having less competence based on ability than men (Ezell, Odewahn, and Sherman, 1980), and by underestimating their abilities and taking less credit for a job well done (Seifert and Miller, 1988).

Another difference between male and female managers regards promotion. Females are not being promoted in many organizations as much as males (Swisher, DuMont, and Boyer, 1985; Freedman and Phillips, 1988). Day and Stogdill (1972) report that for males promotion is related to effectiveness, but for females it is not. Career paths also appear to be different

The author wishes to thank Dr. Fred P. Hilpert, Jr. for his assistance in preparing this paper.

(White, De Sanctis, and Crino, 1981; Markham, South, Bonjean, and Corder, 1985). Kanter (1977) points out that individuals need to develop skills in a broad range of areas in order to be prepared for advancement. She reports that male managers are not giving women the opportunities to develop necessary skills.

A third difference between male and female managers regards inter- action. Females appear to be interacting less often with supervisors, peers, and subordinates. Rosen, Templeton, and Kichline (1981) found that women MBA graduates, after two and a half years on the job, report fewer interactions with supervisors. Donnell and Hall (1980) found no differences in many characteristics of successful male and female managers but did iden- tify that females were less willing to share relevant data with their peers. One laboratory study did find results that are inconsistent with Donnell and Hall's field research. Young (1978) found that females indicated a greater tendency to disclose organizationally relevant data. Glauser (1984) also found that females engaged in more upward communication but distorted messages more than males did.

Women are also interacting less often with supervisors, peers, and sub- ordinates because they are being excluded from the "informal network" of the organization (Kanter, 1977; Bayes and Newton, 1978; Rosen, Templeton, and Kichline, 1981). Brass (1985) found females joined networks with their own sex but were not well integrated into men's networks and had lit- tle access to the dominant coalition that was related to a perception of influence. Other studies indicate that female networks are less effective in building professional reputations (Rose, 1985), and females are less willing to use informal networks for career advancement (Pazy, 1987). Exclusion from important informal contacts often results in women becoming isolates (Kanter, 1977). Staley (1984) stresses that women in upper levels of man- agement are often lone women in mixed-sex groups. These women either achieve low-status membership in the group or become deviants, the results being an "interaction disability."

"Interaction disability" on the part of women provides an explanation, in part, for the low self-confidence of women and the difference in their pro- motability. White, De Sanctis, and Crino (1981) reason that women need to increase their interactions with decision makers both in the formal and infor- mal organization. Increased contact will provide opportunities for females to demonstrate that they have skills necessary for promotion. Increased inter- action will also provide more opportunity for positive evaluation (Taylor and Ilgen, 1980); this should contribute to increased self-confidence. It appears that women are in a negative cycle: They interact less often, which denies them an opportunity to build their self-confidence through positive evalu- ation and which makes them less noticed for promotion by decision mak- ers. The low self-confidence also makes them less desirable as managers.

A variable that is closely linked to interaction is the use of power in the organization. Although the same style of influence was preferred for male and female managers (Izraeli, 1987) and females expressed higher power motives (Chusmir and Parker, 1984), females are identified as having less influence in decisions affecting their work performance (Sherman, Ezell, and Odewahn, 1987). Kanter (1977) suggests that men have a greater opportunity to acquire organizational power because of greater opportunities for sponsorship, visibility, and performing extraordinary tasks. Kanter (1977) links organizational power to interaction. She notes that competent bosses have "more frequent exchanges with superiors" (168). Those who achieve organizational power also develop strong relationships with their peers.

The current research points to the importance of acquiring effective organizational power in order to be a successful manager (Trempe, Rigny, and Haccoun, 1985; Wiley and Eskilson, 1982). Because interaction with superiors and peers is so important to acquiring power, women need to develop their interaction ability.

Because interaction is so important and has been identified as a possible difference between males and females, it would be useful to identify the interaction norms for males and females to better understand this difference. Jackson's (1966) Return Potential Model (RPM) provides the model for describing and measuring norms. This approach is consistent with a General Systems Perspective and Communication Rules Theory.

METHOD

To investigate whether the expected behavior of females is to communicate less often with their supervisors, subordinates, and peers, a questionnaire was designed to obtain data on norms. The items in the questionnaire were designed to elicit responses of approval/disapproval on items regarding supervisor/subordinate and employee/employee relationships. This questionnaire was patterned after the Role Behavior Questionnaire (Jackson, 1963). Other studies advocating this pattern to measure norms are Strom (1963), Tipps (1968), Wicker (1969), Dunkerley (1970), Glick and Jackson (1970), LeCompte and LeCompte (1973), and Santee and Jackson (1977).

The questionnaire items each represent a specific communication behavior. The person responding would indicate the strength of his or her approval or disapproval for each of five alternative ways of behaving. Approval/disapproval will be indicated on a seven-point Likert scale, with 7 representing maximum approval and 1 representing maximum disapproval. An example of an item on the questionnaire is:

An employee is comfortable discussing work problems with his/her co-workers/peers:

a.	*almost always.*	7 6 5 4 3 2 1
b.	*frequently.*	7 6 5 4 3 2 1
c.	*sometimes.*	7 6 5 4 3 2 1
d.	*infrequently.*	7 6 5 4 3 2 1
e.	*almost never.*	7 6 5 4 3 2 1
f.	*does not apply.*	7 6 5 4 3 2 1

The final items for the questionnaire were determined following an expert sort. The final questionnaire consisted of 49 items and is available upon request from the author.

In addition to gathering data for analysis of norms, one of the purposes of the initial administration of the questionnaire was to seek feedback for refining the questionnaire. This initial administration required selection of a sample that had experience in the general work force. College students at two Western colleges were selected because most of them did have experience in the workplace, and because they provided a readily available cross-section with regard to age, sex, and type of organization represented. They also could provide valuable postadministration feedback for questionnaire refinement.

The questionnaire was administered by the instructors of four college communication classes during the spring semester, 1987. There was a total of 65 respondents, 23 males and 41 females; one provided no data. The respondents ranged in age from the categories "20 and under" to "56–60." Thirty-seven respondents were currently working under the immediate supervision of a male, 21 under the immediate supervision of a female, four under the immediate supervision of both a male and a female, and three provided no data. The order of the responses for each item was coded from the most frequent communication (almost always) to the least frequent communication (almost never).

The norms and their structural properties are described and measured as outlined in Jackson's (1966) Return Potential Model (RPM). A norm is designated by a graph with two dimensions: the abscissa is a behavioral dimension, and the ordinate is an evaluation dimension indicating the amount of approval or disapproval an actor would elicit from others for that behavior (see Figure 1).

Points are plotted using the mean of distribution for each point. The line joining each point is the return potential curve representing the potential approval or disapproval for the behavior over the entire behavioral continuum. The return potential model provides a descriptive configuration of the norms for comparison rather than a statistical testing for significance of results. It also provides the basis for which the following structural properties of the norms are described.

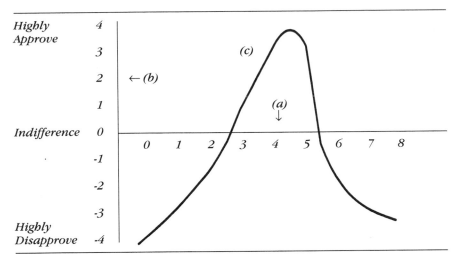

Figure 1. Return potential model for representing norms: (a) A behavior dimension, (b) A return potential dimension, (c) A return potential curve

The intensity of the norm is a measure of the strength of the feeling, whether approval or disapproval, that others have regarding the behavior of an actor in a particular situation. Intensity is developed "by summing the ordinates or height of the curve at each scale position on the behavior dimension" (Jackson, 1960, 142). The intensity value ranges from 1–7.

The crystallization of the norm indicates the amount of agreement others have concerning a norm. Crystallization is calculated "by summing the total variance or dispersion of the return potential for all scale positions on the behavior dimension" (Jackson, 1960, 146). The intensity value ranges from 1–7.

Normative power (NP) refers to "the potential for influencing activity that is inherent in interpersonal identification or shared orientations" (Jackson, 1975, 238). Normative power is calculated by multiplying the crystallization by the intensity. The normative power value ranges from 0–1.

The complementary output to normative power is conflict potential (CP): "the proportion of input of energy, in terms of others' expectations or return potential, that is not available for the regulation of actor's conduct in a given situation...." (Jackson, 1975, 248–49). The conflict potential value ranges from 0–1.

The norms and the property-values for the norms from the questionnaire results were generated from a microcomputer program using Jackson's descriptions (Wright, 1987). The area of male-female interaction norms that will be discussed regards new ideas.

Table 1.   **Summary of Data on Employee Communication with Peers on New Ideas**

Item	N	NP	CP
38			
Males	21	0.135	0.468
Females	37	0.285	0.413
5			
Males	23	0.266	0.484
Females	39	0.372	0.389
44			
Males	21	0.157	0.532
Females	35	0.340	0.368

Note: *The values represent the mean of the values for each point on the RPC.*

RESULTS

Table 1 and Figures 2–4 provide the values and return potential curves (RPC) of results for males and females on the items of employee communication with peers regarding new ideas. The RPC in Figure 2 indicates that females approve of encouraging co-workers/peers to experiment with new ideas. Males are basically indifferent but approve slightly of the occasional occurences of this behavior. This is a particularly weak norm for males and generates higher conflict potential for males than for females.

The RPCs in Figures 3 and 4 address the generating of new ideas with peers in informal conversations in the workplace and at lunchtime. Both males and females approve of this behavior in the workplace (RPC 3), although the approval of males is not as strong as that of females. The normative power (NP) is higher for females, and the CP is higher for males. The RPC in Figure 4 indicates that females approve of generating new ideas at lunchtime. Males are indifferent to the generation of new ideas at lunchtime but approve most strongly when it happens "sometimes." The NP is fairly strong for females, with a midrange value for CP. Males indicate low NP, but high CP.

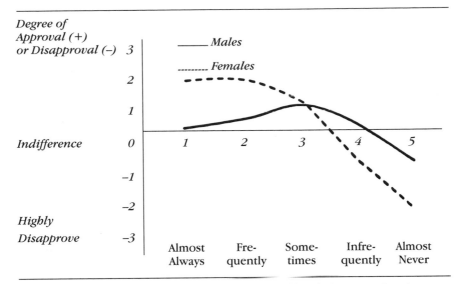

Figure 2. Item 38: Employees are encouraged by their co-workers/peers to experiment with new ideas.

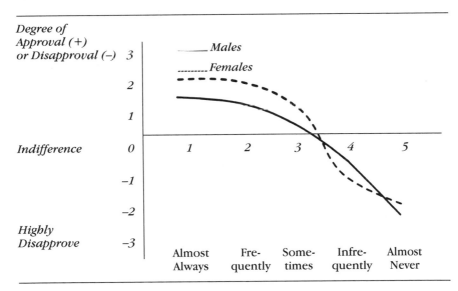

Figure 3. Item 5: Peers/co-workers generate new ideas in informal conversations with each other in the workplace.

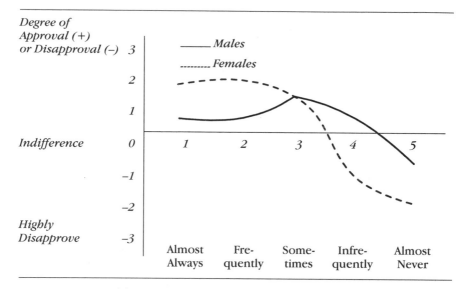

Figure 4. Item 44: Co-workers/peers generate new ideas in conversations with each other at lunch time.

The results in this area of peer communication regarding new ideas show a difference in the norms for males and females. Females approve much more strongly of communication with peers regarding new ideas than do males. Females also view the strength of these norms and the conflict potential to be about equal. Males, on the other hand, view these norms as weak but generating high conflict potential. The items that address location for the discussion of new ideas indicate that females approve of discussing new ideas both at work and at lunchtime. The only time males approve strongly of discussing new ideas is at work. It appears that, regarding the area of new ideas, females approve much more of this interaction with peers and find this interaction less uncertain or conflict-producing.

DISCUSSION

This study demonstrates that analysis of norms contributes to our understanding of gender communication. The research reviewed suggests that females are interacting less often with supervisors, subordinates, and peers. The results of this study reveal that males and females do approve of different amounts of interaction, but males are not the ones approving of more interaction. Females approve more of all types of interaction regarding new ideas. Males indicate the presence of more conflict potential regarding the discussion of new ideas with peers.

One possible interpretation of these results could stem from informal networks. Previous research indicates that females have been excluded from important informal networks. This study does not directly address informal networks but does suggest that males approve of different behaviors than do females. If females do not share the same informal contacts, they may be developing different norms for interaction because they have not had the opportunity to learn the same behaviors as males have. Another explanation is that females choose not to accept and adopt the behaviors that males have adopted.

In analyzing the result that males experience more conflict potential regarding the discussion of new ideas with peers, it would seem that in this area, males view their peers with a greater sense of competition than do females.

It also appears that females use their time away from the workplace differently than males do. Females approve much more than males of using lunchtime for the discussion of new ideas. Only at the workplace does the approval of males for discussing new ideas approximate that of females. Once again this points to the existence of informal networks.

This approach to understanding organizations through the identification and measurement of norms has identified some differences between males and females regarding new ideas. This approach would also be useful in exploring other areas of gender communication, such as the norms of respondents from different age levels, from different positions in the organization, and from different ethnic groups. An analysis of these norms would increase our understanding of male and female interactions in organizations.

REFERENCES

Bayes, M., and P.M. Newton. 1978. "Women in Authority: A Sociopsychological Analysis." *Journal of Applied Behavioral Science* 14:7–20.

Brass, D.J. 1985. "Men's and Women's Networks: A Study of Interaction Patterns and Influence in an Organization." *Academy of Management Journal,* 28(2):327–43.

Chusmir, L.H., and B. Parker. 1984. "Dimensions of Need for Power: Personalized vs. Socialized Power in Female and Male Managers. *Sex Roles* 11(9/10):757–69.

Crandall, B. 1969. "Sex Differences in Expectancy of Intellectual and Academic Reinforcement." In *Achievement-Related Motives in Children,* edited by C.P. Smith, 11–45. New York: Russell Sage Foundation.

Day, D.R., and R.M. Stogdill. 1972. "Leader Behavior of Male and Female Supervisors: A Comparative Study." *Personnel Psychology* 25:353–60.

Donnell, S.M., and J. Hall. 1980. "Men and Women as Managers: A Significant Case of No Significant Difference." *Organizational Dynamics,* 8(4):60–77.

Dunkerley, D. 1970. "The Measurement of Social Norms." *International Journal of Mathematical Education in Science and Technology* 1:291–96.

Ezell, H.F., C.A. Odewahn, and J.D. Sherman. 1980. "Perceived Competence of Women Managers in Public Human Service Organizations: A Comparative View." *Journal of Management* 6:135–44.

Freedman, S.M., and J.S. Phillips. 1988. "The Changing Nature of Research on Women at Work." *Journal of Management* 14(2):231–51.

Glauser, M.J. 1984. "Upward Information Flow in Organizations: Review and Conceptual Analysis." *Human Relations* 37(8):613–43.

Glick, O.W., and J. Jackson. 1970. "Effects of Normative Similarity on Group Formation Among College Freshmen." *Pacific Sociological Review* 13:263–69.

Izraeli, D.N. 1987. "Sex Effects in the Evaluation of Influence Tactics." *Journal of Occupational Behaviour* 8:79–86.

Jackson, J. 1960. "Structural Characteristics of Norms." In *The Dynamics of Instructional Groups, the Fifty-Ninth Yearbook of the National Society for the Study of Education, Part II,* edited by N.B. Henry. 136–63. Chicago: University of Chicago Press.

Jackson, J. 1963. "Role Behavior Questionnaire: A 150-Item, Two Part Inventory." (Copyrighted and available from author.)

———. 1966. "A Conceptual and Measurement Model for Norms and Roles." *Pacific Sociological Review* 9:35–47.

———. 1975. "Normative Power and Conflict Potential." *Sociological Methods and Research* 4:237–63.

Kanter, R.M. 1977. *Men and Women of the Corporation.* New York: Basic Books, Inc.

LeCompte, W.F., and G.K. LeCompte. 1973. "Generational Attribution in Turkish and American Youth." *Journal of Cross-Cultural Psychology* 4:175–91.

Maccoby, E. E., and C.N. Jacklin. 1974. *The Psychology of Sex Differences.* Stanford, CA: Stanford University Press.

Markham, W.T., S.J. South, C.M. Bonjean, and J. Corder. 1985. "Gender and Opportunity in the Federal Bureaucracy." *American Journal of Sociology,* 91(1):129–50.

McCarty, P.A. 1986. "Effects of Feedback on the Self-Confidence of Men and Women." *Academy of Management Journal* 29(4):840–47.

Pazy, A. 1987. "Sex Differences in Responsiveness to Organizational Career Management." *Human Resource Management* 26(2):243–56.

Rendel, M. 1977. "Educating Women for Leadership." *Working Papers: Changing Roles of Women in Industrial Societies.* U.S.A.: The Rockefeller Foundation.

Robie, E.A. 1973. "Challenge to Management." In *Corporate Lib: Women's Challenge to Management,* edited by E. Ginzberg and A.M. Yohalem, 9–29. Baltimore, MD: Johns Hopkins University Press.

Rose, S.M. 1985. "Professional Networks of Junior Faculty in Psychology." *Psychology of Women Quarterly* 9:533–47.

Rosen, B., M.E. Templeton, and K. Kichline. 1981. "The First Few Years on the Job: Women in Management." *Business Horizons* 24(6):26–29.

Santee, R. T., and J. Jackson. 1977. "Cultural Values as a Source of Normative Sanctions." *Pacific Sociological Review* 20:439–54.

Seifert, C. and C.E. Miller. 1988. "Subordinates' Perceptions of Leaders in Task-Performing Dyads: Effects of Sex of Leader and Subordinate, Method of Leader Selection, and Performance Feedback." *Sex Roles* 19(1/2):13–28.

Sherman, J.D., H.F. Ezell, and C.A.Odewahn. 1987. "Centralization of Decision Making and Accountability Based on Gender." *Group and Organization Studies* 12(4):454–63.

Staley, C.C. 1984. "Managerial Women in Mixed Groups: Implications of Recent Research." *Group and Organization Studies,* 9:316–32.

Strom, R.D. 1963. "Comparison of Adolescent and Adult Behavioral Norm Properties." *Journal of Educational Psychology* 54:322–30.

Swisher, R., R.R. DuMont, and C.J. Boyer. 1985. "The Motivation to Manage: A Study of Academic Librarians and Library Science Students." *Library Trends* 34:219–34.

Taylor, S., and D. Ilgen. 1980. "An Investigation of Initial Placement Decisions About Women in Traditionally Male Occupations." *Proceedings of the 40th Annual Meeting of the Academy of Management* (439). Detroit, MI.

Tipps, H.C., Jr. 1968. "An Analysis of the Relationship Between Normative Intensity and Length of Interaction." Paper presented to the University of Oregon at Eugene.

Trempe, J., A. Rigny, and R.R. Haccoun. 1985. "Subordinate Satisfaction with Male and Female Managers: Role of Perceived Supervisory Influence." *Journal of Applied Psychology* 70:44–47.

White, M.C., G. De Sanctis, and M.D. Crino. 1981. "Achievement, Self-Confidence, Personality Traits, and Leadership Ability: A Review of Literature on Sex Differences." *Psychological Reports* 48:547–69.

Wicker, A.W. 1969. "Size of Church Membership and Members' Support of Church Behavior Settings." *Journal of Personality and Social Psychology* 13:278–88.

Wiley, M.G., and A. Eskilson. 1982. "The Interaction of Sex and Power Base on Perceptions of Managerial Effectiveness." *Academy of Management Journal* 25:671–77.

Wood, M.M. 1975. "What Does it Take for a Woman to Make it in Management." *Personnel Journal* 54:38–41.

Wright, R.R. 1987. *Quantitative Analysis of the Return Potential Model* (Micro-computer program). Turlock, CA.

Young, J.W. 1978. "The Subordinate's Exposure of Organizational Vulnerability to the Superior: Sex and Organizational Effects." *Academy of Management Journal* 21:113–22.

Section II
Reconstructing Gender

Unit IV
Interacting with Power

Section Two of this volume looks at how gender roles can be reconstructed through one's interactions with power, culture, and audiences. Power issues are at the base of all interactions, whether they be personal or professional. In turn, how one comes to define power and who is seen as having it affects those interactions. Alice Deakins begins our look at how gender interacts with power by helping us see that men and women use the same linguistic system for divergent meanings. The linguistics of power and solidarity are explored in same sex and mixed sex interaction. Next, Belle Ragins looks at power in organizations. This study investigates how power interacts with the leader's biological sex in subordinate evaluations of male and female leaders. In Chapter 15, Patrice Buzzanell explores research on romance in the workplace and delineates areas in need of further investigation. Chapter 16 is concerned with misuse of power—that is, teasing and sexual harassment. J.K. Alberts argues that women are caught in a double-bind situation insofar as they cannot go along with the tease, ignore the teasing, or leave their jobs without paying a price. This unit on power closes with Mary Monedas's examination of self-esteem levels and sex role attitudes in mixed-sex dyads. The extent to which males use power displays to control interactions is of primary concern.

CHAPTER 13

The *Tu/Vous* Dilemma: Gender, Power, and Solidarity

Alice H. Deakins
William Paterson College

The dimensions underlying the selection of the pronouns *tu* and *vous* in face-to-face interaction—power and solidarity—provide a framework for understanding the ambiguities inherent in single-sex interaction and the conflict found in mixed-sex interaction. Conflicts result from (1) men's orientation to an active speaking style and women's orientation to an active listening style, and (2) the use by men and women of the same linguistic features for different communication functions. In mixed-sex interactions, such conflict can create misunderstandings that can be explained by revealing the operation of power and solidarity in single-sex groups.[1]

LINGUISTIC BACKGROUND

Numerous languages have systems that use the same linguistic signs to code for power and solidarity, two conflicting dimensions which are "fundamental to the analysis of all social life" (Brown and Gilman, 1972). The ambiguity inherent in such systems has been studied in *tu/vous* languages (Fr. *tu/vous*; Sp. *tu/usted*; Ger. *du/Sie*; Ital. *tu/Lei*) by Brown and Gilman, and in the address system of American English by Brown and Ford.

Brown and Gilman posit a pronoun system that originally coded only for power. In medieval Europe, upper-class individuals addressed each other with reciprocal V and lower-class with reciprocal T. When the classes interacted, their pronoun use was nonreciprocal. The upper class gave T downwards and the lower class gave V upwards, resulting in the association of V with high status. This pattern represented the power semantic, reflecting differences between classes. Gradually, another pattern developed to distinguish relationships within the same class, the T of intimacy and the

151

V of formality or distance. This is the solidarity semantic, reflecting like-mindedness or similarity between individuals or groups. As a result of the development of the second pattern, both power and solidarity were signalled by the same linguistic forms: T and V.

All the *tu/vous* languages, which force coding for power/powerlessness and solidarity/distance in pronoun selection in every face-to-face interaction, reveal the ambiguity inherent in pronoun selection. The ambiguity does not occur with reciprocal usage when people are on an equal power or solidarity basis: they use reciprocal *tu* for mutual powerlessness or solidarity/intimacy or reciprocal *vous* for mutual power or distance. Ambiguity occurs when the relationships are not reciprocal. Should superiors who are solidary use the V of superiority or the T of solidarity? Should inferiors who are not solidary use the T of inferiority or the V of formality?

As a result of historical movement toward equality and democracy in Europe, preferred pronoun usage is now reciprocal and generally resolved on the basis of the solidarity semantic. Traces of the power semantic, however, are seen in several ways. First, in moving from mutual V to mutual T in a relationship, the higher-status person retains the right to initiate the change: "The gate to linguistic intimacy is kept by the person of higher status" (Brown and Ford, 1964). Second, native speakers of French retain an awareness of the power semantic in certain interactions. One native speaker of French, who defended his decision to "tutoyer tout le monde," refused to use *tu* in a service encounter. He said it was lack of commonality but was accused by another native speaker of snobbism and classism (Bryan, 1972). So, the power semantic is not far from the consciousness of contemporary French speakers, perpetuating a system that is ambiguous in its very structure.

Although English is not a *tu/vous* language, the power/solidarity ambiguity is clearly visible in English in titles and terms of address. In American English, according to a study by Brown and Ford of modern American plays, actual and reported usage in business offices, and recorded usage in the Midwest, there are two patterns for titles: reciprocal, in which both interactants give and receive title and last name (TLN) or both give and receive first name (FN), and nonreciprocal, in which one gives TLN and receives FN and vice-versa. Nonreciprocal usage in their study was based on age and occupational status. The reciprocal usage reflected the solidarity dimension and the nonreciprocal the power dimension. Again, as with the pronouns, "[o]ne form expresses both distance and deference; the other form expresses both intimacy and condescension" (Brown and Ford, 1964). Thus, ambiguity is built into the address system, and norms are not always clear. Although on most occasions the context, including the relationships of the participants, will indicate which semantic is most salient, some interactions remain ambiguous. A speaker can code for one and be heard for the other. For instance, a boss can say, "Good morning, Mary" to his secretary. He may be coding for familiarity rather than power, but she can interpret it as coding for either one. In most circumstances, she will return not first name but title plus last name, "Good morning, Mr. Jones." Is she coding for lack of power or for distance?

The structure behind a system that uses the same linguistic signs to code for two different interactional dimensions—power and solidarity—provides a model for interpreting other linguistic data as well. The model behind the T/V dilemma can be usefully extended to gender-based interaction, both single-sex and mixed-sex. Such an extension reveals some of the ambiguities of single-sex interaction and some of the conflicts of mixed-sex interaction.

INTERACTIONAL DATA

Gender-based interaction patterns, although studied through a variety of methodologies, have usually been interpreted in similar ways: Men are oriented to competition (power) and women are not; women are oriented to cooperation (solidarity) and men are not. The dimensions of power and solidarity, however, are important for both men and women but operate differently in single-sex and mixed-sex groups. The ambiguity inherent in single-sex interaction is compounded in mixed interaction.

The linguistic features that are salient to gender-based communication can be conceptualized under two main categories: topic selection and topic support. Topic selection includes what overt topics[2] are discussed and how self-disclosure functions. Topic support includes the use of questions, qualifiers, hedges, intensifiers, intonation, quantity of talk, interruptions, stories, humor, expletives and obscenities, confrontation, backchannel cues, and paraverbal and nonverbal behavior. Using these features, interactional research has described communication patterns characteristic of all-male, all-female, and mixed groups.

All-male groups are, as the literature reports, strongly oriented to power, but solidarity is negotiated simultaneously using some of the same features that express power. Power as the basic dimension of all-male groups is seen in their structure, which is hierarchical (Aries, 1976). Although what determines an individual's place in the hierarchy can vary from group to group, in any particular group a dominance order is established. In terms of topic selection, men choose events and facts, which easily lend themselves to competition (Aries, 1976; Deakins, 1986). They tend to self-disclose little about themselves and their feelings, using silence to avoid vulnerability (Aries, 1976; Pearson, 1985; Philipsen, 1975; Sattel, 1983). When men tell jokes, they tend to be competitive and aggressive, using obscene, racial, ethnic, and religious content (Orkin, 1988; van Genderen, 1985), but are not self-deprecatory (Orkin, 1988; Pearson, 1985).

In terms of topic support, the dynamic of competition is continued. In all-male groups men tell stories with either themselves as hero or someone else as victim (Aries, 1976). These stories are competitive: who tells the best one, holds the floor longest, gets more laughter from the audience. The stories can be about pranks and practical jokes (Aries, 1976) or they can be jokes (Kelley, 1986), which also lend themselves easily to competition. The dynamic of competition is continued in the way topics are changed. Men tend to jump abruptly from one story to another, from one joke to another, as they wrest the floor from the previous speaker by topic switch maneuvers (Aries, 1976; Derber, 1979). Competition is also seen in a confrontational style that is forceful and blunt, characterized by strongly expressed opinion. Even disagreements that men try to resolve by compromise reveal the assertion of the self. Finally, quantity of speech in men's groups is determined by who competes most successfully and, as a result, talks more. The less successful talk less and may avoid all-male groups (Aries, 1976).

Several other interactional activities are characteristic of men and relate indirectly to power. Listening is focused on verbal content, not metamessages (Tannen, 1986). This means that men understand *what* is being discussed but not *how* the interlocutors feel about the content, the speaker, and the hearer. Also, men use questions to elicit information, not as a strategy to keep a conversation going, and they use backchannel cues to signal agreement, not interactional support (Maltz and Borker, 1982). These features reveal men's focus on facts, which lend themselves to competition and the "power" dimension.

Although these features of all-male discourse have been used to support power as the most salient dimension for men, many of these same features can also be seen as building solidarity within all-male groups. Discussing events and facts creates a shared community of interests at the very same time that it allows competition to take place. Sharing stories, joking, laughing, and teasing, even the use of expletives and obscenities by some men, build male bonding. "And if the group uses swearing as a marker of identity, then you must swear too—and the more swear-words you use, the stronger your affirmation of solidarity with the group" (Crystal, 1986). Further, confrontation can be a tactic to keep a group going, as well as to show the self as competitive. In summary, some of the very components of interaction that reveal competition and "power" are those used to build all-male solidarity.

Likewise, all-female groups are, as research has pointed out, oriented to cooperation and solidarity, but power is negotiated at the same time using some of the same features. Solidarity is seen in the structure of women's groups, which tend to be lateral, not hierarchical (Aries, 1976; Jenkins and Kramer, 1978). Cooperation is the basic dynamic of all-female groups and is revealed in both topic selection and topic support. In terms of topic selection, all-female groups tend to talk about people: family, friends, lovers (Aries, 1976; Deakins, 1986). The pattern of cooperation characteristic of women's groups, however, is revealed less in terms of overt topics than in terms of self-disclosure. Women self-disclose more about themselves and their feelings than men do, particularly negative and intimate information about themselves (Pearson, 1985). This information is invitational, not competitive, encouraging other women to contribute similar information about themselves. Further, in terms of topics, women's humor tends to be self-deprecatory (Orkin, 1988; Pearson, 1985), revealing vulnerabilities, not strengths. Again, this functions as a cooperative, not a competitive strategy, encouraging similar stories from other women.

In terms of topic support, the dynamic of cooperation is continued. In telling stories, in all-female groups personal narratives begin with a kernel story to which everyone adds by acknowledging the previous contribution and building on it (Kalcik, 1975). The stories are often third-person, not first-person stories, i.e., about other people, not the self. Topic change is gradual, not abrupt. Confrontation is avoided, with problems being settled privately, not in the group. The listening style is also group oriented, focusing on metamessages, those paraverbal qualities that send information about feelings concerned with the self, the listener, and the message (Tannen, 1986). The group dynamic is maintained through a highly active listening style characterized by questions, supportive comments, and numerous backchannel cues, nods, and sustained gaze. Quantity of speech is shared, with active speakers becoming quiet and encouraging quiet ones to speak (Aries, 1976).

Other features of the so-called "women's style" or "powerless style"[3] are also active group-oriented strategies. Hedges, hesitations, qualifiers, and disclaimers encourage the listener to respond because the "last word" has not yet been spoken on the subject. Both intensifiers such as *so* and *such* and the greater pitch range characteristic of women's voices indicate interactional orientation and dynamism.

All these features are used to create a style that is interpreted as cooperative, consensual, and leaderless. As in the men's groups, however, some of these same features are also coding for power. In terms of topics, quantity and accuracy of knowledge about other people and their behavior contributes to a sense of power because it reveals how broad a networking structure a woman has. Self-disclosure not only builds intimacy but gives interactional power to the person who is most thoughtful and analytic. Focusing on metamessages gives assessment not just of verbal content but of feelings about that content. Other aspects of the cooperative style—story chaining, active listening, hedges, qualifiers, disclaimers—make women powerful interactors. Not only do they express themselves, but they make it possible for other women to do so as well. Power in all-female groups is understood as being able to facilitate successful, trouble-free interaction.

To summarize single-sex interaction, both power and solidarity operate in all-male and all-female groups, but they operate differently. Men use some of the same strategies for competition and for solidarity; women use some of the same strategies for cooperation and for power. Power and solidarity are present in both groups but are understood and valued differently. Men understand power as the top position in the hierarchical ladder, whatever it may be. They understand solidarity as a by-product of the power dynamic. Power, indeed, is the more salient dimension, as previous research has indicated, but solidarity is intertwined with it. In contrast, women understand solidarity as their main goal, with power coming from successful interaction. Solidarity is the more salient dimension for women, but power, as women understand it, is intertwined with it. The stage is set for misunderstanding and conflict when the two sexes interact and must struggle to communicate using systems which operate largely unconsciously and which do not always match.

The conflict between the sexes in mixed interaction is rooted in men's basic orientation to power, as reflected by their active speaking style and women's basic orientation to solidarity, as reflected by their active listening style. These differences are seen most clearly in topic support mechanisms, which reveal both differential use of some topic support mechanisms and use of the same linguistic features for different communication functions.

Men's active speaking style and women's active listening style is seen in their differential use of interruptions and of verbal, paraverbal, and nonverbal conversational support mechanisms. Although the number and function of interruptions is complicated, most studies of social/informal interaction report that men interrupt more, resulting in a return of the floor to them. Women, in contrast, as they have learned in all-female groups, wait for the floor to be returned to them by others, which does not happen in a mixed group. Further, women, as active listeners, ask more questions, give more paraverbal support (yeah, mmm, uh-huh), and produce more nonverbal support (nods and eye contact). As a result of these differences, men have more talk time in mixed groups. Indeed, all nonfamily studies of quantity of talk report that men speak longer in mixed groups. Although these data have usually been interpreted as a result of greater male power in mixed-sex interaction, it can also be interpreted as a result of women's orientation to solidarity and to power as facilitating interaction. Thus, women, to the extent that they employ single-sex patterns in mixed-sex groups, unconsciously yield more speaking time to men.

Another differential use of topic support mechanisms resulting from men's basic orientation to power and women's basic orientation to solidarity is seen in connections between turns. Women explicitly acknowledge a previous statement and make a connection before going on. In contrast, men ignore the preceding comment and simply go on. This results in men's topics being narrowly defined and adhered to, with abrupt shifts between topics, whereas women develop topics progressively and shift gradually. As a result, women, accustomed to acknowledgment of their topics from other women, can feel that they have not been heard when they interact with men.

Still another differential topic support strategy between men and women is seen in confrontation. Men, oriented to power and competition, can use verbal aggressiveness as a strategy for maintaining conversational flow. If the conversation is flagging, men can throw out an aggressive comment to get the ball rolling again, as well as to demonstrate their prowess at competition. Women, who avoid confrontation in their all-female groups and sustain interaction by active listening, can interpret this strategy as personally directed, negative, and disruptive.

A further difference related to topics is found in men's orientation to the verbal component of a message and women's orientation to the par-averbal metamessages sent by intonation, pitch, pausing and pacing, and loudness and softness (Tannen, 1986). Men, oriented to power through content, respond to the verbal portion of the message. Women, oriented to solidarity and relationships, hear metamessages containing information about how speakers feel about themselves, the message, and the hearers. Women can respond to the paraverbal message, whereas men respond to the verbal message, creating conflict in mixed-sex interaction. Men and women engaged in the same conversation can appear to be responding to different interactions.

In addition to having some different mechanisms to support topics, which result from men and women's different orientation to power and solidarity and to active speaking and active listening, conflict is also created in mixed-sex interaction by men and women using the same linguistic features for different communication functions (Coates, 1986; Maltz and Borker, 1982). Women use questions as ways to keep the conversation going, furthering their basic goal of smooth interaction but expecting a question to be, at some time, asked of them so that they can respond. Men, on the other hand, hear questions as requests for information, to which they respond by seizing the floor in what sounds to women like a monologue. Similarly, women understand problem sharing and advice giving as opportunities to discuss problems and share experiences, whereas men hear the presentation of a problem as a request for a solution. Further, women use verbal, paraverbal, and nonverbal cues to indicate that they are listening to the speaker and to encourage the speaker to go on. Men use them to indicate agreement with the speaker, not just encouragement. Thus, if a man is not agreeing, a woman feels he is not listening. These three differences continue to reveal men's basic orientation to power and competition and women's to solidarity and relationships.

In summary, the conflicts inherent in mixed-gender interaction are more complicated than the structured ambiguity of single-sex interaction. When men and women talk together, they bring with them patterns developed in the family and during years of socialization in single-sex groups. Although these patterns contain the possibility of ambiguity in the single-sex interactions, in mixed-sex interactions the patterns contain the probability of conflict and misunderstanding.

CONCLUSION

The dimensions of power and solidarity are basic to human social life. The analysis of pronoun selection in T/V languages and of social address systems in American English reveals a system that, in its structure, is ambiguous about whether power or solidarity is being expressed in any given interaction. The structured ambiguity of these linguistic systems provides a useful model in exploring the dimensions of power and solidarity in single-sex and mixed-sex interactions.

In single-sex interaction, the T/V dilemma can clearly be seen. Because power and solidarity are negotiated with the same linguistic signs, the linguistic code is ambiguous about which dimension is more salient in any particular interaction. Further, the T/V model developed from pronouns and terms of address becomes more complicated in single-sex interaction because power and solidarity are valued, understood, and negotiated differently by men and women. Thus, in all-male interaction, power, understood as successful competition, is the dominant dimension, but solidarity is negotiated with the same linguistic features. Based only on the linguistic data, it is not possible to determine whether power or solidarity is being negotiated. Likewise, in all-female groups, solidarity, understood as cooperative interaction, is the dominant dimension, but power, understood as successfully facilitating cooperative interaction, is negotiated with some of the same linguistic features. Again, the linguistic features by themselves do not reveal whether power or solidarity is being negotiated. The system, like the T/V system, is ambiguous in its structure.

Mixed-sex interaction compounds the ambiguity. As a result of men and women differently valuing, understanding, and negotiating power and solidarity, mixed-sex interaction produces conflict, frustration, and misunderstanding. Given their orientation to an active speaking style and their understanding of power as successful competition, men can feel successful in mixed-sex interaction, but they may not feel solidarity. Given their orientation to an active listening style and their understanding of power as facilitating successful interaction, women can feel powerful in mixed-sex interaction at the same time that they feel powerless in terms of access to the floor, which no longer functions in the context of cooperative solidarity. Further confusion results from the use of the same linguistic features for different communication functions.

Much of the communication distress that men and women feel when they interact together in social contexts comes from their different orientation to and understanding of power and solidarity. Such problems are inherent in human communication, which is characterized by indeterminacy. The problems peculiar to gender-based communication provide the challenge of creatively constructing meaning using two mismatched systems. Although the mismatch can result in misunderstanding, frustration, and anger, by revealing some of the linguistic features contributing to the mismatch, the possibility for conscious understanding and action rather than unconscious submission to cultural systems is created.

NOTES

1.   Most research on gendered interaction has been done on white, middle-class, heterosexual, college-age populations. The patterns described in this paper are general cultural molds that influence and shape the behavior of individual women and men in the research groups. However, in addition to the variables of ethnic group, class, sexual orientation, and age, other factors can interact with and override the gender-based patterns discussed in this paper: the setting; the personalities of the interactants; the status of interactants; the degree of intimacy of the relationship; the topic; and the nature of the task.

A further distinction must be made in domains. Three domains, defined by function of interaction, are salient and should not be confused by using evidence from one to describe the others: (1) the world of social/casual (nonfamily) interaction, (2) the world of work, and (3) the world of the family. These "universes of discourse" have different norms and, if the direction of current research is borne out, different orientations to power and solidarity. This paper will discuss M/F interactional dynamics in the world of social/casual interaction.

2.   Overt topics are what people are talking about: sports, family, movies, politics, cars, etc. These overt topics may be used to negotiate covert agendas of interactants: I'm right and you're wrong, etc. This paper refers only to overt topics.

3.   O'Barr and Atkins have suggested that "women's style" is more appropriately identified as "powerless style." Their research, however, was done in the public work domain, where the male orientation to power is arguably the more salient dimension.

REFERENCES

Aries, Elizabeth. 1976. "Interaction Patterns and Themes of Male, Female, and
     Mixed Groups." *Small Group Behavior* 7:7–18.
————. 1987. "Gender and Communication." In *Sex and Gender,* edited by
     P. Shaver and C. Hendrick. Newbury Park, CA: Sage Publications.
Brown, Roger W., and Marguerite Ford. 1964. "Address in American English."
     In *Language in Culture and Society,* edited by Dell Hymes. 234–44.
     New York: Harper & Row.
Brown, R. and A. Gilman. 1972. "The Pronouns of Power and Solidarity." In
     Language and Social Context, edited by Pier Paolo Giglioli. 252–82.
     Harmondsworth, England: Penguin.
Bryan, Anne-Marie. 1972. "Le 'Tu' et le 'Vous'." *The French Review* 45
     (5):1007–10.
Coates, Jennifer. 1986. *Women, Men and Language.* London: Longman.
Crystal, David. 1986. *Grin and Swear It.* English Today 7:34-35.
Deakins, Alice. 1986. "Talk at the Top: Bank Officers at Lunch." Paper presented
     to the Ninth Annual Conference on Communication, Language, and
     Gender. Fairfax, VA.
Derber, Charles. 1979. *The Pursuit of Attention: Power and Individualism in
     Everyday Life.* Cambridge, MA: Schenkman Publishing Company.
Eakins, Barbara, and R. Gene Eakins. 1978. *Sex Differences in Human
     Communication.* Boston, MA: Houghton Mifflin.
Jenkins, Lee and Cheris Kramer. 1978. "Small Group Process: Learning from
     Women." *Women's Studies International Quarterly* 1:67–84.
Kalcik, Susan. 1975. "...Like Ann's Gynecologist or the Time I Was Almost Raped."
     Journal of American Folklore 88:3–11.
Kelley, Denis. 1986. "Communication Patterns: Listening to Barroom
     Conversations." Manuscript.
Labov, William. 1972. "The Social Setting of Linguistic Change." In *Sociolinguistic
     Patterns,* edited by W. Labov, 260–325. Philadelphia: University of
     Pennsylvania Press.
Lakoff, Robin. 1975. *Language and Woman's Place.* New York: Harper and Row.
Maley, Catherine A. 1972. "Historically Speaking, *Tu* or *Vous*?" *The French Review*
     45(5):999–1006.

Maltz, Daniel N. and Ruth A. Borker. 1982. "A Cultural Approach to Male-Female Miscommunication." In *Language and Social Identity,* edited by John J. Gumperz. 196–216. Cambridge, MA: Cambridge University Press.

Nichols, Patricia. 1983. "Linguistic Options and Choices for Black Women in the Rural South." In *Language, Gender and Society,* edited by B.Thorne, C. Kramarae, and N. Henley. Rowley, MA: Newbury House.

O'Barr, William M., and Bowman K. Atkins. 1980. "'Women's language' or 'power-less language'?" In *Women and Language in Literature and Society,* edited by S. McConnell-Ginet, R. Borker, and N. Furman. 93–110. New York: Praeger Publishers.

Orkin, Neil S. 1988. "The Differences Between Male and Female Comedians." Manuscript.

Pearson, Judy Cornelia. 1985. *Gender and Communication.* Dubuque, IA: William C. Brown.

Philipsen, Gerry. 1975. "Speaking 'Like a Man' in Teamsterville: Culture Patterns of Role Enactment in an Urban Neighborhood." *Quarterly Journal of Speech.* 61:13–22.

Sattel, Jack W. 1983. "Men, Inexpressiveness, and Power." In *Language, Gender and Society,* edited by B. Thorne, C. Kramarae, and N. Henley. Rowley, MA: Newbury House.

Tannen, Deborah. 1986. *That's Not What I Meant! How Conversational Style Makes or Breaks Your Relations with Others.* New York: William Morrow and Company.

van Genderen, Karen. 1985. "Language and Topics in Comedy: A Look at Male and Female Comedians." Manuscript.

Zimmerman, Don H. and Candace West. 1975. "Sex Roles, Interruptions, and Silences in Conversation." In *Language and Sex: Difference and Dominance,* edited by B. Thorne and N. Henley. Rowley, MA: Newbury House.

CHAPTER 14

Power and Subordinate Evaluations of Male and Female Leaders

Belle Rose Ragins
Marquette University

The increased number of women in managerial positions (U.S. Department of Labor, 1979, 1984) has amplified the need to evaluate their performance in leadership roles (Powell, 1988; Nieva and Gutek, 1981). Although there are negligible differences in actual leadership behavior (cf. Dobbins and Platz, 1986), subordinates' evaluations of their leaders' behavior appears to be influenced by the leader's gender (Bartol, 1978; Brown, 1979; Jacklin and Maccoby, 1975; Nieva and Gutek, 1981; White, DeSanctis, and Crino, 1981). Subordinate evaluations and support may be an important determinant of upward mobility and power in organizations (Blackburn, 1981; Mechanic, 1962; Mowday, 1978; Pfeffer, 1981). An understanding of the processes and gender differences involved with subordinate evaluation of leadership behavior may therefore help to explain why female managers are not as upwardly mobile as their male counterparts (Stewart and Gudykunst, 1982; Nieva and Gutek, 1981).

Subordinates have been found to evaluate their female leaders inconsistently (cf. Brown, 1979; Terborg and Shingledecker, 1983). In some studies, subordinates gave higher evaluations to male than female leaders (Bartol and Butterfield, 1976; Cohen, Bunker, Burton, and McManus, 1978; Haccoun, Haccoun, and Sallay, 1978; Petty and Lee, 1975);

Portions of this chapter draw upon the author's dissertation, parts of which were published in the *Journal of Management* (1989) and the *Journal of Organizational Behavior* (1991). The author wishes to thank her chair, Jack Larsen, and committee members Mike Rush, John Lounsbury, and H. Dudley Dewhirst. Special thanks to colleagues John Cotton and Ed Inderrieden for their helpful comments on earlier drafts of this chapter.

whereas in other studies subordinates either did not differ in their evaluations (Adams, 1978; Bartol and Wortman, 1975; Osborn and Vicars, 1976; Petty and Bruning, 1980; Rice, Instone, and Adams, 1984; Rosen and Jerdee, 1973; Stitt, Schmidt, Price, and Kipnis, 1983; Terborg and Shingledecker, 1983), or rated female leaders higher than their male counterparts (Bartol, 1975; Petty and Miles, 1976).

These inconsistent findings may be due to subordinates responding to differences between the sexes in power, rather than the leader's sex. Females in organizations generally tend to have less power than their male counterparts (cf. Ragins and Sundstrom, 1989). Since perceived leader power has been found to be positively related to evaluations of leader effectiveness (Pelz, 1952; Trempe, Rigny, and Haccoun, 1985; Wager, 1965), it is reasonable to suspect that female leaders may receive lower evaluations than their male counterparts if they are perceived as lacking the power required to function effectively and provide for their subordinates' needs. To date, no field study has been explicitly designed to explore this explanation. The primary purpose in this study was to explore and compare the effects of perceived leader power and leader's sex on subordinate evaluations of leader effectiveness.

As a foundation for this investigation, it was expected that perceived leader power would be positively related to evaluations of leader effectiveness.

Hypothesis 1: Subordinates' perceptions of their leaders' use of noncoercive power will be positively related to their ratings of leader effectiveness.

Given equivalent levels of perceived power, it was expected that sex-role stereotypes would lead subordinates to rate female leaders lower than their male counterparts.

Hypothesis 2: Holding perceived power constant, female leaders will receive lower leadership evaluations than male leaders.

Although leader's sex was expected to influence evaluations of leader effectiveness, leader power was seen as having a greater impact on the evaluation process.

Hypothesis 3: Non-coercive leader power will account for more of the variance in leader evaluations than leader gender.

Even when female leaders are perceived as being powerful, they may still be penalized for using types of power that are perceived as being incongruent with sex-role stereotypes. Although this is an intriguing proposition, only a few studies to date have directly investigated this sex congruency theory of power, and most of these were conducted in a laboratory setting. In a laboratory study of 95 managers, Wiley and Eskilson (1982) investigated the sex-typing of reward and expert power and found that females received higher evaluations for using reward power, whereas males received higher evaluations for using expert power. These findings were only partially replicated in Rice, Instone and Adams's (1984) two studies of cadets; reward power was not found to be related to sex, whereas expert power, legitimate, coercive, and referent power were found to be male-typed. In a related laboratory study of perceived power, Johnson (1976) found that males were more likely than females to be perceived as having legitimate, expert, and coercive power, whereas females were more likely to be perceived as having reward power based upon liking, affection, and approval. Sex-typing was not found for referent power and reward power based upon money and material possessions.

These findings, although inconclusive, suggest that male and female leaders may receive different reactions for using similar forms of power. Specifically, males may receive higher evaluations when perceived as using male-typed forms of power (expert, legitimate, and coercive), whereas females may receive higher evaluations when perceived as using female-typed power (reward).

Hypothesis 4a: Male leaders perceived as using expert power will receive higher evaluations than female leaders perceived as using expert power.

Hypothesis 4b: Male leaders perceived as using legitimate power will receive higher evaluations than female leaders perceived as using legitimate power.

Hypothesis 4c: Male leaders perceived as using coercive power will receive higher evaluations than female leaders perceived as using coercive power.

Hypothesis 4d: Female leaders perceived as using reward power will receive higher evaluations than male leaders perceived as using reward power.

Since referent power is based upon identification with the leader (French and Raven, 1959), it was not expected to be gender-typed, given equal samples of male and female leaders and subordinates. Accordingly, no hypotheses were developed for referent power.

METHODS

Research Setting, Procedures, and Respondents

The study was part of a larger investigation held at three government-owned, privately operated large research and development organizations in the Southeastern United States. Although the participants were stationed at three different organizations, they were technically employed by one operating company.

To control for sex differences in leaders' positional and departmental power, subordinates were selected from matched sets of male and female managers. Organizational charts were used to match male and female managers on department, rank, and specialization. Confidential questionnaires were mailed to the 717 subordinates of 70 matched pairs of managers; 380 usable surveys were returned.

Since 30 percent of the leaders had only one subordinate responding to the questionnaire, it was necessary to choose one subordinate respondent from each leader to ensure equal representation among leaders. Subordinates were selected on the basis of four hierarchical criteria: (1) sex of subordinate (2) tenure with leader (3) race (4) age. Selection on the basis of gender was first used to obtain equally balanced groups with respect to leader and subordinate gender. In cases where there was more than one subordinate of a given sex, the matching criterion used for selection was the amount of time the subordinates had been supervised by their leaders. Subordinates were excluded from the final sample if their tenure with their leader was less than two months. Given equivalent tenure, subordinates were matched and selected on the basis of race and then age.

The final sample consisted of 110 subordinates of 55 matched pairs of male and female leaders. The primarily Caucasian sample (94 percent) was equally divided by sex and was highly educated; 17 percent held a master's degree and 9 percent held a doctorate degree. The participants' median age was 41, and the median length of time they had been supervised by their leader was 2½ years. The sample was composed primarily of full-time employees (96 percent). The median number of years the participants were employed by their organization was ten years.

Measures

Development of Perceived Leader Power Index.   Given the measurement and scaling problems with existing instruments of leader power (cf. Podsakoff and Schriesheim, 1985), a Perceived Leader Power Index was specifically developed for this study that incorporated recent recommendations for research in this area. A pretest sample of 50 subordinates not in the main study was used to develop the instrument. The initial item pool for the Perceived Leader Power Index was obtained from combining the 15 items from the Leader Power Inventory (Podsakoff, Todor, and Huber, 1980) with 25 modified items from the attributed Power Index (Holzbach, 1974). The final instrument used a seven-point scale [strongly disagree (1) to strongly agree (7)] to measure perceived reward, coercive, legitimate, expert, and referent leader power. The Maximum Likelihood LISREL V Measurement Model (Joreskog and Sorbom, 1981) was used to assess the distinctiveness of the five dimensions of power and to select the final items. The final instrument consisted of 15 items, three for each perceived power subscale. The coefficient alpha for the 15 item Perceived Leader Power Index was .86. The internal reliabilities for the three-item power subscales ranged from .73 to .94 and are listed in Table 1.

Development of Perceived Leadership Effectiveness Measures. Given the potential interaction between leader sex and instruments of leadership effectiveness that measure consideration and initiating structure leadership behaviors (Petty and Lee, 1975; Petty and Miles, 1976), it was necessary to develop a perceived leadership effectiveness instrument.

The pretest sample was used to assess the relationship between five global items (e.g., "my supervisor is an effective leader.") and 46 behaviorally based items of leadership effectiveness. The behaviorally based items focused on nine leadership dimensions: support, motivation, functionality, power, delegation, planning, decision making, problem solving, and team building. All items were based on a seven-point Likert scale [strongly disagree (1) to strongly agree (7)]. The relationship between the global and specific items was assessed by correlating the mean score of the five global items with each of the 46 specific items and then using Fisher Z scores to test the aver-

Table 1. **Means, Standard Deviations, Alphas, and Intercorrelations of Variables**[a]

Variable	M[b]	SD	1	2	3	4	5	6
1. Leader Rating	22.90	9.36	(.97)					
2. Reward power	16.56	4.01	.62*	(.92)				
3. Coercive power	9.28	4.61	−.14	−.20	(.77)			
4. Expert power	16.57	4.57	.82*	.66*	−.13	(.94)		
5. Referent power	15.04	4.48	.83*	.74*	−.22	.84*	(.88)	
6. Legitimate power	17.74	3.22	.41*	.42*	−.07	.52*	.47*	(.73)

[a] $n = 110$. Coefficient alphas are listed on the diagonal.

[b] based on a seven-point scale, ranging from 1 (strongly disagree) to 7 (strongly agree).

* $p < .001$

age correlation. The significant correlation between the specific and global items (.65, p < .001), coupled with the high coefficient alpha of the 51 items (alpha = .98) provided support for using the five global items in lieu of the 46 specific items in the final leadership effectiveness instrument.

Analyses and Results

The descriptive statistics, intercorrelations, and reliability estimates are presented in Table 1. Acceptable internal reliabilities were obtained for the measures of interest (ranging from .73 to .97).

The Pearson product-moment correlation was used to test Hypothesis 1. As expected, noncoercive perceived leader power (measured as the summation of four of the five power subscales) was significantly related to evaluations of leader effectiveness (r = .81, p < .001).

Hierarchical regression analyses were used to test the other hypothesized relationships. As indicated in Table 2, Hypothesis 2 was not supported; leader sex did not significantly affect subordinate evaluations of leader effectiveness when perceived leader power was held constant by entering it first in the hierarchical regression equation. Overall, leader sex had a negligible impact; it accounted for only 1 percent of the variance in subordinate evaluations of leader effectiveness. In line with these findings, Hypothesis 3 was supported in that perceived leader power accounted for more of the variance in evaluations of leader effectiveness than leader sex.

Table 2. **Hierarchical Regression Analyses of the Relationship Between Leader Gender, Leader Power and Evaluations of Leader Effectiveness**

Variable	Step	R^2	R^2 change (per step)[a]	beta	b	t(for beta)
Perceived power	1	.59	.59***	.77	.52	12.22***
Leader gender	2	.59	.0003	.02	.37	.31
Noncoercive power	1	.66	.66***[a]	.81	.54	14.28***
Leader gender[b]	2	.66	.0000	.01	.11	.11
Leader gender	1	.01	.01	−.11	−2.04	−1.13
Noncoercive power	2	.66	.65***	.81	.55	14.09***

[a] *F test performed on R^2 increment.*

[b] *Males = 1, females = 0*

****p<.001*

The interaction terms were used to test the sex congruency hypotheses (Hypotheses 4 a, b, c and d). As discussed earlier, it was expected that males would receive higher evaluations than females when perceived as using expert, coercive, and legitimate power. Females were expected to receive higher evaluations when perceived as using reward power. These differences in evaluations were expected to increase at higher levels of perceived power. Sex differences were not expected at low levels of perceived power; it was expected that both sexes would receive low evaluations when perceived as lacking expert, reward, and legitimate power. In the case of coercive power, both sexes were expected to receive high evaluations when perceived as using low levels of coercive power; at high levels of coercive power males were expected to receive higher evaluations than females.

To control for differences between the sexes in power and the interactions among the subscales of power, leader sex and four of the power subscales were entered as the first step in the hierarchical equation. The power subscale that was included in the interaction term was entered in the second step. The final step consisted of the sex-power interaction term. The results of the four regression analyses are presented in Table 3. Although referent power was not hypothesized to be sex-related, a post hoc analysis of that interaction term was also conducted. Leader sex did not significantly interact with any of the power subscales. Contrary to expectations, male and female leaders received equivalent evaluations when perceived as using equivalent types of power.

Table 3. **Hierarchical Regression Analyses of the Interactions between Leader Gender and Perceived Power Subscales**

Hypo-thesis	Variable	Step	R^2	R^2 change (per step)[a]	beta	b	t(for beta)
4a	Set:	1	.69	.69**[a]			
	Leader Gender[b]				.001	.02	.02
	Reward				.03	.06	.32
	Coercive				.05	.09	.77
	Legitimate				.02	.06	.31
	Referent				.81	1.69	9.28**
	Expert	2	.74	.05**	.45	.93	4.38**
	Expert × Gender	3	.74	.002	.06	.07	.30
4b	Set:	1	.74	.74**			
	Leader Gender				.04	.74	.79
	Reward				−.002	−.004	−.02
	Coercive				.02	.05	.48

Table 3. *continued*

Hypo-thesis	Variable	Step	R^2	R^2 change (per step)[a]	beta	b	t(for beta)
	Expert				.43	.87	4.31**
	Referent				.48	.99	4.37**
	Legitimate	2	.74	.002	−.05	−.16	−.90
	Leg. × Gender	3	.74	.000	.14	.14	.44
4c	Set:	1	.74	.74**			
	Leader Gender				.05	.89	.88
	Reward				.003	.01	.04
	Expert				.46	.93	4.45**
	Referent				.47	.98	4.36**
	Legitimate				−.05	−.16	−.88
	Coercive	2	.74	.001	.03	.05	.49
	Coercive × Gender	3	.74	.003	.15	.26	1.17
4d	Set:	1	.74	.74**			
	Leader Gender				.05	.94	.94
	Coercive				.03	.05	.49
	Expert				.45	.93	4.42**
	Referent				.48	1.01	4.90**
	Legitimate				−.05	−.16	−.90
	Reward	2	.74	.000	.01	.02	.09
	Reward × Gender	3	.74	.004	.28	.30	1.20
Post-Hoc	Set:	1	.69	.69**			
	Leader Gender				.08	1.42	1.29
	Reward				.15	.36	2.01*
	Coercive				−.01	−.01	−.11
	Expert				.76	1.56	9.29**
	Legitimate				−.05	−.16	−.82
	Referent	2	.74	.05**	.48	1.00	4.37**
	Referent × Gender	3	.74	.0004	.07	.09	.39

[a] *F test performed on R^2 increment.*

[b] *Males = 1, females = 0*

* *p< .05*

** *p<.001*

DISCUSSION

The primary finding of this study was that subordinates' ratings of leader effectiveness were influenced more by the subordinate's perception of the leader's power than by the leader's sex. Whereas perceived leader power accounted for 59 percent of the variance in leader evaluations, leader sex accounted for only 1 percent of the variance. There are at least two implications of this finding.

First, the inconsistent research findings on subordinate evaluations of female leaders may be due partly to sex differences in power. In this study male and female leaders were matched on variables related to positional power—rank, department, and specialization—and received equivalent ratings by their subordinates. A closer inspection of previous research reveals that studies that controlled for job level did not find sex differences in leadership evaluations (e.g., Adams, 1978; Osborn and Vicars, 1976; Petty and Bruning, 1980; Rice, Instone and Adams, 1984; Terborg and Shingledecker, 1983). By controlling for job level, these researchers may have inadvertently controlled for some aspects of positional power. Along those same lines, the apparent discrepancy in findings from field and laboratory studies (cf. reviews by Dobbins and Platz, 1986; Osborn and Vicars, 1976) may be a function of differential control for leader power; field studies may be more likely to tap perceived leader power than laboratory studies. This suggests that researchers who fail to control for sex differences in power when comparing male and female leaders in organizations may essentially be comparing high-power leaders with low-power leaders.

Second, if perceived leader power is a critical variable in subordinate evaluations of leader effectiveness, sex differences in power may have important ramifications for the leader-subordinate relationship. In this study, males and females were matched on variables related to positional power and received equivalent evaluations. However, in most organizational realities females tend to have less positional power than males (Hill, 1980; Kanter, 1977; Smith and Grenier, 1982; Wolf and Fligstein, 1979). Female leaders lacking power may receive negative reactions from their subordinates. Since subordinate support has been found to be related to upward mobility and the development of power in organizations (Blackburn, 1981; Mechanic, 1962; Mowday, 1978; Pfeffer, 1981), powerless female leaders may be restricted from gaining power from their subordinate relationships and as a result may be faced with increasing power losses in a "cycle of powerlessness" (Ragins and Sundstrom, 1989).

Another potentially important finding of this study is that subordinates respond favorably to leaders who are perceived as having power, irrespective of the leader's sex. Support was not found for the hypothesis that power is sex-typed; male and female leaders received equivalent evaluations when perceived as using the same forms of power.

This study was limited to investigating subordinates' perceptions of leaders' effectiveness and power. Leadership and power were viewed as perceptual phenomena (e.g., Calder, 1977; Provan, 1980), and were therefore studied through a phenomenological approach. The findings of this study represent perception and have limited generalizability to behavior. Another factor that limits the generalizability of this study is the high educational level of the sample; highly educated samples may be more accepting of powerful females than blue-collar samples. Future investigations may incorporate and compare behavioral and perceptual indices of power and leader effectiveness using a sample with more variance in educational background.

In conclusion, given equivalent perceived power, leader sex may not significantly influence evaluations of leader effectiveness. Subordinates may respond more to their leaders' power than to sex-role stereotypes. Organizational factors that create sex differences in power may have a potentially negative influence on the leader-subordinate relationship.

REFERENCES

Adams, E.F. 1978. "A Multivariate Study of Subordinate Perceptions and Attitudes Toward Minority and Majority Managers." *Journal of Applied Psychology* 63 (3):227–88.

Bartol, K.M. 1975. "The Effect of Male Versus Female Leaders." *Journal of Business Research* 3:33–42.

———. 1978. "The Sex-Structuring of Organizations: A Search for Possible Causes." *Academy of Management Review* 3 (4):805–15.

Bartol, K.M., and D.A. Butterfield. 1976. "Sex Effects in Evaluating Leaders." *Journal of Applied Psychology* 61 (4):446–54.

Bartol, K.M., and M.S. Wortman. 1975. "Male Versus Female Leaders: Effects on Perceived Leader Behavior and Satisfaction in a Hospital." *Personnel Psychology* 28:533–47.

Blackburn, R.S. 1981. "Lower Participant Power: Toward a Conceptual Integration." *Academy of Management Review* 4 (1):127–31.

Brown, S.M. 1979. "Male Versus Female Leaders: A Comparison of Empirical Studies." *Sex Roles* 5 (5):595–611.

Calder, B.H. 1977. "An Attribution Theory of Leadership." In *New Directions in Organizational Behavior,* edited by B.M. Shaw and G.N. Salancik. Chicago: St. Claire Press.

Cohen, S.L., K.A. Bunker, A.L. Burton, and P.D. McManus. 1978. "Reactions of Male Subordinates to the Sex-Role Congruency of Immediate Supervision." *Sex Roles* 4 (2):297–311.

Dobbins, G.H. and S.J. Platz. 1986. "Sex Differences in Leadership: How Real are They?" *Academy of Management Review* 11 (1):118–27.

French, J.R.P., and B.H. Raven. 1959. "The Bases of Social Power." In *Studies in Social Power,* edited by D. Cartwright, 150–67. Ann Arbor, MI: University of Michigan Institute of Social Research.

Haccoun, D.M., R.R. Haccoun, and G. Sallay. 1978. "Sex Differences in the Appropriateness of Supervisory Styles: A Nonmanagement View." *Journal of Applied Psychology* 63 (1):124–27.

Hill, M.S. 1980. "Authority at Work: How Men and Women Differ." In *Five Thousand American Families: Patterns of Economic Progress,* (Volume VII) edited by G.J. Duncan and J.N. Morgan, 107–46. Ann Arbor, MI: Institute for Social Research, University of Michigan.

Holzbach, R.L. 1974. "An Investigation of a Model for Managerial Effectiveness: The Effects of Leadership Style and Leader Attributed Social Power on Subordinate Job Performance." *Dissertation Abstracts International* 35B:565.

Jacklin, C.N., and E.E. Maccoby. 1975. "Sex Differences and Their Implications for Management." In *Bringing Women into Management,* edited by F.E. Gordon and M.H. Strober, 23–38. New York: McGraw-Hill.

Johnson, P. 1976. "Women and Power: Toward a Theory of Effectiveness." *Journal of Social Issues* 32 (3):99–110.

Joreskog, K.G., and D. Sorbom. 1981. *Lisrel,* Chicago: International Educational Resources.

Kanter, R.M. 1977. *Men and Women of the Corporation.* New York: Basic Books.

Mechanic, D. 1962. "Sources of Power of Lower Participants in Complex Organizations." *Administrative Science Quarterly* 7:349–64.

Mowday, R.T. 1978. "The Exercise of Influence in Organizations". *Administrative Science Quarterly* 23:137–56.

Nieva, V.F., and B.A. Gutek. 1981. *Women and Work: A Psychological Perspective.* New York: Praeger.

Osborn, R.N., and W.M. Vicars. 1976. "Sex Stereotypes: An Artifact of Leader Behavior and Subordinate Satisfaction Analysis." *Academy of Management Journal* 19 (3):439–49.

Pelz, D.C. 1952. "Influence: A Key to Effective Leadership in the First-Line Supervisor." *Personnel* 29:209–17.

Petty, M.M., and N.S. Bruning. 1980. "A Comparison of the Relationships Between Subordinates' Perceptions of Supervisory Behavior and Measures of Subordinates' Job Satisfaction for Male and Female Leaders." *Academy of Management Journal* 23 (4):717–25.

Petty, M.M., and G.K. Lee. 1975. "Moderating Effects of Sex of Supervisor and Subordinate on Relationship Between Supervisory Behavior and Measures of Subordinate Satisfaction." *Journal of Applied Psychology* 60 (5):624–28.

Petty, M.M., and R.H. Miles. 1976. "Leader Sex-Roles Stereotyping in a Female Dominant Work Culture." *Personnel Psychology* 29:393–404.

Pfeffer, J. 1977. "The Ambiguity of Leadership." *Academy of Management Review* 2:104–12.

————. 1981. *Power in Organizations.* Boston: Pitman Publishing.

Podsakoff, P.M., and C.A. Schriesheim. 1985. "Field Studies of French and Raven's Bases of Power: Critique, Reanalysis, and Suggestions for Future Research." *Psychological Bulletin* 97 (3):387–411.

Podsakoff, P.M., W.D. Todor, and V.L. Huber. 1980. *Leader Power Inventory.* Unpublished research scale.

Powell, G.N. 1988. *Women and Men in Management.* Newbury Park, CA: Sage.

Provan, K.G. 1980. "Recognizing, Measuring, and Interpreting the Potential/Enacted Power Distinction in Organizational Research." *Academy of Management Review* 5 (4):549–59.

Ragins, B.R., and E. Sundstrom. 1989. "Gender and Power in Organizations: A Longitudinal Perspective." *Psychological Bulletin* 105 (1):51–88.

Rice, R.W., D. Instone, and J. Adams. 1984. "Leader Sex, Leader Success, and Leadership Process: Two Field Studies." *Journal of Applied Psychology* 69 (1):12–32.

Rosen, B., and T.H. Jerdee. 1973. "The Influence of Sex-Role Stereotypes on Evaluations of Male and Female Supervisory Behavior." *Journal of Applied Psychology* 57 (1):44–48.

Smith, H.L., and M. Grenier. 1982. "Sources of Organizational Power for Women: Overcoming Structural Obstacles." *Sex Roles* 8 (7):733–46.

Stewart, L.P., and W.B. Gudykunst. 1982. "Differential Factors Influencing the Hierarchical Level and Number of Promotions of Males and Females Within an Organization." *Academy of Management Journal* 2 (3):586–97.

Stitt, C., S. Schmidt, K. Price, and D. Kipnis. 1983. "Sex of Leader, Leader Behavior, and Subordinate Satisfaction." *Sex Roles* 9 (1):31–42.

Terborg, J.R., and P. Shingledecker. 1983. "Employee Reactions to Supervision and Work Evaluation as a Function of Subordinate and Manager Sex." *Sex Roles* 9, (7):813–24.

Trempe, J., A. Rigny, and R. Haccoun. 1985. "Subordinate Satisfaction with Male and Female Managers: Role of Perceived Supervisory Influence." *Journal of Applied Psychology* 70 (1):44–47.

U.S. Department of Labor, Bureau of Labor Statistics. 1979. *U.S. Working Women: A Databook.* Washington, DC: U.S. Bureau of Labor Statistics.

U.S. Department of Labor, Bureau of Labor Statistics. 1984. *Employment and Earnings.* Washington, DC: U.S. Bureau of Labor Statistics.

Wager, L.W. 1965. "Leadership Style, Hierarchical Influence, and Supervisory Role Obligations." *Administrative Science Quarterly* 9:391–420.

White, M.C., G. DeSanctis, and M.D. Crino. 1981. "Achievement, Self-Confidence, Personality Traits, and Leadership Ability: A Review of the Literature on Sex Differences." *Psychological Reports* 48:547–69.

Wiley, M.G., and A. Eskilson. 1982. "The Interaction of Sex and Power Base on Perceptions of Managerial Effectiveness." *Academy of Management Journal* 25 (3):671–77.

Wolf, W.C., and N.D. Fligstein. 1979. "Sex and Authority in the Workplace: The Causes of Sexual Inequality." *American Sociological Review* 44:235–52.

CHAPTER 15

Sex, Romance, and Organizational Taboos

Patrice M. Buzzanell
Marquette University

Anecdotes and critical incidents about romance in the workplace display several prominent themes in the extant literature and in the typical approaches to organizational relationships. First, most of the published accounts are derived from case studies, consultants' reports, and organizational advice columns. Though highly interesting and descriptive, these materials lack the rigor and thorough analysis that scientific scrutiny and theoretical frameworks provide. Second, most of the literature dichotomizes the issues into two camps—those touting the positive aspects of affectionate and romantic relationships at work and those depicting a plague of organization woes descending upon the lovers. Third, most of the popular magazine features offer simplistic advice that belies the complexity of issues and obscures the factors contributing to the growth, effects, and implications of organizational romance.

Journal articles have investigated a number of variables including power, intimacy, attractiveness, organizational size, participativeness, mentor-protégé relationships, sex role spillover, and proximity (Anderson and Hunsaker, 1985; Crary, 1987; Dillard and Witteman, 1985; Gutek, 1985; Mainiero, 1986). Few have investigated interpersonal and contextual factors, catalysts to romance, long-term career and organizational effects of romance, and reasons behind diverse responses to and attitudes about romance in the workplace. In this paper, the significance of romance in the workplace is explored. Available research is critiqued and, finally, some areas for programmatic research are presented.

DEFINITIONS OF, REASONS FOR, AND SIGNIFICANCE OF ROMANCE IN THE WORKPLACE

Most definitions of romance focus on elements of physiological arousal, sexual tension, attraction, and intimate behaviors between heterosexuals (Anderson and Hunsaker, 1985; Berscheid and Walster, 1978; Crary, 1987; Dillard and Witteman, 1985; Jamison, 1983; Mainiero, 1986; Peele, 1988; Quinn and Lees, 1984). Some writers add components such as: third-party reports of romantic partners' actions (Anderson and Hunsaker, 1985; Mainiero, 1986; Quinn, 1977); courtship behaviors (Cohen, 1982); and degree of physical attractiveness (Dillard and Witteman, 1985). Because of the organizational setting for romance, these romantic relationships are differentiated from sexual harassment and sexism. The former focuses on victims' vulnerabilities, harassers' needs to control and exercise power, and compliance-gaining techniques; the latter pivots around discriminatory behaviors and desires to diminish victims (Jamison, 1983; Mainiero, 1986; Quinn and Lees, 1984). The final key component that distinguishes romance in the workplace is the context; namely, that these romances usually occur between individuals who are employed by the same organization. However, relationships between members of supplier-client firms and industry rivals can also be considered romances in the workplace. Therefore, romance in the workplace is defined as intimate relationships between heterosexual partners employed by the same or by resource-sharing organizations. No degree of intimacy is stipulated in this definition.

These romances are similar to those outside the workplace with regard to participants' motives and relationship forms (Anderson and Hunsaker, 1985; Horn and Horn, 1982; Mainiero, 1986; Quinn, 1977; Quinn and Lees, 1984). Workplace romances develop because of shared interests or projects, physical proximity, boredom at work, loneliness and alienation from others at work, changing social mores, and convenience or little time for outside interests (Berscheid and Walster, 1978; Graham, 1986; Horn and Horn, 1982; Kole, 1988; Quinn and Lees, 1984). Organizational romances are distinguished from other romances because organizational attractions are often based on power, have profitability and productivity issues, connote illicitness or taboo notions, and engender severe negative consequences for careers, especially for women (Collins, 1983; Crary, 1987; Gutek, 1985; Gutek and Dunwoody, 1986; Harragan, 1977; Jamison, 1983; Josefowitz, 1982; Mainiero, 1986; Spruell, 1985).

Despite the increasing percentages of women and romantic relationships in the workplace (Gutek, 1985, 18–19; Quinn, 1977, 30), the significance of organizational romances is downplayed by the scant research in this area. One reason for the neglect in this area is the stigma against those who investigate love and intimacy (Berscheid, 1988, 360). Other reasons include the sensitive nature of the topic and the potential problems with invasion of privacy (Gutek, 1985; Mainiero, 1986). Not only are few organizations willing to demarcate clearly what are private and what are professional concerns, but few wish to enter the controversy over whether they should "support, ignore, or punish participants in such relationships" (Mainiero, 1986, 750). Fairhurst (1986) commented that "this is unfortunate because the implications of an office romance are far reaching" (91). The "very little solid empirical evidence" that is available focuses on "eliminating the problem" (Dillard and Witteman, 1985, (99–100) rather than the emergence of intimate relationships in the workplace and the romantic participants themselves (Crary, 1987, 27).

However, the significance of relational issues in the workplace needs to be addressed because romance can be a significant problem for organizations if not managed effectively. Some writers and researchers (Collins, 1983; Schein, 1984) propose that organizations develop norms and rules against emotional and intimate expressions to forestall negative consequences. Others advise organizational human resource managers to develop avenues for the expression of affection and intimacy in the workplace (Jamison, 1983; Josefowitz, 1982; Horn and Horn, 1982; Spelman et al., 1986). These researchers argue that the expression of feelings in the workplace is beneficial because individuals can interact as mature, full human beings. They contend that positive results include supportive/open workplace climates and both output and process measures of effectiveness, such as increased productivity, efficiency, and creativity.

Thus, little research is available that focuses on the emergence of romantic relationships and variables enhancing the successes and failures of romances in the workplace. Although many of the power, productivity, relational, career, and taboo issues are fundamentally communicative, organizational and interpersonal communicologists have ignored this topic.

AREAS FOR FUTURE RESEARCH
ON ROMANCE IN THE WORKPLACE

In brief, few surveys have been conducted on organizational romance. What researchers and practitioners know about romance in the workplace is that: proximity and opposite-gender supervisors enhance the probability of organizational romances in any type of organization (Anderson and Hunsaker, 1985; Gutek, 1985; Quinn, 1977; Quinn and Lees, 1984); romances are primarily superior-subordinate relationships, especially boss-subordinate, with women usually in the subordinate category (Josefowitz, 1982); and romances engender a range of negative consequences perceived as detrimental to participants' (particularly women's) careers, communication networks, displays of competence, and to the future of the relationship itself (Collins, 1983; Crary, 1987; Henely, 1987; Horn and Horn, 1982; Quinn, 1977; Spruell, 1985).

What researchers and practitioners do not know can be roughly classified in the following four divisions: interpersonal, structural and contextual, antecedent conditions or catalysts to romance, and individual or personal factors.

First, research would benefit from examination of the interpersonal dynamics involved in power issues and of the communication competency and enactment ability of romantic partners. Mainiero (1986) concluded that power is the critical variable in all interpersonal relationships at work, but is particularly salient when organizational members perceive exploitation, imbalance, coalition formation, and inappropriate disruption and obstruction of formal lines of authority and communication. However, this researcher argues that power per se, that is, the ability to influence others and procure limited resources, is not critical in and of itself. Rather, it is the perceived imbalance of power that engenders undesirable repercussions. This is the reason why boss-subordinate relationships are so deadly and why peer relationships have a better survival rate.

Determining differences in individual and organizational power quotients and factors may provide a fruitful area for research, but not the most productive avenue. Indeed, cases appear in anecdotal accounts in which individuals and/or couples survive unscathed despite vast power differences. What may distinguish these relationships is each individual's communicative skill.

Typically, people do not know how to manage their attractions to others at work, and they dissociate themselves from other organizational members who could provide needed guidance. Westoff (1986) noted that "people don't know how to behave [in romantic relationships at work].... There is a lot of fear and uncertainty about how to deal with the situation" (50; see also Collins, 1983; Fernandez, 1984). Despite partners' need for information and feedback, they rarely seek formal or informal counseling (Quinn and Lees, 1984, 44). Compounding these problems are a widespread lack of organizational guidelines, an inability to broach and discuss issues of intimacy at work, and a common sense approach to keep intimate relationships secret.

Crary (1987) discussed issues of attraction with professional men and women in six different industries and found that the more skilled in communication organizational participants were, the better able they were to manage their romantic relationships. Although she did not clarify what communicative dimensions this skill entailed, it seems likely that self-monitoring is one key to successful management of workplace romances. Specifically, high self-monitors should be less likely to incur perceived and actual negative outcomes of romantic and intimate relationships in the workplace. The self-monitoring construct is based on the premise that some individuals, namely high self-monitors, vary their presentational styles as a function of the situations in which they find themselves. Low self-monitors maintain consistent presentational styles, relying on their internal dispositions for guidance, and seem to display little concern for appropriateness, for examination of others' behaviors, and for monitoring of their self-presentation (Eichenhofer, Gerstein, Valutis, and Jankowski, 1987; Snyder, 1974). Hence, the self-monitoring construct emphasizes both awareness of appropriate behavioral cues and ability-competence-skill in enacting appropriate responses. Self-monitoring is a pragmatic ability to tailor behaviors to enhance communication accuracy and adaptive concealment of emotions.

Of importance to this particular study is the finding that an individual's self-monitoring is stable across a variety of situations, namely, that high self-monitors are not responsive to inner states and that they consistently perform based on situational, rather than internal, cues (Eichenhofer, Gerstein, Valutis, and Jankowski, 1987). Hence, high self-monitors should behave appropriately when involved in workplace romances and should incur fewer negative consequences despite power differentials.

Second, structural and contextual factors offer another research area. Whereas structural elements are both formal organizational characteristics and emergent, informal patterns of interaction, contextual factors are frameworks that imbed behavioral and structural aspects of organizations (Jablin, Putnam, Roberts, and Porter, 1987, 123, 287–301). Formal structural dimensions include: configuration (span of control, hierarchical level, organizational size, and sub-unit size); complexity (vertical and horizontal); formalization; and centralization (Jablin, 1987). Context includes information environment, climate, and culture.

Of the structural elements that have been investigated, organizational size, rank or vertical differentiation, and participativeness have yielded little explanation as to why some organizational romances are more likely to occur than others. Supposedly, small organizations respond warmly to office romances, but larger organizations contain larger candidate pools and abilities to transfer out of divisions if relationships falter. However, these suppositions have not been supported in research. Dillard and Witteman (1985) found no support for the hypotheses that participativeness is positively related to the likelihood of organizational romance and that formalization is negatively related to romance. In addition, they found no support for the hypothesis that a positive organizational climate was associated with a greater likelihood of organizational romance occurrence. This is con-

trary to practitioners' assertions that supportive climates not only breed intimate relationships, but forestall negative effects of romances (Horn and
Horn, 1982; Josefowitz, 1982; Kantrowitz, 1988; Spelman et al., 1986).

Rather than concentrating on structural elements, this researcher
believes that contextual factors, such as task interdependence and cohesion,
are more critical variables in both stimulating the occurrence of organizational romances and in anticipating consequences of these relationships.
Spelman et al. (1986, 86–87) found that job design, especially jobs with inter-
connected tasks, directly affected opportunities for people to interact in the
workplace and thus initiate romances. Yet, high interdependence may also
correspond with satisfaction if the interdependence promotes strong ties to
friendship, power, and task accomplishment networks. Changes in these
networks and routines may be met with resistance if they do not further individual and network goals.

In addition, work group cohesion, "the extent to which employees have
close friends in their immediate work units" (Price, 1986, 250), may also be
a factor in the inception and results of workplace romances, although
there are no clear directions in research to determine the nature or direction of this relationship. Spelman et al. (1986) suggested that cohesion may
breed romance, but reactions to these relationships will be intense.
Employees who derive great satisfaction from intact work group relationships
would probably view disruptions of their routines negatively.

The critical issues in both task interdependence and work group
cohesion are the degrees to which individuals affect each other's jobs. In
cases where close working relationships are mandatory for effective task
accomplishment, co-workers may fear possible dissolution of established and
effective interpersonal patterns. They may lose productivity because of
time spent gossiping and watching the couple. They may feel a personal loss
if participation in the work group has been especially rewarding for them
and if they view the romance as a threat to or intrusion in the group's interpersonal patterns. Even if they do not react negatively to the individuals
themselves or to the idea of workplace romance, they may anticipate an even-
tual backlash against themselves and/or work group estrangements if the relationship ends (Kantrowitz, 1988). Thus, high task interdependence and work
group cohesion should correlate with negative consequences of romances
in the workplace.

The third major research focus investigates antecedent conditions or
catalysts to romance. Researchers and practitioners have not developed a tax-
onomy of conditions most likely to correspond with romance in the workplace, nor have they attempted to dichotomize situational factors into categories most likely to produce negative and positive consequences for
romantic participants. As noted earlier, proximity, long hours, organizational

socializing, male-female workplaces, and opposite-gender supervisors contribute to the development of organizational romance. But why do some people succumb to these relationships and others not? What situational factors promote organizational romance? What makes some people able to forestall negative repercussions? Are these reasons primarily situational or personal, or a mixture of both?

With regard to antecedent environmental conditions and their effects, Gutek (1985) discussed two issues; namely, the role of external factors and the concept of sex-role spillover. First, she stated that the importance of environmental and situational factors is underestimated. Gutek found that people generally do not blame the hierarchy or the sexualized environment for sexual relationships at work; rather, they blame the persons.

Second, Gutek described the sex-role spillover effect as the degree to which one's gender enters into varied life roles. Based on Gutek's (1985) and Gutek and Dunwoody's (1986) findings on sex-role spillover, one possible conclusion is that women will incur negative consequences in the workplace whenever their gender becomes prominent. Sex-role spillover is problematic for romances because these relationships focus on individuals' gender in a situation in which women, in particular, often attempt to downplay their sexuality. Once gender is the characteristic at the forefront, is it possible for women to revert to a basically "asexual" nature? Do men continue to react to women in stereotypical ways (see Kanter, 1977; and Harragan, 1977)?

Fourth, individual and personal factors may affect the development and results of romances in the workplace. First, one's ability to compartmentalize work and romance may be critical in developing and maintaining romantic relationships in the workplace. As Spelman et al. (1986, 750) noted, "...we are apt to view our jobs and our love lives as occupying two separate worlds," yet most people cannot view these aspects of their lives as mutually exclusive if they are involved in a romance. Those who are able to compartmentalize them in separate realms while at work may be able to weaken or alleviate negative consequences.

Second, individuals with an internal locus of control may be better able to guide their romances at work. Internally controlled persons view events as being under their own control, whereas externally controlled persons picture events as being beyond their control and due to outside forces. Dion and Dion (1988) found that internally controlled people viewed their romantic relationships as "rational, calculated, nonreciprocal," which reduced the "positive attachment between the partners" and resulted in the relationship being "perceived in pragmatic rather than idealistic terms" (267). Thus, internally controlled individuals may be able to objectify their relationships and map out effective strategies for dealing with outcomes.

Third, past relationship history influences an individual's willingness to enter into a romantic relationship and a person's anticipation of possible relational effects. It seems likely that past relationships have effects on the outcomes of organizational romances and on the willingness of organizational members to engage in these romances (Crary, 1987). However, this area has been neglected in discussions of romantic love (Berscheid, 1988, 371), so little in direction and magnitude of these associations can be presented.

Finally, organizational naiveté, the lack of sophistication and critical insight into the dynamics of organizational relationships, manifests itself in a failure to account for varied reactions to male-female work interactions and in the unilateral avoidance of issues of attraction. As Quinn and Lees (1984, 44) remarked, "not only are...judgments impaired by emotions, but they [romantic partners] fail to understand the interpersonal and organizational dynamics." This inability to foresee varied reactions to their romance and to select the optimal path for defusing undesirable effects is not necessarily associated with organizational tenure or status in an organization. Organizational naiveté is problematic for situations in which male-female relationships are friendships or mentor-protégé relationships because others immediately assume that there is a sexual relationship (Josefowitz, 1982, 91). The naive individual might assume that others would see that the relationship is friendship-based or work-based and might maintain high visibility of the relationship to forestall (but actually fuel) rumors.

Finally, naiveté may lead to avoidance of issues of attraction. Spelman et al. (1986) wrote that "avoidance of attraction issues leaves participants unprepared (77)." Spelman et al. concluded that an examination of beliefs about relationships may enable individuals to better anticipate others' reactions and to determine possible courses of action. Thus, organizational naiveté may correspond with a greater willingness to enter into romances in the workplace, but may also be associated with increased negative effects.

In summary, organizational researchers and practitioners need to develop greater insight into four main areas insofar as these areas affect and are affected by romances in the workplace. A brief overview of the interpersonal, structural and contextual, antecedent conditions or catalysts to romance, and individual or personal factors yielded several hypotheses for future research.

CONCLUSION

The paucity of quality research on romance in the workplace is detrimental to the formation of reality-based and people-centered organizational policies and guidelines. One point is indisputable; namely, that romance is inevitable and organizational members need to confront and manage these issues collectively and individually. None of the issues surrounding romance in the workplace is readily resolved, nor is the necessary research easily conducted. Nonetheless, investigation into personal, structural, and environmental factors yields insights into male-female relationships in the workplace.

REFERENCES

Anderson, C., and P. Hunsaker. 1985. "Why There's Romancing at the Office and Why It's Everyone's Problem." *Personnel* 62 (February):57–63.

Berscheid, E. 1988. "Some Comments on Love's Anatomy: Or, Whatever Happened to Old-Fashioned Lust?" In *The Psychology of Love,* edited by R.J. Sternberg and M.L. Barnes, (359–74). New Haven: Yale University Press.

Berscheid, E., and E.H. Walster. 1978. *Interpersonal Attraction.* Reading, MA: Addison-Wesley.

Cohen, L.R. 1982. "Minimizing Communication Breakdowns Between Male and Female Managers." *Personnel Administrator* 27 (October):57–60, 89.

Collins, E. 1983. "Managers and Lovers." *Harvard Business Review* 61 (September/October):142–53.

Crary, M. 1987. "Managing Attraction and Intimacy at Work." *Organizational Dynamics* 15 (Spring):27–41.

Dillard, J.P., and H. Witteman. 1985. "Romantic Relationships at Work: Organizational and Personal Influences." *Human Communication Research* 12:99–116.

Dion, K.L., and K.K. Dion. 1988. "Romantic Love: Individual and Cultural Perspectives." In *The Psychology of Love,* edited by R.J. Sternberg, and M.L. Barnes, (264–89). New Haven: Yale University Press.

Driscoll, J.B. and R.A. Bova. 1980. "The Sexual Side of Enterprise." *Management Review* 69 (July):51–54.

Eichenhofer, D., L. Gerstein, W. Valutis, and J. Jankowski. 1987. "Effects of Anxiety on Self-Monitoring." *Psychological Reports* 61:831–36.

Fairhurst, G.T. 1986. "Male-Female Communication on the Job: Literature Review and Commentary." In *Communication Yearbook 9,* edited by M.L. McLaughlin, (83–116). Newbury Park, CA: Sage.

Fernandez, J.A. 1984. Letters to the Editor. *Harvard Business Review* 84 (January/February):150–51.

Graham, E. 1986. "My Lover, My Colleague." In *The Wall Street Journal.* 67, 23D and 26D.

Gutek, B.A. 1985. *Sex and the Workplace.* San Francisco, CA: Jossey-Bass.

Gutek, B.A., and V. Dunwoody. 1986. "Understanding Sex in the Workplace." In *Women and Work: An Annual Review, Volume 2,* edited by A.H. Stromberg, L. Larwood, and B.A. Gutek, (249–69). Newbury Park, CA: Sage.

Harragan, B.L. 1977. *Games Mother Never Taught You: Corporate Gamesmanship for Women.* New York: Warner.

Henely, C.F., Jr. 1987, (May 15). "Marital Status and Employment—Another Protected Class." *CUE: An Organization for Positive Employee Relations.* Washington, DC: CUE Legal Alert.

Horn, P.D., and J.C. Horn. 1982. *Sex in the Office.* Reading, MA: Addison-Wesley.

Jablin, F.M. 1987. "Formal Organizational Structure." In *Handbook of Organizational Communication,* edited by F.M. Jablin, L.L. Putnam, K.H. Roberts, and L.W. Porter. (389–419). Newbury Park, CA: Sage.

Jablin, F.M., L.L Putnam, K.H. Roberts, and L.L. Porter. 1987. *Handbook of Organizational Communication.* Newbury Park, CA: Sage.

Jacobs, B. 1981 (February 9). "Sex in the Office." *Industry Week* 208:32–38.

Jamison, K. 1983 (August). "Managing Sexual Attraction in the Workplace." *Personnel Administrator* 28:45–51.

Josefowitz, N. 1982 (March). "Sexual Relationships at Work: Attraction, Transference, Coercion or Strategy." *Personnel Administrator* 27:91–96.

Kanter, R.M. 1977. *Men and Women of the Corporation.* New York: Basic.

Kantrowitz, B. 1988 (February 15). "Love in the Office." *Newsweek* 111:48–52.

Kole, J.W. 1988. "Office Relationships Get Support from New Study." *The Milwaukee Journal,* 9D.

Mainiero, L.A. 1986. "A Review and Analysis of Power Dynamics in Organizational Romances." *Academy of Management Review* 11:750–62.

Peele, S. 1988. "Fools for Love: The Romantic Ideal, Psychological Theory, and Addictive Love," in *The Psychology of Love,* edited by R.J. Sternberg and M.L. Barnes. (159–88). New Haven, CT: Yale University Press.

Price, J.L. 1986. *Handbook of Organizational Measurement.* Marshfield, MA: Pitman.

Quinn, R.E. 1977. "Coping with Cupid: The Formation, Impact, and Management of Romantic Relationships in Organizations." *Administrative Science Quarterly* 22:30–45.

Quinn, R.E., and P.L. Lees. 1984 (Autumn). "Attraction and Harassment: Dynamics of Sexual Politics in the Workplace." *Organizational Dynamics* 13:35–46.

Schein, E.H. 1984 (Winter). "Coming to a New Awareness of Organizational Culture." *Sloan Management Review* 26:3–16.

Snyder, M. 1974. "The Self-Monitoring of Expressive Behavior." *Journal of Personality and Social Psychology* 30:526–37.

Spelman, D., M. Crary, K.E. Kram, and J.G. Clawson. 1986. "Sexual Attraction at Work: Managing the Heart." In *Not As Far as You Think,* edited by L. Moore. (69–91). Lexington, MA: Lexington.

Spruell, G.R. 1985 (February). "Daytime Drama: Love in the Office." *Training and Development Journal* 39:21–23.

Westoff, L.A. 1986 (October). "Mentor or Lover." *Working Woman* 11:116–19.

CHAPTER 16

Teasing and Sexual Harassment: Double-Bind Communication in the Workplace

J.K. Alberts
Arizona State University

Several studies have concluded that a majority of all working women have at one time been subject to sexual harassment. The Equal Employment Opportunity Commission defines sexual harassment as "unwelcome sexual advances, requests for sexual favors, and other verbal or physical conduct of a sexual nature" (Bureau of National Affairs [BNA], 1981). A survey conducted by the Working Women's Institute, a research and advocacy center, reported that 70 percent of the women contacted had experienced sexual harassment, and a joint study by *Harvard Business Review* and *Redbook* magazine indicated that 88 percent of the more than 9000 respondents had suffered such treatment (Neugarten and Shafritz, 1980, 4, 5).

Despite the wide coverage sexual harassment has received by the media (*Los Angeles Times,* 1988; *New York Times,* 1977) and the research that has been conducted from both psychological and sociological perspectives, it is not an issue that has been examined extensively as a communicative phenomenon. Certainly both the psychological and sociological ramifications of sexual harassment are essential to an understanding of it and give rise to it as a communicative event, but the failure to examine how sexual harassment is communicated and responded to verbally is a failure to get at the heart of *what* is going on, rather than why.

Much of the recent research on sexual harassment argues that sexual jokes and teasing are a primary form of harassment. In fact, several studies indicate that between 40 and 60 percent of all complaints are in response to this form of harassment (BNA, 1981; Neugarten and Shafritz, 1980, 4). Thus, it seems a most frequent and troublesome form of harassment may not be the direct "come-on," but rather the tease and sexual play that passes between men and women. This is a more difficult problem to examine, but also more clearly a communicative one.

One might wonder why teases and jokes are so frequently enacted in the organizational setting and why they might often be perceived as harassing, for one normally thinks of teasing as play or humor. The answer lies with the fact that teases contain elements of humor and insult and can function as either play or punishment (or both).

To clarify, a tease is an utterance that includes playfulness/joking and derogation/aggression. Generally, it is an aggressive verbalization couched in some situational qualifiers that indicate play is occurring. The verbal element of a tease is derisive (to varying degrees), and the content of the communication is frequently insulting or counts as assault. It is humor with a bite (Alberts and Hopper, 1983). As Drew explains in his seminal article on teasing (1987), "...recurrently, teases attribute some kind of *deviant* activity or category to the person who is teased." He further explains that "Something which is normal, unremarkable, etc., is turned into something abnormal" (244). Thus, teases, though supposedly offered in the spirit of play, include some verbal, negative comment about the recipient. In the tease, then, there is a contradiction between what is explicitly said and what is implied by the nonverbal and paraverbal signals that indicate play.

Because teasing possesses this dual nature, its interpretation is important—and often in doubt. Consequently, when a man offers a sexual tease to a woman, the meaning of the tease as well as its intent is highly uncertain. The woman may feel harassed, whereas the man believes he is engaging in play. In fact, men as a group are less likely to consider sexual innuendo and joking as sexual harassment (Tangri et al., 1982; U.S. Office of Merit Systems, 1981). Or the woman may believe it was a joke, only to discover that the perpetrator was serious indeed. Finally, the woman may feel harassed and this could be exactly what the perpetrator intended. This type of interaction creates considerable ambiguity and is therefore ripe for misunderstanding and abuse. The perpetrator can harass a recipient, then deny culpability; teasing can be an expedient form of sexual harassment because the harasser can masquerade it as "only joking."

This chapter examines teasing and sexual harassment as communication acts, analyzes the context for such interactions, and then examines the conversational strategies/responses recipients invoke to respond to such events. Finally, why recipients feel so unhappy with both the sexual teases and their own responses is examined. It is intended that through this effort will emerge a clearer understanding of what is occurring and why most women feel their responses have been failures.

TEASING: SEXUAL HARASSMENT
AS A COMMUNICATIVE EVENT

Traditionally, discussions of sexual harassment treat it primarily as a power move—involving aggression and dominance (Backhouse and Cohen, 1981; Crull, 1980; Kanter, 1977). However, the set of circumstances out of which sexual harassment arises is more complex than the power issue alone.

In discussing sexual harassment with men and women one is struck by the differing attitudes men and women have toward the subject. Often men indicate they believe sexual teasing in the workplace is merely "fun and games" (Tangri et al., 1982; U.S. Office of Merit Systems, 1981), whereas women more often view it as a serious violation and threat. Of course, it can be both. The problem seems to lie in part with the different interpretations men and women have for the event. Men more often view it as normal inter-action between men and women; women often argue that sexual teasing is inappropriate in the workplace—they wish to be viewed as co-workers and for their sex and sexuality to be irrelevant to their performance on the job. However, when men and women interact, even in the workplace, it is difficult to leave these issues out.

Part of the ideology of male and female roles and relationships includes the issues of sexuality and courtship. These factors also play a part in sexual harassment. Sexual teasing and harassment spring from a social real-ity in which men have been the sexual initiators and women frequently sex-ual objects/recipients (Brownmiller, 1984; Freud, 1960). Much of the inter-action between men and women, historically, has been sexual in nature. That is, men and women have not generally been reared as playmates, friends, teammates, and co-workers; instead, their interactions have predominately been through dating, mate selection, and marriage. Consequently, they have viewed one another first, and often foremost, as potential sexual or marriage partners. So it is not surprising that these habitual patterns reemerge and interactions are heavily colored by sexuality or sexual interest. It is men and women's most accustomed mode of interaction.

Participants may view sexual teasing as a form of courtship behavior. Because men and women have interacted throughout most of their lives in the courtship schema, it is not surprising that the schema is transported into the organizational setting. This is not necessarily a harmful situation; how-ever, when the schema is overlaid with a power/dominance relationship in the workplace, it takes on different overtones. In a woman's personal life, if she does not like the courtship interaction being played out, she is rela-tively free to end the interaction. However, in the work setting where men more often have power and can initiate courtship interactions, the woman is often tied to her job for economic and career reasons, and she is not so easily able to walk away from the interaction. Thus, the woman is caught in a relationship fraught with the potential for coercion.

Because the woman does feel trapped by her circumstances and the power relationship between the perpetrator(s) and herself, she may interpret sexual teasing and other courtship behavior as a threat, whether the perpetrator intended it as sexual harassment or playful quasi courtship. However, once the event is interpreted as harassment, it generally counts as such, and further interactions are interpreted in light of this.

As well as a courtship issue, sexual teasing and harassment is a power issue. Sexual harassment arises out of a context in which men traditionally have exerted power over women, both at home and, to an even greater extent, on the job. This situation to some extent still holds: women are still to a large degree dependent on men for their material survival—for the most part women are hired and fired by men. Since they are in a subordinate position, if their male boss decides to treat their desirability/sexuality as a job-related issue, they are prime candidates for sexual harassment. Thus, sexual harassment reflects both the issues of power and sexuality.

FUNCTIONS OF TEASING AND SEXUAL HARASSMENT

Teasing, the communication that often serves as the vehicle for expressing sexual harassment, also is a strongly power-related issue. In terms of preconditions, the single overriding factor that controls the form teasing takes is status: it is the most essential element for determining who may be teased by whom. Teasing is often a sign of power or intimacy—that one has the right or privilege of insulting/joking with another. Because it is the privilege of the powerful, teasing is generally directed downward (Coser, 1960; Urban, 1976). This downward teasing in organizational settings reinforces the organizational hierarchy by informally delineating status boundaries, thereby maintaining or increasing social distance. It also enhances the image of the dominant party at the expense of the subordinate.

Since women tend to hold positions on the lower rungs of the organizational ladder, they are likely recipients of such communicative events. In addition, they are subordinated by virtue of their femaleness, so they are even more likely to receive such treatment than men who are low in the hierarchy. For example, among the data collected for this study is an instance where a lower status traffic officer sexually harassed his female superior, a sergeant. After she completed giving him his orders, he replied, "You know I'd do anything for you, darling." Here, even though she held hierarchically superior status, he felt free to respond familiarly to her by virtue of her lower status as a female.

The tease itself is frequently a power move on the part of the perpetrator. By putting oneself in the position of teasing/insulting another, one establishes a claim of superiority, if even only for the moment. One also puts the recipient down by making him/her the butt of laughter for oneself and the audience. It is a one-up move. Freud argues that by making our enemy "small, inferior, despicable, or comic, we achieve in a roundabout way the enjoyment of overcoming him, to which a third part person, who has made no effort, bears witness by his laughter" (1960, 103). Thus, through sexual teasing, a male can establish his superiority and the woman's subordination, and enhance his image in the eyes of his fellow workers.

Of course, not all teases or humorous interactions in the organization are harmful. Teasing serves some useful purposes by increasing cohesion and comraderie and by helping to ease conflict through safe dissipation (Alberts, 1982; Coser, 1960; Martineau, 1972). However, teasing and sexual harassment do serve some very real and harmful functions in the workplace. In general, they can create conflict and control; but they may also serve some specific functions: to prevent subordinates from participating equally in the organization, to punish subordinates for their attempts at acquiring status, and to maintain the superior's dominance and power (Alberts, 1982; Coser, 1960; Kanter, 1977; Urban, 1976).

Sexual harassment, and especially teasing, can be an effective means of control and expressing conflict or venting hostility. As a means of social control, teasing may act to express disapproval of social forms and actions, it can express group sentiments (especially negative ones), develop and perpetuate stereotypes, and express collective approbation for actions not explicitly approved (Stephenson, 1951, 573). All of these purposes are served by sexual teasing and harassment of women.

One way sexual teasing may function to control women is to prevent them from rising in status. When a woman appears to be violating stereotypical expectations, a sexual tease is an effective reminder to her, and any audience, that she is, after all, still a woman and primarily evaluated in terms of her sexuality. This control mechanism of teasing is demonstrated in a recurring incident reported by one female interviewee on an otherwise all-male staff. The interviewee had access to potentially useful information to other staff members because of her acquaintance with a higher-status male in the organization. In a meeting with her male colleagues, when she shared this information and acknowledged the source, the males would tease her by implying that she got the information only because she was having an affair with the higher status male. This subtly denigrated her professional position, while reminding others of her main social function—as a sexual object.

In much the same manner, sexual harassment and teasing may be used as conflict weapons. Teasing is well-adapted to this because it can conceal malice or allow it without the consequences of overt behavior (Burma, 1946; Stephenson, 1951). Through teasing, a punishing force is allowed to emerge without risking harm, or often any sanctions, to the perpetrator. If the perpetrator is called to task for the tease he or she can always beg off as "only teasing."

Related closely to these two functions is that fact that sexual harassment and teasing can also prevent women from participating equally and fully in the organization. By repeatedly sanctioning women for their attempts to rise in status and to be full members in the company, sexual teases help train women into passivity and nonparticipation. If women accept this definition of themselves, provided by both cultural ideology and the harassment/teasing experience, they will be less likely to compete and participate.

Sexual harassment can occur largely because women do occupy inferior roles and job positions while men have power positions; at the same time, sexual harassment functions to keep women in subordinate roles by further defining them as inferior and by interfering with their job performance. Thus, sexual teasing and harassment both use and create women's structurally inferior status (Mackinnon, 1979).

METHOD

The data for this paper were collected in three different ways. Forty women in a variety of private and public organizations were surveyed regarding their experiences with and opinions on sexual harassment. The four-page questionnaire contained one section that focused on sexual harassment which had occurred through sexual jokes and teasing. In addition, a sample of ten women from the survey population were questioned in follow-up interviews to further explore their attitudes and experiences. Finally, male and female participant observers collected examples of sexual harassment that occurred in their work environments. It was hoped that through this variety of approaches it would be possible to more accurately collect concrete examples of sexual harassment so that the communicative nature of the event could be analyzed. This material was used both to explicate a theory of sexual teasing and harassment and to reveal the specific forms the teases and responses manifest.

THE FORM OF SEXUAL TEASING
Structure of Sexual Teases

In his discussion of joking and humor Freud (1960) delineates essentially two types of jokes: innocent jokes and tendentious jokes. *Tendentious jokes* are those that serve a particular (generally negative) aim. Freud further categories tendentious jokes into two groups: *hostile jokes* and *obscene jokes*. (Though he does not offer a separate category of hostile, obscene jokes, he does recognize the possibility of a joke serving this dual function.)

In his discussion of obscene jokes, Freud discusses smut, "the intentional bringing into prominence of sexual facts and relations by speech" (97). He explains that among educated people smut tends to be "elevated" through its transformation into a joke. By framing smut as a joke, it becomes tolerated. He goes on to explain that such jokes are originally directed at women and that the person who laughs at such humor is laughing as though he were the spectator "of an act of sexual aggression" (Freud, 1960).

Thus, one would anticipate that in organizations much of the harassment of women would be sexual aggression in the guise of humor, and that it would take as its subject matter women's sexuality and their sexual relationships to men. Furthermore, as Drew (1987) indicated, the tease generally imputes that the butt of the humor is deviant in some way. Consequently, it may also be expected that sexual teasing will most often have as its form some explicit or implicit comment upon the woman's sexual self and often some imputation of deviance.

In terms of its form, Freud goes on to say that such humor most often requires three participants: (1) one who makes the joke, (2) one who is taken as the object of the hostile or sexual aggression, and (3) one in whom the joke's aim of producing pleasure is fulfilled. And in fact, in her 1977 study of organizational relationships, Kanter discovered that a substantial portion of sexual harassment is directed by several males to one female or by one male to a female in the presence of other males. Consequently, one would more often expect such types of sexual harassment to occur in front of an audience.

The data reveal that these expectations were fulfilled in women's and observers' reports of sexual teasing and harassment. Of the 50 incidences studied, 31 involved some form of joking and/or teasing. Fifty-two percent of the 40 women surveyed claim they have been sexually harassed through teasing and joking, and all of the observed incidences involved teasing behavior. Furthermore, of the women who reported they were harassed through teasing, 42 percent indicated that the event occurred in the presence of an audience. What was surprising, however, was that 13 percent of the incidences were perpetrated by the woman's subordinate, 31 percent by her peers, and 56 percent by her superior. Notably, though, when the woman was teased by her peers, there tended to be an audience. For example, the following interaction occurred among three male and one female colleagues of equal status.

(1) Male: You know, we should get together. We'd make real cute babies.

    Female: (Walked by with no comment.)

    Males: (Began to laugh and talk in Spanish.)

As anticipated, many of the examples of sexual harassment involved the imputation by the perpetrator that the woman was sexually available and willing. For example, the following interaction was reported in the survey data.

(2) Male: You've got a great body.

    Female: (Ignored)

    Male: I bet you're great in bed.

Also, as Drew (1987) indicated in his research on teasing, teases frequently suggest that there is something deviant about the recipient. This held true with regard to the sexual teases collected for this study. For example, in the following interaction, the male teaser suggests the female is somehow deviant sexually.

(3) Male: How come you don't have a boyfriend—maybe it's because you're frigid.

    Female: (Ignored)

    Male: What you need is sex—and I'd be glad to give it to you.

COPING: THE COMMUNICATIVE RESPONSES WOMEN INVOKE

Thus far, sexual teases and harassment have been examined predominantly as communicative events perpetrated by men toward women. But women also participate communicatively in the interaction. In examining sexual teasing episodes, one of the more interesting aspects of that interaction is women's responses or coping strategies. Numerous responses are recommended and employed, but there is a prevailing sense that most of them are ineffective.

A number of coping strategies are given by women for dealing with sexual harassment. They are: ignore it, request that it stop, tease back, complain, quit one's job, get therapy or a support group, or file a legal complaint. What is important is that those which are most frequently recommended and used are the ones that further victimize the victim—ignore it, quit, or go into therapy. What is also significant is that none of the reported strategies is claimed to be very successful.

More often, women respond with some communicative strategy. Probably the strategy most frequently invoked first is the pass; that is, women choose to ignore the sexual tease. However, the Working Women's Institute's report states that 70 percent of the women surveyed had experienced sexual harassment at least once; of these, the majority ignored it, only to find that the behavior continued or worsened (Neugarten and Shafritz, 1980). Of the women in this sample, 69 percent chose to ignore the behavior.

Another, more direct communicative response is to request that the behavior stop. Of another group of women surveyed, 76 percent attempted to resolve the dilemma by explaining to the perpetrator or someone in authority that they wanted the behavior to stop. This tactic was generally useless; in only 9 percent of the cases did the harassment stop. In 26 percent of the cases the complaint led to retaliation (Crull, 1980). Eighteen percent of our sample confronted their harasser, and only 10 percent made any type of formal complaint.

If the recipient does complain of the treatment, *she* is often blamed. The perpetrator is likely to accuse her of "not having a sense of humor." Also, when women protest they are frequently answered with an attack to an even more vulnerable area of their psychological anatomy—their caring. The attack often begins, "I was only being friendly, you're too sensitive." The woman is made to feel she has misinterpreted the interaction and now has hurt someone's feelings and made the person feel rejected; she is forced to back down in her analysis of the situation and her own self-defense. Another form of attack is to call the woman "frigid" (Henley, 1977).

A number of women will respond to sexual teases, or suggest that others respond, by teasing back. (Thirteen percent of this sample tried this tactic.) However, this too, is generally an unsuccessful response. Women often are prevented from or sanctioned for participating in the teasing/joking activity itself. As Coser (1960) has noted, women are not expected (or sometimes allowed) to be witty. Their humor may be acceptable in some situations, but it is disapproved of in those social situations in which there is danger of subverting implicit or explicit male authority. If a woman attempts to tease, the inherent aggressive nature of it is recognized and men perceive it as a challenge to which they must rise; the tease is perceived as humiliating and unbecoming to their dignity. The woman who teases back is likely to find herself punished—perhaps even out of a job.

Finally, some women report that they "go along" with the teasing behavior. Although they may not like the behavior, they found it problematic to refuse to participate. Of the women surveyed for this study on their response to sexual harassment and teasing, approximately 60 percent claimed that at times they "had" to laugh and respond to sexual teasing—it was dangerous and unproductive to do otherwise.

What these coping strategies do, for the most part, is cause women to quit their jobs, produce poorly due to stress, and remain victimized, which reinforces and further justifies the ideological basis of their harassment—that they are inferior workers and weak.

Generally, women do feel that their responses have been ineffective and would like to have responded differently, but usually they are not sure how they should have responded.

COPING STRATEGIES AND THE DOUBLE BIND

For the most part, there is a general lack of understanding of why the verbal methods (teasing back, complaining, ignoring) have been so ineffectual and why women have responded with severe physical and psychological symptoms (Backhouse and Cohen, 1981) to what many consider mere play. Some researchers have attempted to determine ways of dealing with sexual teasing that will be more successful, though there are no indications that any of the recommendations do, in fact, help. What such research has failed to consider is the possibility that there is no fully successful method of coping.

Gregory Bateson's (1972) research on the double bind delineates how the communicative "catch-22" operates in familial relationships and serves to induce schizophrenia. This double-bind theory can be extended to explain how paradox functions in other interpersonal relationships and is particularly productive for analyzing and understanding sexual teasing and women's reactions to it. If the sexual tease is a double-bind situation, then one can more clearly understand why women do not cope well; they do not because they cannot. The double bind does not offer an easy method of coping or escape.

The double bind generally requires that there be two or more persons involved (one of which is the "victim") and that the event be a repeated experience. Both of these factors, obviously, are congruent with the environment of sexual harassment.

As has been discussed, in the sexual tease, generally the woman is a lower status organizational member who is the victim of one or more higher-status male perpetrators. If the experience were to happen only once, it would not be a significant concern. However, the interactions tend to be repeated, and often worsen over time (Crull, 1980; Neugarten and Shafritz, 1980).

The double bind tends to be composed of three parts:

1. *A primary negative injunction.* (This may have either the form of "Do not do so-and-so, or I will punish you," or "If you do not do so and so, I will punish you.")

2. *A secondary injunction conflicting with the first.* This injunction requires either that the victim not recognize that the first injunction exists, or it may require that the victim not obey the primary injunction.

3. *A tertiary negative injunction prohibiting the victim from escaping the field* (Bateson, 1972).

In sexual teasing, the injunctions offered are implied and are in direct opposition. When a man subjects a woman to a sexual tease, he is putting her in a situation that demands that she respond in a sexual manner (the primary negative injunction). The woman is aware that if she does not respond in a sexual way and thereby validate the perpetrator, she runs the risk of punishment, by continued harassment, increased work load, or repercussions on her promotions/retention. However, if she does, she knows that she will likely suffer loss of professional status and reputation. She also faces possible censure by her colleagues. So although the sexual tease demands by its nature that she respond sexually, at the same time, by virtue of the work context, it also demands that she *not* respond in a sexual way (the secondary injunction).

All this is made worse by the tertiary injunction that prevents her from leaving the field—the fact that it occurs in a work context and she is in a powerless position. The woman is not in a position to call her harasser to task because she could be accused of not being able to take a joke or of misunderstanding the interaction (which puts her in the wrong); she can be punished by virtue of her status, and she cannot leave the field because she is tied to it for economic reasons. Thus, the woman who suffers sexual teasing and harassment is effectively caught in a double bind from which there are limited opportunities for escape.

Once the sexual teasing and harassment issue is examined as a communicative event and from the perspective of the double bind, it is easier to understand why it has continued to be perpetuated with little change in men's and women's interaction patterns. With this awareness, perhaps researchers could turn to more useful ways of examining these interactions and how the participants enact them. Interest needs to focus on helping women understand the bind in which they are caught and on helping men and women create new ways of interacting that are more healthful and productive.

REFERENCES

Alberts, J. 1982. "The Form and Functions of Teasing." Unpublished paper.

Alberts, J. and R. Hopper. 1983. "The Nature of Teasing: A Conversational Analysis." Paper presented at the International Communication Association Convention, Dallas, Texas.

Athanassiades, P. 1980. *Women and Work.* Bombay, India: Somiaya Publications.

Backhouse, C. and L. Cohen. 1981. *Sexual Harassment on the Job: How to Avoid the Working Woman's Nightmare.* Englewood Cliff, NJ: Prentice-Hall.

Bateson, G. 1972. *Steps to an Ecology of Mind.* San Francisco, CA: Chandler Publishing Co.

Baudelaire, C.P. 1956. *The Essence of Laughter and Other Essays, Journals, and Letters.* New York: Meridian Books.

Berger, A. 1976. "Anatomy of a Joke." *Journal of Communication* 25:113–15.

Brownmiller, S. 1984. *Femininity.* New York: Fawcett Columbine.

Bureau of National Affairs Editorial Staff. 1981. *Sexual Harassment and Labor Relations.* Washington, DC: Bureau of National Affairs.

Burma, J.H. 1946. "Humor as a Technique in Race Conflict." *American Sociological Review* 11:710–15.

Coser, R.L. 1960. "Laughter Among Colleagues." *Psychiatry* 23:81–95.

Crull, P. 1980. "The Impact of Sexual Harassment on the Job: A Profile of the Experiences of 92 Women." In *Sexuality in Organizations: Romantic and Coercive Behaviors at Work,* edited by D.A. Neugarten and J.M. Shafritz. 67–71. Oak Park, IL: Moore Publishing Co.

Dallea, Georgia. (August 23, 1977). "Women Win Fight for More Construction Jobs, Less Harassment." *New York Times,* 30.

Drew, P. 1987. "Po-Faced Receipts of Teases." *Linguistics* 25:219–53.

Fine, G.A. 1976. "Obscene Joking Across Cultures." *Journal of Communication,* 26:134–39.

Freud, S. 1960. *Jokes and Their Relation to the Unconscious.* New York: W.W. Norton.

Henley, S. 1977. *Body Politics.* New York: Harper and Row.

Kanter, R.M. 1977. *Men and Women of the Corporation.* New York: Basic Books.

Los Angeles Times. (August 16, 1988). "Bradley Demands Strict Response to Sex Harassment." 2, 3.

Mackinnon, C.A. 1979. *Sexual Harassment of Working Women.* New Haven, CT: Yale University Press.

Martineau, W.H. 1972. "A Model of the Social Functions of Humor." In *The Psychology of Humor,* edited by J.H. Goldstein, and P.E. McGhee. New York: W.W. Norton.

Neitz, M.J. 1980. "Humor, Hierarchy, and the Changing Status of Women." *Psychiatry* 43:211–23.

Neugarten, D.A. and J.M. Shafritz. *Sexuality in Organizations: Romantic and Coercive Behaviors at Work.* Oak Park, IL: Moore Publishing Co.

Stephenson, R.M. 1951. "Conflict and Control Functions of Humor." *American Journal of Sociology* 56:569–74.

Tangri, S., M. Burt, and L. Johnson. 1982. "Sexual Harassment at Work: Three Explanatory Models." *Journal of Social Issues* 36:33–54.

Urban, R.L. 1976. "Joking in a Volunteer Fire Department; Combining Fun and Work." *Sociological Abstracts.*

U.S. Office of Merit Systems Protection Board. 1981. "Sexual Harassment in the Federal Workplace: Is it a Problem?" Washington, DC: USGPO.

CHAPTER 17

Men Communicating with Women: Self-Esteem and Power

Mary Monedas
University of Kansas

Changing norms in male-female relationships are causing confusion and frustration (Kimmel, 1987). A man may think a woman is progressive, only to learn that she still expects him to open doors for her. A woman may find that, however liberal a man may seem, he misinterprets her telephone call as an aggressive overture, and treats her with less respect than she had anticipated. Because each is not sure of the sex-role orientation of the other, interaction between women and men is often problematic (Bate and Taylor, 1988). To compound the confusion, men and women do not always act consistently within the same style. As a result, traditional sex stereotypes are no longer reliable guides for behavior.

Many interpersonal problems between the sexes relate to men's socialized tendencies to dominate, control, and subordinate women to maintain their traditionally held power. Uncomfortable in situations that do not proceed according to the old, established rules, they fall back on familiar mannerisms and routines in an attempt to appear confident in their roles. The man who controls is "manly" (Nichols, 1975).

The dominating man is frightened by the self-confident woman because he is accustomed to being in control and "making his moves" at a time he chooses (Nichols, 1975). Astrachan (1986) repeatedly points out that "fear is so frequent a male emotion in the confrontation with women who claim authority or any other aspect of power (197)." In the face of feminism, males lose energy, initiative, and joy due to loss of power and control (Kaufman and Timmers, 1985).

The appeal of the independent woman presents a unique problem for

The author wishes to thank Dr. Ken Johnson for his guidance in completing this chapter.

the traditional man who is bored with traditional, passive, and dependent women, because he can neither give up the conquest of more interesting women, nor commit himself to anyone he cannot control (Fasteau, 1975). In the presence of sharp, assertive women, he feels "less than whole" (Nichols, 1975). Farrell (1974) states, "It takes a secure man to want a liberated woman" (191). Even for this type of man, a traditional upbringing creates conflicts (Dickstein, 1986).

The 1980s focused on communication problems that men face as a result of their upbringing (Bate and Taylor, 1988; Dailey and Rosenzweig, 1988). Many men are now realizing that they, too, have been oppressed by rigid sex roles, and have been limited in developing as whole human beings (O'Neil, 1981b; Lott, 1987). Their use of control and power, and their inability to express their own feelings or to allow others to express themselves cause internal conflicts and problems in interpersonal relationships (O'Neil et al, 1982). *Power* refers to the extent to which a person can impose his or her will on others, whereas *control* refers to the regulation or restraint one individual holds over another through the use of that power.

Biological differences have not proven conclusive in explaining interaction between the sexes. Thus, we might consider attitude toward self as an explanatory variable, because it affects our interaction with others. According to Festinger (1954), self-perception is largely a function of one's social frame of reference. Nichols (1975) criticizes male socialization based on sex roles as being central to the problem of male self-concept. "Men are supposed to be *sure* of themselves in relation to women" (174) whereas the "pressure on a man to appear successful compels him to make others appear unsuccessful" (Farrell, 1974, 57). Masculinity has been found to be a significant predictor of mental health, particularly of self-esteem (Long, 1989). Therefore, it seems reasonable to assume that self-esteem (self-evaluation of one's worth) plays an important part in the use of power to control interactions.

According to O'Neil (1981b), control and power for the traditionally socialized male are based on rigid gender-role stereotypes and beliefs about men and masculinity. For the traditional male, "power, control, and competition are essential to proving one's masculinity," and consequently vital to his self-image (O'Neil, 1981b, 207). Yet, the controlling man is so intent upon monitoring the relationship that he loses self-awareness, spontaneity, honesty, and emotional freedom (Nichols, 1975). The woman loses as well, because she interprets his power as self-seeking ego. Machismo, devoid of sensitivity and insight, says Whitaker (1987), is destructive to the self and to others.

Power struggles cause relational problems between men and women, distorting the messages each receives (Patton and Ritter, 1976). In relationships in which one person always has control, defensive, manipulative styles of interchange are inevitable (Millar and Millar, 1976). One who never shares the control of the relationship stunts his or her own maturity and development, and becomes unaccustomed to thinking for him or herself and exploring his or her own feelings. In essence, this person is forfeiting the right to be a responsible individual. Millar and Millar comment that in today's society parallel transactions seem most likely to bring out mutual satisfaction and actualization.

The purpose of this study is to examine male self-esteem levels and sex-role orientation and how they influence perceptions of different conversational styles used by males and females in mixed-sex dyads. Examining self-esteem levels in conjunction with sex-role attitudes in mixed-sex dyads should reveal how self-esteem affects the degree of power displays males exert to control the interaction. If, indeed, self-esteem affects power displays in mixed-sex dyads, then we have open to us the possibility of new avenues to explore in the explanation of communication between women and men.

REVIEW OF LITERATURE

Past research of male/female communication focused on sex and gender differences to explain communication behavior. Women have been classified with children, servants, convicts, idiots, and the incompetent (Adler, 1927; Key, 1972). They have been referred to in terms of weakness and decoration, the inferior, the negative, and the trivial. Men have been associated with intellect and power (Thorne and Henley, 1975). Because women speak with more emotional variability, they are seen as less stable (Lakoff, 1973). Male speakers, on the other hand, are more outgoing, animated, and confident (Mulac et al., 1985). They use more forceful, persuasive, demanding, and blunt language (Kramarae, 1981). Profanity in a man's speech is seen as power and dominance (Selnow, 1985).

Control of the flow of conversation directions reflects both power and status. Those who speak more and initiate talk more have the greatest power and status. It has been said that men initiate, change and drop topics, and interrupt more than women do in all social situations (Zimmerman and West, 1975) and that they talk longer than do women (Ayres, 1980). However, research by Aries (1982) suggests that bright, motivated women are equally adept at controlling conversation, and that attitudes regarding verbal women may be changing.

The amount and type of power exerted by each of the sexes is influenced by our culture and social organization (Lips, 1981). Women tend to facilitate relationships, whereas men control them by not disclosing (Rosenfeld, 1979). Men tell jokes; women laugh (Kramarae, 1981). Women allow men to make decisions, and tend to conform to their opinions. (Aries, 1977, in Sargent, 1977).

The nonverbal communication patterns of women and men also indicate differences. Male power displays and status may be indicated by stance, an unsmiling countenance, raised head, or touch (the dominant one has the "right" to touch the subordinate), as well as staring and using loud, dominating speech (Henley, 1977; Dovidio et al., 1988). Submissive gestures of females are seen in lowering the head, averting the gaze, and smiling (Henley, 1977). Women smile more than men do (Dovidio et al., 1988). Men look more as they talk and less as they listen. The person who looks more while talking and less while listening has the greater power (Dovidio et al., 1988). Since men speak more, we would expect women to do most of the looking (Henley and Thorne, 1977). Keeping one's distance, sitting or standing in a more "closed" position, using soft, deferential speech, and cuddling to the touch are other demonstrations of submission (Henley, 1977).

The significance of gestures changes according to the sex of the gesturer. No matter what they do, women find that their behavior may be taken to symbolize inferiority (Henley, 1977). If a woman stares, touches, or relaxes her posture, her gestures are interpreted not as power plays such as the male's, but as bold sexual invitations (Henley, 1977).

Gender-Role Conflict and Self-Esteem

Gender-role conflict, the result of the discrepancies between the real self and the ideal self-concept culturally associated with gender (Garnets and Pleck, 1979), restricts the ability of a person to actualize his or her human potential or restricts the potential of another (O'Neil, 1981a). The resultant gender-role strain, "excessive mental or physical tension caused by gender-role conflict and rigidly socialized masculine and feminine roles," leads to "poor psychological adjustment, particularly of self-esteem" (O'Neil et al, 1982, 3). Consequently, the strain may affect personal relationships (Daily and Rosenzweig, 1988).

The changing male attitude is related to ego strength and self-concept (Miller and Swift, 1976), whereas male "fear of femininity," defined as a "strong concern that one possesses or is seen as having feminine values, attitudes and behaviors and that these will reflect negatively upon oneself," is a view of self-esteem (O'Neil et al, 1982). O'Neil's *Fear of Femininity* (1982) is central to this study because it deals with self-esteem, gender-role conflict, and gender-role strain. Low self-esteem in men related to traditional attitudes toward women is associated with maladjustment (Pleck, 1978).

Gender ideals that require males and females to "achieve" masculinity and femininity cause frustrations that strain both the individual and the relationship (Bate, 1988). The traditional male sees power as necessary for his masculinity, and the controlling man pays the high price of forfeiting interpersonal and emotional flexibility (O'Neil, 1981a,b). Kahn (1984) argues that male power is critical to the masculine stereotype. It increases self-esteem and is addictive. Yet, male supremacy can cause interpersonal and intrapersonal problems for men (Werrbach and Gilbert, 1987). The man who believes in this system fears that changes such as those in the work world will transfer power to women (Astrachan, 1986).

Research Problems

Past studies of male and female differences only seem to have compounded the confusion, leaving us with inadequate answers and contradictions. Assumptions on which research is based often reflect obvious sex stereotypes (Henley and Thorne, 1977). Androgyny (the balance between masculine and feminine traits) as a measurement of sexuality may create problems because of the ambiguity of defining what is masculine and what is feminine. Whether or not these differences are innate remains controversial today. Researchers now caution against making generalizations about extensive differences between women and men (Kramarae, 1981). Supporters of socialization effects claim that there are no innate differences between the sexes, and that rearing boys and girls the same, without discrimination, will produce androgynous adults. Birdwhistell (1970) concludes that many sex differences in nonverbals (posture, gestures, expressions) are culturally learned.

The interaction styles of women and men are affected by the situational sex-role demands (Key, 1975). Whatever heredity may provide, experience alters drastically, claims Deaux (1976). For women and men working in groups, particularly those who are highly educated, stereotypic beliefs about men and women communicating may not hold (Bate and Taylor, 1988). Nichols (1975) argues that adaptability suggests that sex-role behavior is not innate. Similarly, Lips (1978) believes that "...male dominance is...amenable to change in response to variations in the social structure," suggesting that our social organization and culture dramatically influence the amount and type of power used by each of the sexes (239). The first three coed classes at West Point did not reveal differences in educational or career aspirations of men and women (Adams, 1984). As values regarding male and female roles continue to change, it is becoming even more important to reorient our perspective in examining what is happening and why problems exist. Rather than to pursue gender differences, it seems more productive to look for characteristics within the individual that might account for some of the communication problems women and men are encountering.

This research examines the effects of sex-role orientation and self-esteem in communication, exploring the possibility that, along with stereotypic sex-role views, low self-esteem affects power displays of certain males in interaction with females. The general hypothesis of this study states that males of low self-esteem having a traditional sex-role orientation will evaluate a dominant communication style of a male toward a female differently than will males of high self-esteem having a nontraditional sex-role orientation.

METHODS AND PROCEDURES

Sex-role orientation and self-esteem levels of the subjects made up the antecedent variables. These were measured by means of the Personality Inventory questionnaire, composed of the Bem Sex Role Inventory and a short version of the Tennessee Self-Concept Scale. Conversations between men and women comprised the independent variable, and evaluations by the subjects of the conversations formed the dependent variable.

Design of the Study

The design of the study was a $2 \times 4 \times 3$ analysis of variance design: two levels of self-esteem (high and low), four sex-role orientations (undifferentiated, masculine, feminine, and androgynous) and three conversational styles (traditional male/traditional female, traditional male/nontraditional female, nontraditional male/nontraditional female.

Subjects

The sample consisted of 53 single college males in introductory courses in communication studies classes at a large midwestern university. Class members were invited to participate in a study about communication between women and men. There were no restrictions other than single status.

Procedure

The Personality Inventory was administered to determine the subjects' sex-role orientation and the self-esteem levels. Each subject then read three conversations of (1) a man using a dominant style of communication toward a female using a traditional style of communication, (2) a man using a dominant style of communication toward a female using a nontraditional style of communication, and (3) a male using a nontraditional style of communication toward a female using a nontraditional style of communication. These scripts, reconstructed from actual conversations, had been taped, recorded, and adjusted to the three conversational styles, which then became the stimulus material. They were then counterbalanced to control for order effects. Subjects recorded their impressions of the communication styles of the actors in each dyad on the Conversation Evaluation form, using seven-point Likert-like scales, indicating their perceptions of the styles as appropriate/inappropriate, influential/noninfluential, confident/lacking in confidence and social attractiveness/unattractiveness. These evaluations were then examined in relation to sex-role orientation and self-esteem level to determine whether a relation existed. Subjects were instructed not to refer back to make changes once they had begun the next conversation.

RESULTS

According to the Bem Sex Role Inventory, 24.5 percent (13) of the subjects were of undifferentiated sex-role orientation, 45.3 percent (27) were of masculine sex-role orientation, 7.5 percent (4) subjects were of feminine sex-role orientation, and 22.6 percent (12) subjects were of androgynous sex-role orientation.

The mean for self-esteem, as measured by the Tennessee Self-Concept Scale, was 111.4, with a standard deviation of 15.0. Of the 53 subjects, 67.9 percent (36) revealed average self-esteem, whereas the remainder of the population sample was split about equally between high self-esteem (15.1 percent or 9), and low self-esteem (15.1 percent or 8).

Self-esteem was the significant factor in male evaluations of communication styles. Males of high or average self-esteem felt that the dominant male in a traditional dyad had a greater degree of influence than did males of low self-esteem.

Significant interaction between sex-role orientation and self-esteem in male perceptions of the degree of influence of the nontraditional female using a dominant communication style toward a traditional male did not produce any main effects. Androgynous males of high self-esteem perceived the female as having greater influence than did androgynous males of low self-esteem. Androgynous males saw the females as more influential than did the males of masculine sex-role orientation.

Self-esteem was the significant factor in male perceptions of the appropriateness of the dominant communication style of the nontraditional female toward the traditional male. High self-esteem males saw the female's style as more appropriate than did the males of low or average self-esteem.

A significant difference for sex-role orientation was indicated in the appropriateness of the nontraditional female's nondominant communication style toward a nontraditional male. However, it was not supported by the one-way analysis of variance.

Self-esteem was the significant factor in the perceptions of males in evaluating the self-confidence of the traditional male's dominant communication style toward the traditional female. Males of low or average self-esteem perceived him as having a higher degree of self-confidence than did males of high self-esteem.

Significant two-way interaction between sex-role orientation and self-esteem affected perceptions of males evaluating the self-confidence of the nondominant communication style of the nontraditional male toward a nontraditional female. Androgynous males of high self-esteem perceived the nondominant male as less self-confident than did androgynous males of low self-esteem or males of feminine or of masculine sex-role orientation with high self-esteem.

DISCUSSION

According to O'Neil (1981a,b; 1982), fear of femininity leads to gender-role conflict and strain. Nichols's *Men's Liberation* (1975) also asserts that interpersonal problems relate to men's socialization, which teaches them to dominate and to maintain power to validate their masculinity. Socialization is central to the male self-concept, and resistance to change is linked to self-concept. Poor self-esteem is rooted in gender-role conflict, and can manifest itself in male-female communication (O'Neil, 1981b). Although many men want change, they are reluctant to give up privilege or power, even though maintaining these comes at a price (Astrachan, 1986).

The general hypothesis of this study states that males of traditional sex-role orientation and low self-esteem will evaluate the dominant communication style of a male toward a female differently than will males of nontraditional sex-role orientation and high self-esteem.

Some of the hypotheses were supported, although not as many as had been expected in light of the O'Neil and Nichols literature. Perhaps this is an indication that variables other than sex-role orientation and self-esteem are involved, or that changing sex-role perceptions may have cancelled out significant differences.

The hypotheses supported involved either self-esteem alone, or both self-esteem and sex role orientation. Males of low self-esteem perceived the male's dominant communication style as being more influential than did males of high self-esteem. Low self-esteem males perceived the dominant communication style of the traditional male toward the traditional female as exhibiting more confidence than did males of high self-esteem. Males of high self-esteem saw the non-traditional dominant female style of communication as more appropriate than did those of low self-esteem.

Significant two-way interaction between sex-role orientation and self-esteem emerged when the nontraditional female used a dominant communication style toward a traditional male. The androgynous male saw the female as more influential than did males of masculine sex-role orientation. Androgynous males of high self-esteem perceived her style as being more influential than did males of low self-esteem.

Some significant differences emerged with respect to sex role orientation in relation to the appropriateness of the nontraditional female's nondominant style toward the nontraditional male. The fact that there was no significant pattern may also reflect changing perceptions.

No differences were predicted in the perceptions of males of low self-esteem with traditional sex-role orientation or of males of high self-esteem having a nontraditional sex-role orientation in evaluating the traditional female's communication style toward a traditional male.

Some surprising results emerged. Significantly, a two-way interaction between sex-role orientation and self-esteem affected perceptions of males in evaluating the self-confidence of the nondominant communication style of the nontraditional male toward the nontraditional female. Males of high self-esteem would have been expected to perceive a male who did not resort to dominance as being more confident. The results indicated the reverse. Androgynous males of high self-esteem perceived the nondominant male as having less self-confidence than did androgynous males of low self-esteem. Androgynous males of high self-esteem perceived the nondominant male as less confident than did males of feminine sex-role orientation or males of masculine sex-role orientation with high self-esteem. This generates an interesting question, since neither the theory nor the literature led us to expect this.

There were surprises as to what did not show up that would have been anticipated. The literature would lead us to expect that a dominant communication style by a nontraditional female would be perceived as socially unattractive to the traditional male of low self-esteem. However, results indicate that she was not viewed as a threat. According to O'Neil and Nichols, traditionally-oriented males of low self-confidence would feel threatened by the assertive female because they are accustomed to being in control, and would feel that she would be encroaching on their territory. The fact that social attractiveness was not a factor in any of the conversations poses questions. Perhaps it is because these men find independent women fascinating (Fasteau, 1975) but not threatening, since they are not dealing with them personally. Possibly the conversation style differences were not extreme enough to bring out this variable.

The literature implies that self-esteem lies at the base of power interchanges. At the same time, gender roles are considered flexible (Lips, 1981), and women are encouraged to change submissive behavior. Astrachan (1986) comments that, although now more men would like to make changes, it is not the majority. He says, "It is not at all clear that the 'new' or 'emerging' egalitarian values will be adopted by a majority of men, or that if they are, performance will catch up with attitudes" (223). Perhaps the changes in perceptions regarding acceptable norms in male-female interchanges have affected the results of this study. It may be that males of masculine sex-role orientation and males of feminine sex-role orientation of high self-esteem evaluated the nondominant communication style of the nontraditional male as exhibiting more confidence than did the nontraditional males of high self-esteem because of socialization, which teaches them that males are, by nature, confident.

The results of this study must be viewed tentatively. More data are needed to buttress the findings. Some of these do support the notion that self-esteem plays a role in displays of dominance in communication styles, and that significant interactions exist between sex-role orientation and self-esteem. However, since sex role perceptions are in a state of flux, longitudinal data may be needed.

REFERENCES

Adams, J. 1984. "Women at West Point: A Three-Year Perspective." *Sex Roles* 11 (5–6):525–41.

Adler, A. 1927. *Understanding Human Nature.* New York: Greenburg.

Aries, E. 1977. "Male-Female Interpersonal Styles in All Male, All Female, and Mixed Groups." In *Beyond Sex Roles,* edited by A. Sargent. New York: West.

Aries, E. 1982. "Verbal and Nonverbal Behavior in Single-Sex and Mixed-Sex Groups: Are Traditional Sex Roles Changing?" *Psychological Reports* 51:127–34.

Astrachan, A. 1986. *How Men Feel: Their Response to Women's Demands for Equality and Power.* Garden City: Doubleday.

Ayres, J. 1980. "Relationship Stages and Sex as Factors in Topic Dwell Time." *Western Journal of Speech Communication* 44:253–60.

Bate, B. 1988. *Communication and the Sexes.* New York: Harper and Row.

Bate, B. and A. Taylor, eds. 1988. *Women Communicating: Studies of Women's Talk.* Norwood, NJ: Ablex.

Birdwhistell, R. 1970. "Masculinity and Femininity as Display." *Kinesics and Context.* Philadelphia: University of Pennsylvania.

Dailey, D. and J. Rosenzweig. 1988. "Variations in Men's Psychological Sex Role Self-Perception as a Function of Work, Social and Sexual Life Roles." *Journal of Sex and Marital Therapy* 14(3):225–40.

Deaux, K. 1976. *The Behavior of Women and Men.* Belmont, CA: Wadsworth.

Dickstein, L. 1986. "Social Change and Dependency in University Men: The White Knight Complex Unresolved." *Journal of College Student Psychotherapy* 1(1):31–41.

Dovidio, J.F., K. Heltman, C.E. Brown, S.L. Ellyson, and C.F. Keating. 1988. "Power Displays Between Women and Men in Discussions of Gender-Linked Tasks: A Multichannel Study." *Journal of Personality and Social Psychology* 580–87.

Farrell, W. 1974. *The Liberated Man.* New York: Bantam Books, Random House.

Fasteau, M. 1975. *The Male Machine.* New York: Dell.

Festinger, L. 1954. "A Theory of Social Comparison Processes." *Human Relations* 7:117–40.

Garnets, L., and J. Pleck. 1979. "Sex Role Identity, Androgyny, and Sex Role Transcendence: A Sex Role Strain Analysis." *Psychology of Women Quarterly* 3:270–83.

Henley, N. 1977. *Body Politics: Power, Sex, and Non-Verbal Communication.* Englewood Cliffs, NJ: Prentice-Hall

Henley, N. and B. Thorne. 1977 "Womanspeak and Manspeak: Sex Differences and Sexism in Communication, Verbal and Non-Verbal." In *Beyond Sex Roles,* edited by A. Sargent. New York: West.

Kahn, A. 1984. "The Power War: Male Response to Power Loss Under Equality. *Psychology of Women Quarterly* 8:234–47.

Kaufman, J. and R.L. Timmers. 1985–86. "Searching for the Hairy Man." *Women and Therapy* 4(4): 45–57.

Key, M. 1972. "Linguistic Behavior of Male and Female." *Linguistics* 88:15–31.

Key, M.R. 1975. *Male-Female Language.* Metuchen, NJ: Scarecrow Press.

Kimmel, M. 1987. "Real Man Redux." *Psychology Today* 21(7):48–52.

Kramarae, C. 1981. *Women and Men Speaking.* Rowley, MA: Newbury House.

Lakoff, R. 1973. *Language and Woman's Place.* New York: Harper and Row.

Lips, H. 1981. *Women, Men, and the Psychology of Power.* Englewood Cliffs, NJ: Prentice-Hall.

Lips, H. and N. Colwill. 1978. *The Psychology of Sex Differences.* Englewood Cliffs, NJ: Prentice-Hall.

Long, V. 1989. "Relation of Masculinity to Self-Esteem and Self-Acceptance in Male Professionals, College Students, and Clients." *Journal of Counseling Psychology* 36(1):84–87.

Lott, B. 1987. *Women's Lives: Themes and Variations in Gender Learning.* Monterey, CA: Brooks/Cole.

Millar, D., and F. Millar. 1976. *Messages and Myths.* New York: Alfred.

Miller, C., and K. Swift. 1976. *Words and Women.* Garden City, NY: Anchor Press, Doubleday.

Mulac, A., J.J. Bradec, S.K. Mann. 1985. "Male/Female Language Differences and Attributional Consequences in Children's Television." *Human Communication Research* 11(4):481–506.

Nichols, J. 1975. *Men's Liberation: A New Definition of Masculinity.* New York: Penguin Books.

O'Neil, J. 1981a. "Male Sex Role Conflicts, Sexism, and Masculinity: Psychological Implications for Men, Women, and the Counseling Psychologist." *The Counseling Psychologist* 9(2): 61–80.

————. 1981b. "Patterns of Gender Role Conflict and Strain: Sexism and Fear of Femininity in Men's Lives." *The Personnel and Guidance Journal* December 203–10.

O'Neil, J., et al. 1982. *Fear of Femininity Scale (FOFS): Men's Gender Role Conflict.* University of Kansas. Presented at the American Psychological Association Annual Convention, Washington, DC.

Patton, B. and B. Ritter. 1976. *Living Together...Male/Female Communication.* Columbus, OH: Merrill.

Pleck, J. 1978. "Men's Traditional Perceptions About Women: Correlates of Adjustment or Maladjustment." *Psychological Reports* 42:975–83.

Rosenfeld, R.A. 1979. Women's Occupational Careers: Individual and Structural Explanations. *Sociology of Work and Occupations* 6:283–311. (In Stewart, et al.)

Sargent, A., ed. 1977. *Beyond Sex Roles.* New York: West.

Selnow, G.W. 1985. "Sex Differences in Uses and Perceptions of Profanity." *Sex Roles* 12 (3-4):303–12.

Stewart, L.P., P.J. Cooper and S.A. Friedley. 1986. *Communication between the Sexes: Sex Differences and Sex-Role Stereotypes.* Scottsdale, AZ: Gorsuch Scarisbrick.

Thorne, B., and N. Henley, eds. 1975. *Language and Sex: Difference and Dominance.* Rowley, MA: Newbury House.

Werrbach, J. and L. Gilbert. 1987. "Men, Gender Stereotyping, and Psychotherapy: Therapists' Perceptions of Male Clients." *Professional Psychology Research and Practice* 18(6):562–66.

Whitaker, L. 1987. "Macho and Morbidity: The Emotional Needs vs. Fear Dilemma in Men." *Journal of College Student Psychotherapy,* 1(4):33-47. Abstract.

Zimmerman, D., and C. West. 1975. "Sex Roles, Interruptions and Silences in Conversation." In *Language and Sex: Difference and Dominance,* edited by B. Thorne and N. Henley. Rowley, MA: Newbury House.

Unit V
Interacting with Culture

Although considerations of power have long been a staple of gender research, the role of culture has not. An analysis of gender that ignores other influences suffers from causal oversimplification. Gender research has only begun to attend to the complex interactions among gender, class, race, and culture. However, the research that has been done shows the value of a sophisticated causal analysis. Gender is not simply a function of sex, power, and class. It also takes on different flavors within different cultures.

In this section, the authors address the ways in which one's culture affects gender construction. Freedman explores the rich resources of the metaphor of "border crossing." "Writing in the Borderlands" considers the role played by the Mexico/Texas border in the writings of Gloria Anzaldúa and Susan Griffin. That border is a metaphor of the connections and divisions between poetry and prose, poetry and politics, lesbians and straights, writing and living. Freedman shows how border crossing develops women's tolerance and flexibility. Riley's article acquaints readers with popular and scholarly work that blends gender with cultural concerns. And Rossi, Todd-Mancillas, and Apps carefully match Brazilian and American businesspeople's perceptions on stress, indicating some ways in which gender and culture—in this case, Latin American and North American—interact with each other.

CHAPTER 18

Writing in the Borderlands: The Poetic Prose of Gloria Anzaldúa and Susan Griffin[1]

Diane P. Freedman
Skidmore College

Living in a state of psychic unrest, in a Borderland, is what makes poets write and artists create....[A Mestiza] is subjected to a swamping of her psychological boundaries.

Gloria Anzaldúa, Borderlands/La Frontera

Many contemporary writers, but especially those women occupying a marginalized position in American society and its literature, employ the central trope of border-crossing as both theme and compositional mode. Mixing genres and disciplines in an autobiographical literary-critical amalgam enables such feminist writers as Gloria Anzaldúa and Susan Griffin to celebrate a self-expressive literature of mosaics and margins as they defy dominant culture's "voice of order."

Gloria Anzaldúa's *Borderlands/La Frontera: The New Mestiza,* like its title, crosses from English to Spanish.[2] For Anzaldúa, being a self-identified "queer," "half-breed," and writer both complicates and replicates what it is to be a woman in North America. The Texas-Mexico borderland is more than a personal, geographical reality for Anzaldúa. More, too, than a metaphor for Anzaldúa's experience as woman/writer/lesbian/Chicana, it describes the compositional strategy of her collection. Her textual hybrid of feminist-auto-biographical-anthropological essays and poems crosses genres and disciplines along with languages and cultures. For Anzaldúa, writing from and through borders results in an unbounded fecundity, a powerful, poetic hybrid where the personal, poetic, and political are joined. She vows:

I will have my voice: Indian, Spanish, White. I will have my serpent's tongue—my woman's voice, my sexual voice, my poet's voice. I will overcome the tradition of silence. (59)

Susan Griffin, author of *Made from this Earth* and other books, is also a lesbian feminist poet-critic crossing several realms—private and public, poetic and academic. Since, in Anzaldúa's view, homosexuals are the "supreme crossers of cultures" (84), Griffin too lives as though in the borderlands, even in a kind of war zone, a "shock culture" (Anzaldúa 11). Like *Borderlands/La Frontera, Made from this Earth* is an anthology, a collection of prose, poetry, and poetic prose, an amalgam of journal, autobiography, history, anthropology, and aesthetic manifesto. Both Griffin and Anzaldúa challenge the centrality of patriarchal power and institutional prose styles with their prose stylistically bordering on, or textually bordered by, poetry. They have engendered a linguistic version of the "hybrid progeny, a mutable, malleable species" that Mexican philosopher Jose Vascocelo claims is possible with "racial, ideological, cultural, and biological cross-pollination" (Anzaldúa 77).

Yet as each writer documents, danger lurks in the borderlands. Living as a *mestiza* (woman of mixed Indian and Spanish blood) in the borderland between Texas and Mexico may mean living with transition, uncertainty, even the threat of death. Anzaldúa reports:

> *Gringos in the U.S. Southwest consider the inhabitants of the borderlands transgressors, aliens—whether they possess documents or not, whether they're Chicanos, Indians or Blacks. Do not enter, trespassers will be raped, maimed, strangled, gassed, shot. (3)*

Less dramatically, writing in the borderlands—suspended between academic and creative writer, published or perished author, dominant and minority cultures—can mean personal and aesthetic uncertainty. Anzaldúa confides that "writing produces anxiety. Looking inside myself and my experience, looking at my conflicts, engenders anxiety in me" (72). She continues:

> *Being a writer feels very much like being a Chicana, or being queer—a lot of squirming, coming up against all sorts of walls. Or its opposite: nothing defined or definite, a boundless, floating state of limbo. (72)*

Griffin notes that she had been worried by an aesthetic problem in *Women and Nature:* "[H]ow was I to convey scientific attitudes in...very personal, emotional language...what I experienced...was a split. I was both censor and poet" (*Earth* 17).

The image of life on the border has force even for women writers not consciously torn by cultural or aesthetic splits: Women writers in general are limited to writing on the borders of their days, writing around childcare or another job, or constant interruptions, rarely given ample time and money for their words. And if women don't find writing a forbidden zone, their past conditioning often makes it one, especially if they seek to avoid the mono-lithic monotony of dominant discourse. Griffin speaks of being assaulted by the patriarchal voice within her:

> *All the time I wrote that book* [Woman and Nature: The Roaring Inside Her],
> *the patriarchal voice was in me, whispering to me (the way the voice of*
> *order whispers to me now) that I had no proof for any of my writing, that*
> *I was wildly in error, that the vision I had of the whole work was absurd.*
> *(*Earth *231)*

Anzaldúa feels similarly assaulted by a "voluntary (yet forced) alien-ation," complaining, "I have so internalized the borderland conflict that sometimes I feel like one cancels out the other and we are zero, nothing, no one" (63).

In order to combat their mutual sense of prohibition and unrest as writ-ers, both Anzaldúa and Griffin use the ways they have been circumscribed or closed out as raw material for what Mary Daly, another poet-critic, calls a process of alchemy. In *Gyn/Ecology*, Daly suggests women "transmute the base metals of man-made myth by becoming unmute, call forth from our-selves and each other the courage to name the unnameable" (34). Poets are especially suited to this transformative task. According to Patricia Hampl, another poet-critic-autobiographer:

> *the golden light of metaphor, which is the intelligence of poetry, was*
> *implicit in alchemical study To change, magically, one substance into*
> *another, more valuable one is the ancient function of metaphor, as it was*
> *of alchemy. (219)*

Anzaldúa's early prose clarification of "border" seems a picture of poetry as it looks on the page, poetry as it is created and received:

> *a border is a dividing line, a narrow strip along a steep edge. A borderland*
> *is a vague and undetermined place created by the emotional residue of*
> *an unnatural boundary. It is in a constant state of transition. (3)*

Like borders of countries and the geographical features—such as rivers—that define them, poetry by its very definition is in a "constant state of transition." It is full of "emotional residue," often perceived as more "vague and unde-termined" than prose, at least conventional prose. Griffin and Anzaldúa's free-verse poems, with their enjambed lines, both contain and disdain "unnatural boundaries." Like the *mestiza*, a poet is a "crossroads," linking literal to figurative, stanza to stanza, life to art. And borderlands, full as they are of the ambiguity of poetry, can yield a similar kind of transformative power. Anzaldúa confesses she dreams about shifts: "thought shifts, reality shifts, gender shifts...I change myself, I change the world" (70). To Griffin, "poetry is a secret way through which we can restore authenticity to ourselves" ("Poetry as a Way of Knowledge" 245). Oscillating or weaving from poetry to prose, American poet-critics like Anzaldúa and Griffin discover a discursive no-man's land, with all the dangers and delights of any "wild-zone"—to use Elaine Showalter's term for women's writing (262).

By pouring the power of poetry for change and connection into prose, women writers find an authentic voice, taking the best from tradition and innovation, old realms and new. In "Transformations," Griffin affirms that "we do battle, not only with the ghosts of patriarchy within us, but with reality again: we see men are still in power and to survive we transform, re-tell old stories, listen, hear again" (221). Anzaldúa claims the new *mestiza* copes by turning ambivalence into something else (79). These writers are alchemists, transforming their lives into prose, their prose into something else.

As all these quotations suggest, these writers tend towards metadiscursive commentary on the forms they explore. Such metadiscourse is another kind of border-crossing. The writer loops inside to outside as she describes her compositional motivations, even her work-in-progress, to her readers. Often these statements themselves employ border imagery, as when Anzaldúa and Griffin assert there is no division between their writing and themselves. "I cannot separate my writing from any part of my life. It is all one," insists Anzaldúa (73). Griffin declares that "why we write, as feminists, is not separable from our lives," and further, "I have always felt myself to be...a medium in which the many voices...are melted, mixed and transformed. Yet I have always written out of the experience of my own life" (3). Griffin's statement implies not only that she and her writing are one, but that she and other women merge in her words; the boundaries of her ego are fluid as those of her text(s). Her practice and claim seem to substantiate both Judith Kegan Gardiner's notion that women's writing "may blur the public and private and defy completion" (185) and Thomas J. Farrell's view of a "female mode" which obfuscates the boundary between the self of the author, the subject of her discourse, and her audience (910).[3]

Griffin uses the image of weaving to talk about how women move beyond the borders of their own experience, closely connecting writer to reader, speaker to hearer, creating new real-life and discursive possibilities:

> *Our writing, our talking, our living, our images have created another world than the man-made one we were born to, and continuously in this weaving we move, at one and the same time, towards each other, and outward, expanding the limits of the possible. (220)*

Many women writing from, about, or through borders deliberately hark back, as Griffin has, to the homespun, to women's traditional talent for bridging home and community, private and public spheres, the artistic and the functional.

Borders can thus evoke a cozy, domestic scene. Think of cloth borders appearing at the loom, in quilts. I connect the alchemical amalgams of *Borderlands* and *Made from this Earth* with quilts, collage, and mosaic. So does Anzaldúa:

> *In looking at this book that I'm almost finished writing, I see a mosaic pattern (Aztec-like) emerging, a weaving pattern...Numerous overlays of paint...make me realize I am preoccupied with texture as well. Too, I see the barely contained color threatening to spill over the boundaries of the object it represents...and over the borders of the frame. I see a hybridization of metaphor. (66)*

As Mary Daly tells us, the Latin term *texere*, meaning to weave, is the origin and root for *textile* and for *text* (4). She observes that "'texts' are the kingdom of males"; in patriarchal tradition, sewing and spinning are for girls whereas books are for boys (5). Nonetheless, feminist poet-critics, who seek to bridge poetry and criticism, the personal and the professional, writer and reader, seek also to weave together home and books, all kinds of borders with/in all kinds of writing. Moreover, they teach their craft, inspire their readers to weave connections among all women writing in the borderlands.[4]

Griffin, corroborating other feminist analyses, writes that it seems obvious that a culture which has created "dualisms between mind and body, intellect and emotion, and spirit and matter would also produce, in its individual members, a divided self" (17). Anzaldúa calls for a "massive uprooting of dualistic thinking" in order to heal the splits she maintains we experience at the root of "our" culture, language, and thought (80). She then labels herself cultureless because, as a feminist, she challenges collective cultural/religious, male-derived beliefs of Indo-Hispanics and Anglos; yet she is cultured because she is participating in the creation of another culture (81). The way to a new culture is through a transformed view of what ails the old. In her poem, "To live in the Borderlands means you," Anzaldúa sums up:

> *To live in the Borderlands means to*
> *   put* chile *in the borscht...*
> *   speak Tex-Mex with a Brooklyn accent...*
> *To survive the Borderlands*
> *   you must live* sin fronteras
> *   be a crossroads. (195)*

Anzaldúa and Griffin become both/either, straddling and striving beyond borders, the limits of genre, language, culture, gender. They refuse to deny or limit their identities, their refusals enacted in a weaving or crossing from land to land, language to language, genre to genre, self to words. What Anzaldúa recognizes as necessary for the *mestiza* might be said to be necessary for all women writing:

*Rigidity means death...*La mestiza *constantly has to shift out of habitual formations...*

The new mestiza *copes by developing a tolerance for contradictions, a tolerance for ambiguity...She learns to juggle cultures. She has a plural personality, she operates in a pluralistic mode ...she turns the ambivalence into something else. (79)*

Like life, poetry calls for a tolerance, even celebration, of ambiguity and plurality. But life and poetry also rely on those other essentials—connection and transformation. These, too, are the essence of textual handicraft, of women's work, of these women's work.

NOTES

1.   This essay has also appeared, in a slightly different form, in *Women and Language* (1989).

2.   To be more accurate, I should note that Anzaldúa refers to, if not employs, some eight languages spoken by her people. They are: standard English, working class and slang English, standard Spanish, standard Mexican Spanish, northern Mexican Spanish dialect, Chicano Spanish with its regional variations, Tex-Mex, and *Pachuco* or *calo.* Anzaldúa points to the Chicano penchant for "switching codes": "We speak a patois, a forked tongue, a variation of two languages" (55).

3.   I am indebted to Gardiner—and to Nancy Chodorow, whom she quotes extensively—for this notion. Gardiner tells us Chodorow portrays "female personality as relational and fluidly defined" (184). See Chodorow's *The Reproduction of Mothering.*

4.   For a mixed-genre (poetry and prose, literary criticism and autobiography) discussion of a range of border-crossing feminist critics—including Adrienne Rich, Cherrie Moraga, Marge Piercy, Tess Gallagher, Alice Walker, and others—see Freedman, "An Alchemy of Genres: Cross-Genre Writing by American Feminist Poet-Critics."

REFERENCES

Anzaldúa, Gloria. 1987. *Borderlands/La Frontera: The New Mestiza.* San Francisco, CA: Spinsters/Aunt Lute.

Chodorow, Nancy. 1978. *The Reproduction of Mothering: Psychoanalysis and the Sociology of Gender.* Berkeley: University of California Press.

Daly, Mary. 1978. *Gyn/Ecology: The Metaethics of Radical Feminism.* Boston: Beacon.

Farrell, Thomas J. 1979. "The Male and Female Modes of Discourse." *College English* 40:922–27.

Freedman, Diane. 1992. "An Alchemy of Genres: Cross-Genre Writing by American Feminist Poet-Critics." Charlottesville: University Press of Virginia.

Gardiner, Judith Kegan. 1982. "On Female Identity and Women." In *Writing and Sexual Difference,* edited by Elizabeth Abel, 177–91. Chicago: University of Chicago Press.

Griffin, Susan. 1982. *Made from This Earth.* New York: Harper.

Hampl, Patricia. 1981. *A Romantic Education.* Boston: Houghton.

Showalter, Elaine. 1985. "Feminist Criticism in the Wilderness." *The New Feminist Criticism: Essays on Women, Literature, and Theory,* edited by Elaine Showalter, 243-270. New York: Pantheon.

CHAPTER 19

Gender in Communication: Within and Across Cultures

Margaret Riley
St. Norbert College

When the issue of gender is discussed in most literature and in classroom and social settings, it is generally understood that the references made apply to gender issues in Western culture, specifically, in the United States. As noted by Pearson, inquiry into sex and communication began in 1908, though the bulk of the research dealing specifically with *gender* and communication has been done in the past fifteen years (1988, 154). It should be evident, however, that there is an entire world from which to draw references and in which research might be conducted. This potentially broad research base, if explored, no doubt could render a bountiful crop of revealing discoveries. Researchers should not be content to dwell on the idiosyncracies of gender issues in the United States culture, but should expand their horizons to incorporate the globe. Through expanded access resulting from increased use of telecommunications and travel, the world is becoming a much smaller place. If we expect to coexist peacefully with our international neighbors, we must work as hard at understanding them as we work at understanding ourselves.

In attempting to locate information regarding gender differences in cross-cultural communication, there appears to be a paucity of research. Liberman (1984) suggests that there is little empirical research in intercultural communication as a whole because of the unique problems that evolve when trying to assess communication across cultures. The epistemology used to report specific structural communication differences includes strange discourse, clear understanding, the ongoing character of the talk, sequential organization, gratuitous concurrence, repetition, strange silences, inquests, and political strategies. This epistemology was applied specifically in a comparison between Anglo-Australians and Aboriginal people, though the points are transferable. A list of potential areas of study is suggested, which, interestingly enough, does not include the gender issue.

Philipsen and Carbaugh (1986) claim to set forth a comprehensive listing of "fieldwork published since 1962 which is responsive to [Dell] Hymes' call for ethnographic studies in communication (387). Hymes coined the term "ethnography of communication"—which he suggested would serve a similar purpose to comparative politics, religion, etc. The impetus for producing this list was the criticism that work being done in the ethnography of communication has consisted primarily of descriptive fieldwork, leaving behind the important concept of comparative analysis. Through the development of this comprehensive bibliography the authors hoped to remove the impediment posed by the lack of such. They even went so far as to suggest areas of comparative analysis that would be ripe for exploring, based on the results of their research. Some of these include the universal conditions for silence behavior, speech acts, self-presentation, and content organization. Gender issues in communication were not mentioned, though the authors admitted that their suggestions are not exhaustive.

This indeed is a valuable resource for those concerned with virtually any aspect of intercultural communication. The wide range of topics that have been investigated must surely include something from just about any arena. The lack of information about gender issues in cross-cultural communication, however, is an oversight that needs to be remedied.

RESEARCH TO DATE

The following is a brief review of articles that have appeared in journals and books that address the issue of gender communication in non-Western cultural settings. It is the contention of the author that cross-cultural communication takes place *within* cultures as well as across cultures. A resident of Spanish Harlem communicating with an individual from Westchester County, New York, is communicating cross-culturally; hence there are articles dealing with specific sub-cultures of the United States as well as those dealing with cultures other than those found within the United States.

Professional journals were a primary source of information regarding the topic of gender and communication. Because the topic is so broad, it cuts across numerous disciplines, hence the subdivision here into different classifications of journals.

Sociologically/Anthropologically Based Journals/Texts

Remarks by Philipsen in the opening statement in an article written in 1975 indirectly summarize the need for studies in cross-cultural communication issues, which are interpreted here to apply specifically to gender issues:

> *Talk is not everywhere valued equally; nor is it anywhere valued equally in all social contexts....Cultures are not only varied but are also internally diverse in the emphasis they place on the value of talk; in all communities there are some situations in which "silence is golden" and some in which talk is the most valued mode of social behavior. Each community has its own cultural values about speaking... (13)*

"Teamsterville" is the speech community upon which this study focuses. It is located on the Near South side of Chicago, and is a neighborhood in which the residents share a cultural outlook on communication. This outlook, although not written, and not easily verbalized by the members, is sharply delineated and detected without much difficulty. The author proceeds to describe the cultural idiosyncracies of this speech community, particularly as they relate to men. The real value of the study is that it confirms the necessity to pursue cultural studies of communication differences.

Philipsen observes, "This suggests the importance of understanding the diversity of cultural outlooks on speaking in contemporary America" (22). We should not be satisfied with just contemporary America, however. The only way we will ever reach the point where we can truly think of the world as a global community will be when we recognize and understand the cultural differences (and similarities) of which Philipsen speaks not only in our geographically confined area, but globally.

The Old Order Amish of Lancaster County, Pennsylvania, were the subjects of a study done by Ericksen and Klien in 1981. It reveals the role of women in a subculture of the United States, and discusses the effects that role plays in communication. The authors analyze the position of Amish women through viewing their role in production, public and private spheres of influence, and childbearing. There is a distinction between public and private spheres because power in one domain does not necessarily lead to power in the other.

The men in the community basically deal with any public communication, hence the women's power in that sphere is secondary. The predominance of men in the public sphere is not as important as it might seem, however, because of the emphasis on the private sphere in the Amish culture. Since family is the central Amish institution, on the homefront, "the wife's opinion takes precedence, and she is consulted on farm matters. In many ways the Amish ideology supports equality" (285). Regardless of sex, humility is an important value, and the ideal person remains quietly in the background. This allows women equal opportunity for respect for the role they play domestically. Men and women are equally dependent on each other economically—the man contributes the money, and the women contribute the indispensable rare goods—children (a work force) and subsistence production—"A kitchen garden provides a considerable proportion of the yearly produce eaten by the family" (284). The egalitarian nature with which the women are treated provides a contrast to the rest of the United States, where there has been an espoused egalitarian ideology, yet much less than that in actual practice.

Previous research on the pastoral societies of the Middle East has been conducted predominantly by male ethnographers falsely assuming a dichotomous nature of those societies—the male's dominant world centering on the public world of the camp, and the women subjugated to their world in the tent, with the separation of the two worlds accepted as a given. The negative impact this has on studies in pastoral societies is no surprise. As Pearson comments, "the investigations of women in male-dominated cultures have been, at the very least, biased" (1988, 160). It is a problem faced not only by pastoral societies in Iran, but in the United States as well.

This assumed dichotomy is disproved in an article by Fazel (1977). The private and public domains of nomadic women are explored, as well as their power and rank, their position in the political hierarchy and the elite, and the effects of external change on their status. Based on field research conducted by the author in southwest Iran among the Boyr Ahmad nomads, this report relies heavily on first-hand observations, yet also integrates (often for the sake of refuting) prior ethnographic work that has been done in this and similar societies. Previous work has not explored the role of the women, and the author primarily addresses this fault. The conclusion states that, contrary to previously held notions, women play a significant role not only in the domestic economy, but through the use of the informal association and loyalties built up through their private communication, "a public expression of the woman's domestic power and authority" (87) is facilitated as well. These informal female communication linkages bear further exploration in a manner that avoids the male bias that has previously contaminated such studies.

Linguistically Based Journal/Texts

The complicated nature of the relationship between the status of women and the politeness or formality of their speech was the focus of a study conducted by Brown (1980). An attempt was made to analyze language usage so that the features differentiating the speech of men and women can be related in a precisely specifiable way to the social-structural pressures and constraints on their behavior (112). The author has three basic complaints about previous work on women's speech: the randomness with which linguistic features differentiating women's and men's speech have been treated; the randomness and arbitrariness of the sociological concepts utilized in the studies of women's speech; and the fact that there is no explicit connection drawn between the linguistic facts and sociological facts in the analyses that have been done (113). This study attempts to remedy those complaints. The conclusions drawn from the report are that studies such as this allow social scientists to predict universals in linguistic usage based on universals in women cross-culturally, to the extent that they occupy similar social-structural positions. Along with this conclusion, the author cautions that the generalizations that one might arrive at as a result of such a study may only be generalized to similar situations (i.e., the use of politeness between women in a small farming community in Mexico should not be generalized to high-caste women in India or a Western African woman). An expansion of empirical research in the gender/language arena is encouraged by Brown.

Gal (1978) conducted a study that focused on an area in Austria where the residents are bilingual in both Hungarian and German. It described the language shift taking place in this community and the role women are playing in this language shift. German is the more widely used in the industrialized world, whereas Hungarian is the language of the peasants in the farming community. The males in the community remain in their farming positions, whereas the women have expanded their horizons, choosing jobs and husbands in the more socially acceptable industrial area where German is the language that prevails. This is leading to social problems within the Hungarian-speaking community, because as the title implies, "peasant men can't get wives" (1). Hence, women are causing a shift not limited to the linguistic concerns of the community but including the social concerns as well.

This is one of the few studies that actually focused specifically on gender issues in communication. Significantly, women play the innovative role in this community. The fact that this study was done, and done successfully, is indicative that the seemingly unconquerable hurdles that cross-cultural gender/language studies are not insurmountable, and in fact significant conclusions can be drawn from investigations done by those who do not let those hurdles stand in their way.

An anthropological-linguistic study conducted by Tannen in 1983 was done as a follow-up to previous work done by the author in 1979 and 1980. In the earlier studies, 20 Greek women and 20 American women watched films and wrote descriptions of what had happened, and those descriptions were compared. Conclusions drawn from those works indicated a discrepancy between American and Greek narrative styles. This study focused on those differences, in an effort to determine what the discrepancies were, and why they existed. The women in this study were asked to relate experiences they had had in being molested—with the Americans, it revolved around New Yorkers on the subway systems, and with the Greeks, it involved any molestations, whether in a transportation situation or not, whether in Greece or not. The Americans had a tendency to approach the narrative task as a memory text, showing that they remembered details accurately, in correct temporal sequence, and objectively.

The linguistic features that typified the Greek narrative focused on the involvement of the listener in the story through repetition, direct quotations in reported speech, historical present verbs, ellipsis, sound-words, second person singular, "now" for time frame "then" and minimal external evaluation (362). They were concerned with telling a good story. This is an interesting distinction to make between females of different cultures. The natural follow-up would be to do a similar study comparing males between the two cultures, and then, males and females within the same culture. Do only Greek females desire to be good storytellers, or is this a cross-gender cultural trait? Do American males relate narratively in the same fashion as American females? There is certainly room for further study.

In a classic book that deals with the subject of women and language, Nichols's chapter analyzes the speech community upon which language studies are focused and the effect that speech community differences can have on the context of their language usage (1980). A relatively new area of study, sociolinguistics, recognizes language variability as playing an essential role in language change (141), yet Nichols feels that most gender studies on language differences fail to take this into consideration. She reports on three actual studies that have taken place in different cultures, and the effect gender has had on these sociolinguistic studies. The results of one study on a small speech community in rural South Carolina indicate the role sex-related choice can play in linguistic change (143).

In this particular community, an English-related creole known as Gullah has predominated since the 1700s. Language patterns have shifted because of increased mobility, particularly among the females in the community. Although both men and women are leaving the island for employment opportunities these days, the men tend to work in groups of other Gullah speakers, whereas the women work independently in jobs that require Standard English. With women switching to Standard English, there appears to be a significant negative impact on the overall usage of Gullah, which in turn will have an impact in language shift and change in this particular community. As in the study by Gal, the women are the innovators of change. Similar sociolinguistic studies in an African and a European nation were described, with the overall conclusion that women potentially have a tremendous effect on speech communities.

Code-switching among bilingual Mexican-American women and the effect that sex has on the alteration of language use was the topic of interest for a study conducted by Valdes-Fallis (1978). The report attempted to answer the following questions:

> *Is there a difference between speech alternatives chosen by women when involved in a communicative act with other women as opposed to their interaction with men? For Mexican-American women, are these differences reflected by language choice? And finally, what do these differences, if any, reveal concerning less obvious differences in the speech choices of monolingual women in their interactions with members of their own sex and of the opposite sex? (65)*

The overall conclusion of the research indicated that "Mexican-American women do reflect their traditional social conditioning and their view of themselves as having lesser status than males in general" (72). The author encouraged additional research that focuses on the implications that might exist regarding monolingual women and their perceptions of their roles and relationships with and to the opposite sex.

Communication Based Journals/Texts

In an article that relates well to the Ericksen article on Old Order Amish and the Fazel report on pastoral nomad societies, Rothstein looks at three different Mexican communities—one that was the author's fifteen-month field research site, and two others that had been subjects of studies in the 1940s. Rothstein's main contentions are that variation in the reports can be attributed to stressing the "ideal" (male dominated production) versus the "real" behavior, and that the family unit is slighted in its description and analysis because of limitations placed on the description by the "ideal" model. The 1970 study netted similar results to the Amish study: the "real" behavior in peasant communities is much more egalitarian than researchers working with the "ideal" model would have us believe. The women's role as a primary producer of the subsistence economy puts them in a position that contradicts the traditionally assumed subordinate role. The concept of "powerless authority" is discussed as it applies to men who have public power, but no real power. That rests with the women who are primary producers.

Rothstein's final statement: "Unless we rid ourselves of Western notions of male dominance and women's work, the family economy will be hidden and we will continue to be deceived by the superficial similarities we ourselves impose" (1983, 21). This accusatory comment could well hold true for any and all efforts to research gender issues cross-culturally. Unless we can throw off the traditional Western approaches to research and models of behavior, attaining some kind of androgynous or generic approach that avoids limitations, research efforts will be worthless.

CONCLUSION

In several of the articles, there were recommendations of how the research in that area could be expanded or augmented. These recommendations just scratch the surface of the potential that exists for research in the field of cross-cultural communication in gender issues.

A newsletter entitled *World Goodwill* had as a recent title article "The Voice of Women." This newsletter is devoted to the promotion of goodwill internationally and its conclusions reinforce the argument of this paper:

> *The "Voice of Woman" calls for a transformation of our society so that we move towards a world where women and the feminine principle are justly represented at all levels of life. Then women and men will both have the opportunity of full participation and the opportunity to give of their best....the women's movement...is emerging as a movement for equality, for life, for peace, for justice, for the earth. The new era depends upon the "voice of woman" being heard and acted upon. This new era depends more than anything else upon the united action of women and men of goodwill and understanding in every part of the world, serving creatively together in equal partnership. (3)*

It is only through research and dedication that the "voice of woman" will be heard and recognized in its rightful place, in full equality with that of its male counterpart.

REFERENCES

Brown, P. 1980. "How and Why are Women More Polite: Some Evidence from a Mayan Community." In *Women and Language in Literature and Society*, edited by S. McConnell-Ginnet, R. Borker and N. Furman. 111–35. New York: Praeger Publishers.

Ericksen, J., and G. Klien. 1981. "Women's Roles and Family Production Among the Old Order Amish." *Rural Sociology* 46(2):282–96.

Fazel, R.G. 1977. "Social and Political Status of Women Among Pastoral Nomads: The Boyr Ahmad of Southwest Iran." *Anthropological Quarterly* 50(2):77–89.

Gal, S. 1978. "Peasant Men Can't Get Wives: Language Change and Sex Roles in a Bilingual Community." *Language in Society* 7:1–16.

Liberman, K.B. 1984. "The Hermeneutics of Intercultural Communication." *Anthropological Linguistics* 26(1):53–83.

Nichols, P.C. 1980. "Women in Their Speech Communities." In *Women and Language in Literature and Society,* edited by S. McConnell-Ginnet, R. Borker and N. Furman, 140–49. New York: Praeger Publishers.

Pearson, J.C. 1988. "Gender and Communication: Sex is More Than a Three-Letter Word." In *Intercultural Communication: A Reader,* edited by L.A. Samovar and R.E. Porter, 154–62. Belmont, California: Wadsworth Publishing.

Philipsen, G. 1975. "Speaking 'Like a Man' in Teamsterville: Culture Patterns of Role Enactment in an Urban Neighborhood." *Quarterly Journal of Speech* 61:13–22.

Philipsen, G. and D. Carbaugh. 1986. "A Bibliography of Fieldwork in the Ethnography of Communication." *Language and Society* 15:387–98.

Ross, C.E., J. Mirowsky, and P. Ulbrich. 1983. "Distress and the Traditional Female Role: A Comparison of Mexicans and Anglos." *American Journal of Sociology* 89(3):670–82.

Rothstein, F. 1983. "Women and Men in the Family Economy: An Analysis of the Relations Between the Sexes in Three Peasant Communities." *Anthropological Quarterly* 56(1):10–23.

Tannen, D. 1983. "'I Take Out the Rock-Dok!': How Greek Women Tell About Being Molested (and Create Involvement)". *Anthropological Linguistics* 25(3):359–73.

Valdes-Fallis, G. 1978. "Code-Switching Among Bilingual Mexican-American Women: Towards an Understanding of Sex-Related Language Alternation." *International Journal of the Sociology of Language* 17:65–72.

"The Voice of Woman." 1988. *World Goodwill Newsletter* 1:1–3.

CHAPTER 20

An Investigation of Gender Differences in Brazilian versus American Managers' Perceptions of Organizational Stressors

Ana Rossi
The Stress Management Clinic, Porto Alegre, Brazil

William R. Todd-Mancillas, and Barbara Apps
California State University, Chico

Stress has become recognized as one of the most serious occupational health hazards of our time (Bateman and Strasser, 1983; Davidson and Cooper, 1983). During the past three decades numerous books and research articles on organizational stress have emphasized the complexity of the problem and the need for research (Bateman and Strasser, 1983; Parker and DeCotiis, 1983; Schuler, 1980). Work-related stress jeopardizes the organizational member's health, with 50 to 80 percent of all diseases being psychosomatic or of a stress-related nature (Pelletier, 1984). Thus far, the evidence indicates that the job setting, corporate structure, and numerous other job/employee interactions contribute to individual stress and strain responses. As a consequence, the organization experiences problems with employees' dissatisfaction, withdrawal, high turnover and absenteeism, and attendant low productivity, at an estimated annual cost of $10 to $20 billion (Schuler, 1980).

Organizations have begun to realize that work-related stress is a contributing factor in the development of functional disorders, psychosomatic problems, and degenerative disease. This realization has led organizations to develop an increasing number of stress management programs for their employees (Parkinson, 1982). In spite of this growing awareness, however, there has been a paucity of research differentiating between men and women regarding occupational stress. One missing element is an analysis of how the organizational member actually perceives his or her on-the-job stressors. Further, there is a great need for combined cross-gender research in order to understand how culture may mediate organizational and individual variables linked with occupational stress (Beehr and Newman, 1978; Parasuraman and Alutto, 1984). Accordingly, the purpose of this study was to compare and contrast organizational stress as perceived by male and female American managers and their Brazilian counterparts. The Brazilian cohort was selected because it represents a third-world culture with extreme economic constraints, and therefore poses an interesting contrast with the United States.

METHOD

The American sample consisted of 220 professionals (110 men and 110 women) randomly selected from the directories of four professional organizations in a Midwestern city. Letters of explanation and questionnaires were mailed to all respondents. Ten days later, follow-up requests were mailed to individuals not having yet returned their questionnaires. A second follow-up request was mailed 14 days after the first. These procedures resulted in response rates of 77 percent for females and 57 percent for males.

The Brazilian sample consisted of 220 professionals (110 men and 110 women) randomly selected from the directories of four professional organizations in Porto Alegre (a Brazilian coastal city). Because of time constraints, some aspects of the data-collection procedure were changed. Respondents were contacted initially by phone and requested to complete the questionnaire. The questionnaire was then personally delivered by one of the researchers. If the respondent missed the appointment a follow-up call was made. The return rates were 96 percent for females and 67 percent for males.

Completing the questionnaire involved two tasks. The first was to circle all those factors appearing on a list of 18 items, which previous research (Rossi, 1986) had identified as potentially related to job-related stress. The second task was then to rank order (1 = most stressful) all the previously circled factors.

Using Kendall's tau coefficient (Siegel, 1956), a series of nonparametric, rank-order correlations were computed to determine the degree of similarity among the sample groups with respect to types of stressors identified and perceptions of the intensity of their impact. Specifically, Kendall's tau was computed comparing American men's and women's responses, Brazilian men's and women's responses, Brazilian men's and American men's responses, and Brazilian women's and American women's responses. Kendall's tau was used because it is an appropriate nonparametric statistic to use when computing measures of agreement among sets of ordinal-level data (Hays, 1963). These analyses allowed us to determine the independent and conjoint impact of gender and nationality on affecting perceptions of stress enhancing factors.

RESULTS

Of the 220 questionnaires mailed to Americans, 131 usable questionnaires were returned (57 from males, 74 from females). Most respondents reported having managerial and supervisory positions. Manufacturers, banks, human service and government agencies, hospitals, and educational institutions were the most typical organizations represented. Of the 220 questionnaires distributed to Brazilians, 180 were returned (70 from males, 98 from females). The Brazilian respondents held positions comparable to those held by American respondents.

In comparing American men's and women's responses, a nonsignificant tau coefficient was obtained (tau = .34, p > .05). Thus, although inspection of Table 1 indicates that American men and women identified the same 11 factors as causing stress, their rankings of the relative importance of these factors differed.

For women, stress caused by others (Item 18) ranks second in importance, but it ranks as one of the least important factors for men, indicating that men are better able to withstand stress emanating from others ("stress carriers," as they are referenced in the literature) than are women. On the other hand, men identified lack of resources (Item 13) as one of the most debilitating stressors, whereas for women it was one of the least important.

A difficulty immediately presented itself when attempting to compute a tau coefficient between Brazilian men's and women's responses. To ensure against spurious results, it was decided a priori that coefficients would be computed only among those factors identified as important by at least 20 percent of each respondent group. However, as indicated in Table 2 (and contrary to results obtained for American men and women), 20 percent or more of the Brazilian women identified three stress factors not also identified by 20 percent or more of the men. These factors were conflict, ambiguity, and changes in one's job description (Items 15, 5, and 4 respectively). Accordingly, one concludes that Brazilian women differ from Brazilian men in that they have a broader understanding of factors causing stress.

Table 1. **Frequency and Rank of Stress Related Factors as Reported by American Men and Women**

| Stress Item | American Sample | | | |
| | Men | | Women | |
	Freq	Rank	Freq	Rank
1. Uncertainty	29	3	35	4
2. Lack of control	27	2	35	1
3. Environmental change	3		10	
4. Job change	5		8	
5. Ambiguity	18	8	23	11
6. Heavy work load	24	1	46	3
7. Insufficient work load	5		7	
8. Inability of managing your time	18	5	38	6
9. Incomplete job information	14	6	24	8
10. Preparedness	6		13	
11. Nonparticipation	6		4	
12. Lack of feedback	22	11	25	10
13. Inadequate resources	18	4	21	9
14. Interpersonal stress	24	7	37	5
15. Conflict	20	9	28	7
16. Dealing with emotional issues	6		11	
17. Trying to express ideas	3		8	
18. Other people	26	10	32	2
Total frequency	274		405	
Total number of respondents	57		74	

Note: The Frequency column records the total number of instances when given factors were identified as significantly associated with stress. The Rank column indicates the overall ranking given to each factor identified by at least 20 percent of a given sample group as stress-producing.

However, an interesting finding obtains if one computes tau on the basis of those eight factors mutually identified by Brazilian men and women. A moderate and significant correlation (tau $= .50, p < .05$) obtains, indicating that although Brazilian women have, for whatever reasons, a more complicated view of factors common to both groups, they have a similar understanding and appreciation of mutually perceived stress factors.

Accordingly, whereas American men and women agree perfectly on the factors associated with stress, they tend to disagree on the relative importance assigned to them; contrarily, Brazilian men and women agree less on the factors associated with stress (with women having a more extensive perceptual set than the men), but tend to agree on the relative importance assigned common factors. Thus, American men and women have similar

Table 2. **Frequency and Rank of Stress Related Factors as Reported by Brazilian Men and Women**

| | Brazilian Sample | | | |
| | Men | | Women | |
Stress Item	Freq	Rank	Freq	Rank
1. Uncertainty	44	32	62	1
2. Lack of control	16	3	24	7
3. Environmental change	3		6	
4. Job change	11		22	6
5. Ambiguity	13		21	5
6. Heavy work load	35	1	45	3
7. Insufficient work load	17	8	23	9
8. Inability of managing your time	10		12	
9. Incomplete job information	22	6	39	11
10. Preparedness	6		16	
11. Nonparticipation	6		9	
12. Lack of feedback	19	9	20	12
13. Inadequate resources	20	4	44	10
14. Interpersonal stress	18	5	30	8
15. Conflict	11	22	4	
16. Dealing w/ emotional issues	4		16	
17. Trying to express ideas	6		10	
18. Other people	15	7	37	2
Total frequency	277		458	
Total number of respondents	70		98	

Note: The Frequency column records the total number of instances when given factors were identified as significantly associated with stress. The Rank column indicates the overall ranking given to each factor identified by at least 20 percent of a given sample group as stress producing.

mental pictures of factors contributing to stress, but disagree on the relative importance of those factors. By contrast, Brazilian men and women have somewhat dissimilar mental pictures, but share clearer overlapping structures than is obtained among American men and women.

Interesting findings are obtained when comparing American with Brazilian responses. Both American men and women identified "inability to manage time" as a significant stress factor, but neither Brazilian men nor women did so; contrarily, both Brazilian men and women identified "insufficient work load" as a significant stress factor, whereas neither American men nor women did so. These differences may reflect some of the national and widespread concern that has recently been given by American social scientists and authors to the subject of time management, hence its readily being identified as a stress factor by Americans but not Brazilians. Brazilians, on the other hand—as a function of working in a somewhat more patriarchal and nepotistic culture—may occasionally find themselves in "make-work" positions requiring too little challenge, hence their identifying insufficient work load as a stress factor.

Further, as previously indicated, American men and women each identified the same set of 11 factors as principal stress-causing agents, whereas Brazilian men identified only nine and Brazilian women 12 factors. Strictly speaking, under such circumstances it is not permissible to compute Kendall's tau. However, some indication of the relative similarity in viewpoints may be obtained by computing tau among those factors for which there is agreement. In this manner, Kendall's tau was computed among the eight stress factors mutually identified by Brazilian and American men (tau = .86, p < .05). This impressive coefficient indicates that although American men may have a slightly broader understanding of or somewhat greater sensitivity for factors causing stress, there are nonetheless striking similarities in their perceptions of most of the factors causing stress.

By implementing a similar procedure, and computing tau for Brazilian women's and American women's responses, a less impressive though still significant coefficient was obtained (tau = .42, p < .05). This would indicate that Brazilian and American women overlap somewhat in their perceptions of the factors and intensities of factors associated with stress, but that they agree substantially less than their male counterparts.

Taken together, these findings suggest that among the four sample groups: Brazilian men have the most parsimonious understanding of factors affecting stress and that the bulk of these factors are essentially task-related; that although somewhat more complicated in viewpoint, American men also identify task-related factors as predominantly associated with stress (in this respect, there is essential agreement between Brazilian and American men); that both Brazilian women and American women evidence greater sensitivity for interpersonal factors than do men from either culture (women from both cultures assigned, for instance, greater importance to conflict and stress caused by others than did their male counterparts). However, despite Brazilian and American women's agreement on interpersonal factors causing stress, the differences in their culture accounted for a few interesting differences: for Brazilian women, changes in job descriptions and insufficient work load were troubling factors—not so for American women; conversely, for American women, time management was a problem—not so for Brazilian women.

In conclusion, these findings indicate that both culture and gender interact to account for differences in understanding stress-associated factors.

REFERENCES

Bateman, T.S., and S. Strasser. 1983. "A Cross-Lagged Regression Test of the Relationships Between Job Tension and Employee Satisfaction." *Journal of Applied Psychology* 68:439–45.

Beehr, T.A., and J.D. Newman. 1978. "Job Stress, Employee Health and Organizational Effectiveness: A Facet Analysis, Model and Literature Review." *Personnel Psychology* 31:665–99.

Davidson, M., and C. Cooper. 1983. *Stress and the Woman Manager.* New York: St. Martin's.

Hays, W. 1963. *Statistics.* New York: Holt, Rinehart, and Winston.

Parasuraman, S., and J.A. Alutto. 1984. "Sources and Outcomes of Stress in Organizational Settings: Toward the Development of a Structural Model." *Academy of Management Journal* 27 (2):330–50.

Parker, D.F., and T.A. Decotiis. 1983. "Organizational Determinants of Job Stress." *Organizational Behavior and Human Performance* 32:160–77.

Parkinson, R. 1982. *Managing Health Promotion in the Workplace: For Implementation and Evaluation.* Palo Alto, CA: Mayfield.

Pelletier, K.R. 1984. *Healthy People in Unhealthy Places: Stress and Fitness at Work.* New York: Delacorte.

Rossi, A.M. 1986. "Work Related Stress: An Investigation of Gender Differences." *Biofeedback Society of America Annual Meeting Proceedings:* 133–36.

Schuler, R. 1980. "Definition and Conceptualization of Stress in Organizations." *Organizational Behavior and Human Performance* 25:184–215.

Siegel, S. 1956. *Nonparametric Statistics for the Behavioral Sciences.* New York: McGraw-Hill.

Unit VI
Interacting with Audience

The five chapters in Unit Six illustrate the position that gender, like communication, is an ongoing process. Thus, gender changes through transactions with others. In a real sense gender is the cocreation of speaker and audience. This unit operates from an interactional perspective and posits that gender is an evolving construct. Gender changes as a result of perceived expectations and constraints emanating from an audience.

These chapters address the complex mix of sender and audience that affects gender development in slightly different ways. Judi Beinstein Miller's article and the one by Mary-Jeanette Smythe and Bill Huddleston both examine transactions with conversational partners. Beinstein Miller analyzes women's and men's generation of conflict scripts, a subject that necessitates a sensitivity to the responses of a conversational partner. Smythe and Huddleston focus on differences among male-female, female-female, and female-male conversational pairs. John Schmitt's textual analysis of the gender of language in the Bible examines the interactions among text, reader (as audience), and historical context. Judith Bowker and Pamela Dunkin's chapter and the essay by Mari Boor Ton both center on how gender is negotiated between a public speaker and her audience. Bowker and Dunkin examine the classroom context, whereas Boor Tonn's analysis focuses on the interplay between labor leader Mary Harris "Mother" Jones and her audiences of various labor groups. Each article defines audience in a slightly different manner, but all are concerned with the exchanges between partners. These exchanges and the cognitions that precede and accompany them are seen as fundamental to an emerging definition of gender.

CHAPTER 21

Conflict Scripts of
Men and Women

Judi Beinstein Miller
Oberlin College

According to traditional sex role stereotypes, men and women manage conflict differently. Men are believed to be more aggressive and competitive than women; women are believed to be more yielding and cooperative than men (Bem, 1974; Spence et al., 1975; and Williams and Best, 1982). These beliefs appear to have behavioral counterparts. Studies of conflict tactics indicate that, at least among college students, women prefer and use more integrative, compromising, or tactful responses than do men, whereas men prefer and use more competitive and unyielding responses than do women (e.g. Fitzpatrick and Winke, 1979; Kimmel et al., 1980; Shockley-Zalabak and Morley, 1984; Miller, 1987). Differences such as these can be explained by a variety of theoretical perspectives, including women's greater communal focus (Bakan, 1966), permeability to the feelings of other (Chodorow, 1978), sense of care and responsibility for others (Gilligan, 1982), and interpersonal orientation (Swap and Rubin, 1983). Common to these explanations is that women may be more constrained than are men to take the other's point of view into consideration, even while expressing their own. If such explanations are correct, then we might find differences in the mental representations that men and women have for conflict and/or the extent to which they use these representations as guidelines for their behavior. This study investigated men's and women's "scripts" for interpersonal conflict and the influence of these scripts on their preferences for conflict responses.

The term "script" has been used to refer to our generalized beliefs about the standard components of an event and their organization (Schank and Abelson, 1977; Abelson, 1981). "Going out to dinner," for example, has an ordered set of general components (e.g., waiting to be seated, being seated, ordering from the menu, and so forth) that vary in detail from situation to situation but that nonetheless make specific instances of going out to dinner meaningful. That we have scripts for interpersonal conflict is implied by research on schemata for persuasion (e.g., Rule et al., 1985). It is also suggested by certain regularities in the conflict behavior of intimates.

Peterson (1983), for example, organizes findings on interpersonal conflict into three developmental stages and provides a limited number of trajectories through which most conflicts appear to move. The beginnings of conflict are marked by some precipitating event (e.g., criticism, rebuff, illegitimate demand, or cumulative annoyance) and decision to engage the partner in discussion about it. Once conflict has been engaged, in the middle stages, it may take one of two turns. Partners may be able to state their positions and obtain validation from each other. If they do, they will generally solve their problem in a direct and constructive way. Or, partners may not stick to the issue at hand but instead expand it by, for example, disparaging each other, steamrolling, or crucializing (Raush et al., 1974). If they do, they will generally escalate the conflict and not resolve it unless some conciliatory act is made later on. Finally, conflict is terminated when partners withdraw without reaching a resolution or when a resolution is reached, either because one gives in to the other or because they discover a compromise or integrative agreement.

Peterson's review suggests that there may be a limited number of generalized scripts for interpersonal conflict and that these scripts may serve as guidelines for conflict behavior. If the scripts of men and women differ, then differences could occur in their components (e.g., the kinds of events that precipitate conflict) or the organization of their components (e.g., the extent to which escalation of conflict is contingent upon the precipitating event).

The following three research questions were therefore posed by this study.

1. What are the common components of people's schemata or scripts for interpersonal conflict and how are these components organized?
2. Do the components and/or organization of interpersonal conflict scripts differ among men and women?
3. In what ways do conflict scripts provide guidelines for conflict behavior?

METHOD

These questions were addressed by a questionnaire study in which undergraduate men and women wrote scripts depicting conflict between friends and also indicated the likelihood of using certain types of responses in a series of hypothetical conflicts with friends.

Subjects

One hundred twenty-one students (50 men and 71 women) from introductory psychology courses agreed to participate in a study of interpersonal conflict in return for supplementary course credit. Each student who agreed to participate received a questionnaire packet that he or she filled out in his or her spare time and returned in the following class session.

Stimulus Materials

The questionnaire packet included one instrument to estimate the subjects' preferred responses to interpersonal conflict and another to elicit their schemata for interpersonal conflict. The first instrument contained ten hypothetical situations of interpersonal conflict. In each situation a "friend" expressed disagreement with the subject, criticized the subject, or was interfering in some way with the subject's achievement of goals. Four responses—an aggressive assertion, a tactful assertion, a direct, simple assertion, and an acquiescent response—were written for each situation. In one situation, for example, the "friend" was critical of a joke that the subject had told. The four responses that were written for this situation were as follows.

> I would say that he or she didn't have a very good sense of humor or must be in a bad mood today (aggressive assertion).
> I would say that I was sorry he or she didn't like the joke but would indicate that I liked it (tactful assertion).
> I would say that I thought it was a good joke (direct, simple assertion).
> I would just say "I'm sorry" (acquiescent response).

Responses to each situation were counterbalanced in random order. Subjects were asked to indicate, on a five-point scale, the likelihood of their responding in each way to each situation (i.e., very unlikely, somewhat unlikely, neither likely nor unlikely, somewhat likely, or very likely). At the end of this instrument, subjects were asked to reread each situation and rate, on another five-point scale, how comfortable they would be in each.

The second instrument contained one open-ended question. Subjects were asked to imagine two friends who were having an argument. One had made several promises to the other and had not kept these promises. Subjects were asked to imagine the encounter from beginning to end and to write down a script or scenario that depicted the argument.

Analytic Procedures

Conflict response preferences were estimated by summing the subjects' likelihood ratings for aggressive, tactful, and direct assertions and for acquiescent responses in the ten conflict situations. These scores were then divided by the total likelihood of responding in any of the possible ways and multiplied by 100, to reflect the subjects' preference for one type of move in relation to the others. As in previous work with this scale (Miller, 1987), greatest preference was indicated for direct assertions ($\overline{X}$ = 30.39; SD = 2.75) and tactful assertions ($\overline{X}$ = 29.42; SD = 3.41) and least preference for aggressive assertions ($\overline{X}$ = 16.24; SD = 3.78). Acquiescent responses ranked in between ($\overline{X}$ = 23.94; SD = 3.86). Women indicated greater preference for tactful assertions (t = 3.59; df = 116; p = .000) than did men and lesser preference for aggressive assertions (t = -2.75; df = 116; p = .007).

Schemata for interpersonal conflict were derived from the conflict scenarios that the subjects had written. Each scenario was coded according to the type of promise that had been broken (i.e., the initiating event) and the stages through which the conflict developed. Preliminary analysis of approximately one-third of the scenarios indicated three general types of broken promises. The first included promised favors or services, such as lending a car or money, helping with schoolwork or housecleaning, and shopping for things. The second included promises to share one's time and self, but without performing specific services; for example, meeting for lunch or dinner, going to a movie together, spending time together in general, and keeping confidences. The third type of promise was nonspecific. Significant numbers of subjects referred to "things" that the friend had promised to do and not done. Since these generic promises seemed similar to promised favors and services, they were grouped together. This left two categories of broken promises, one for favors/services and the other for sharing time/self.

The development of conflict was captured by three stages that are comparable to those outlined by Peterson (1983). The first or beginning stage concerned the way in which the offended party brought the broken promise to his or her friend's attention. In most cases the offended party simply accused the friend of breaking the promise (e.g., "You promised to do this and you didn't"), but in a significant number the offended party questioned the friend about the promise (e.g., "Why didn't you have my bike back when you told me you would?") rather than making an accusation. The conflict was therefore coded as starting with either an accusation or a question.

The middle stage included the promise-breaker's response to the accusation or question and the offended party's reply to the promise-breaker. Since the promise-breaker, in general, either accepted responsibility for the broken promise (e.g., by apologizing) or did not accept responsibility for it (e.g., by justifying his or her behavior), his or her behavior was coded accordingly. The offended party sometimes replied by accepting this response, regardless of whether or not it was apologetic. More often, however, he or she either accepted the response grudgingly and continued to dwell on the broken promise (e.g., by saying why the promise was important to keep) or did not accept the response and instead escalated the argument (e.g., by castigating the friend's personality, threatening the friend, or accusing the friend of not caring for the relationship). Although the response of the offended party should therefore have been coded into one of three categories, it was not always easy to decide whether an acceptance should be coded as a simple or grudging one. Due to significant intercoder disagreement with regard to these two categories they were collapsed into one, with the result that the offended party's response was coded as either "accepts the friend's response" or "escalates the argument without accepting the friend's response."

Finally, the outcome or final stage of the conflict was coded as minimally resolved, somewhat resolved, or completely resolved. Once again, intercoder disagreement necessitated the collapsing of two categories. Specifically, conflicts that were somewhat and completely resolved were coded together as "conflicts that had at least some resolution." Once the necessary categories had been collapsed, agreement between two independent coders ranged from 93 percent (Scott's pi = .88) for the response of the offended party to 96 percent (Scott's pi = .94) for the outcome of the conflict.

RESULTS

Components of the Conflict Scripts and Their Organization

Nearly as many subjects wrote about promises to share time or self (47.5 percent) as about promises to perform favors or services (52.5 percent). The developmental components of the scripts were not as evenly balanced, however, and suggested greater prominence for some forms of conflict than for others. Most subjects (73.3 percent) imagined the offended party starting the conflict with accusations rather than questions. A majority (61.5 percent) depicted the promise-breaker taking responsibility for the broken promise by apologizing, rather than not taking responsibility. A majority (60.7 percent) also indicated that the offended party would escalate the conflict rather than accept the response of the friend. Even so, an equal proportion (60.7 percent) indicated at least some resolution of the conflict rather than minimal resolution of it. Apparently, for most of these subjects, a broken promise was forgivable but not to be taken lightly. It was a serious enough violation of the friendship for the offended party to be upset and make his or her upset explicit.

A series of contingency analyses were performed to study the patterning of the scripts' components. These analyses revealed four constraints on the development of conflict. First, if the promise-breaker apologized, this increased the probability of a better resolution (chi square = 5.24; df = 1; p = .02). Second, if the offended party accepted the promise-breaker's response instead of escalating the conflict, this also increased the probability of a better resolution (chi square = 8.95; df = 1; p = .003). Third, if the offended party started the conflict with an accusation rather than a question, then he or she also tended to escalate the conflict rather than accept the promise-breaker's response (chi square = 5.34; df = 1; p = .02). And fourth, if the promise was to share time or self rather than to perform a favor or service, then there was a marginally significant tendency for the offended party to escalate the conflict rather than accept the promise-breaker's response (chi square = 3.20; df = 1; p = .07).

The Scripts of Men and Women

There were no statistically significant differences between the components of the men's and women's scripts. Men and women were equally likely to write about promises to share self or time and promises to perform favors or services. Neither tended more than the other to start the conflict with a question or with an accusation. Roughly equal proportions depicted the promise-breaker apologizing for his or her behavior and roughly equal proportions depicted similar replies by the offended party. The outcome of the conflict was as often good for men as for women, and as often bad for one as for the other.

The development of the men's and women's scripts did differ somewhat, however. Outcomes in the men's scripts appeared to be more contingent on the behavior of the offended party than were outcomes in the women's scripts. When men started the conflict with a question, for example, they tended to resolve it more often than when they started with an accusation (chi square = 4.53; df = 1; p = .03). Women wrote good endings (i.e., resolutions) when they started with an accusation as often as when they started with a question. Similarly, initial accusations were associated with later escalation of conflict in the men's scripts and initial questions with acceptance of the promise-breaker's response (chi square = 5.45; df = 1; p = .02). This tendency was statistically insignificant and weak at best in the women's scripts. Men also tended to write better endings when they depicted the offended party accepting the promise-breaker's response rather than escalating the conflict (chi square = 8.64; df = 1; p = .003). Among the women, this contingency was only marginally significant (chi square = 2.69; df = 1; p = .10).

In contrast, outcomes in the women's scripts appeared to be more contingent on the behavior of the promise-breaker than were outcomes in the men's scripts. When women depicted the promise-breaker apologizing, they were significantly more likely to write good endings than when they depicted the promise-breaker only justifying his or her behavior (chi square = 5.72; df = 1; p = .02). Although a similar trend occurred in the men's scripts, it was weaker and statistically insignificant. The men, then, appeared to be writing scripts that kept outcomes under the control of the offended party, whereas the women appeared to be writing scripts that placed control of outcomes in the hands of the promise-breaker.

The tendency for men in general to establish somewhat more contingent responses resulted in their writing scripts that were either all good or all bad more often than did women. Thirty percent of their scripts were either all good (i.e., questioning starts, apologies, acceptance of apologies, and resolution) or all bad (i.e., accusatory starts, no apologies, escalation, and minimal resolution), in contrast to only 17 percent of the women's (chi square = 2.90; df = 1; p = .09).

Guidelines for Behavior Provided by the Scripts

Comparison of the subject's conflict response preferences according to their conflict scripts required a summary measure of their conflict scripts. This measure was obtained by summing the occurrences of prosocial or "good" components in each script. A script with a questioning start, apology, acceptance of apology, and resolution, for example, received a score of 4, whereas a script with an accusatory start, no apology, escalation of conflict, and minimal resolution received a score of 0. The subjects' scripts were normally distributed according to this scoring procedure, with an average occurrence of 1.9 prosocial or "good" components (SD = 1.15).

Among the men, correlations between these scores and their conflict response preferences yielded two statistically significant trends. The more prosocial were the scripts of these men, the greater was their preference for acquiescent responses (r = .29; p = .02) and the less was their preference for aggressive assertions (r = −.43; p = .001). Similar correlations among the women produced only one marginally significant tendency. The more prosocial were their scripts, the more they tended to prefer tactful assertions ($r = .18$; $p = .07$). One other trend occurred among the women but not the men. The less comfort they reported in the conflict situations, the more prosocial their scripts tended to be ($r = -.23$; $p = .03$).

DISCUSSION

Three research questions were posed initially by this study. The first concerned the general content and organization of people's schemata for interpersonal conflict. Would scripts for conflict over broken promises, for example, yield a common set of components? Would these components be related to each other in a predictable way? As in Peterson's (1983) review of marital conflict, it was possible to summarize the conflicts portrayed by these scripts with reference to their precipitating event (here, the nature of the broken promise), beginning stages (here, the start of conflict by the offended party), intermediate stages (here, the response of the promise-breaker and reply of the offended party), and termination (here, the outcome). The most commonly occurring components suggested the following general scenario for conflict. The offended party accuses the promise-breaker of not keeping his or her word. The promise-breaker accepts blame for his or her behavior and apologizes. The offended party escalates the conflict nonetheless, particularly if the promise was to share time or self. And, in the end some resolution is reached. Of course, this kind of summary does not capture the richness of detail in many of the scripts. Nor does it reflect the cycling of apologies and accusations that occurred in the middle stages of many. The following script, provided by a young woman, illustrates the kind of detail and cycling of apology and accusation that were included in many of these scripts.

> *B:* You promised me that you would be here an hour ago so we could finish this project!
>
> *A:* I'm sorry. My class was running late....
>
> *B:* Fine.
>
> *A:* It's not my fault if my pro—
>
> *B:* I'm sick of it. I'm tired of all your excuses. You are always breaking your promises to me! Am I so low on your list of priorities that you feel you can just blow off any promises you made to me?
>
> *A:* Well, I'm sorry if I'm so busy, but don't try to give me a guilt complex. If you were my friend you'd try to understand.
>
> *B:* If you were my friend you would at least consider my feelings and tell me or send a message that something came up. I understood the first few

times, but I refuse to be trampled. I'm busy too, I can think of better ways to spend my afternoons than waiting around for you.

A: I'm sorry. It's just that it never occurs to me that I'm supposed to meet you at a certain time. You know how forgetful I am.

B: Then write it down. I'm sorry I yelled, but you know how I hate to wait.

A: Let's try this again.

B: Okay.

A: Hi! Sorry I'm late. It will never happen again! If I make you wait ever again you can chop off my fingers—

B: (Sarcastically) Ha, ha.

A: —you can cut out my tongue—

B: You would die if you couldn't talk.

A: —you can hang me upside down and smear honey all over my body to attract the bees—

B: What bees?

A: The killer bees imported from Africa.

B: (Laughing) I forgive you already! Just please, no more.

Each script, just as this one, had its unique aspects. From the standpoint of generalized stages and components, however, the scripts had much in common with each other.

Not surprisingly, the form that conflict took at one stage depended in part on what had happened at the preceding stage. In general, prosocial or "good" acts early on increased the likelihood of good outcomes, whereas problematic or "bad" acts early on increased the likelihood of bad outcomes. These contingencies were particularly apparent in the scripts of the men, who tended to write outcomes in accord with the initial and later behavior of the offended party. Consequently, their scripts were somewhat more often all good or all bad than those of the women. The major contingency in the women's scripts was between the outcome of conflict and the promise-breaker's responses.

The second research question concerned differences in the scripts of men and women. Surprisingly, differences were not found in the components of their scripts. However, the tendency for outcomes in the women's scripts to be influenced more by the promise-breaker's behavior and in the men's scripts more by the offended party's behavior suggests somewhat different criteria for forgiveness among men and women. Men apparently viewed the offended party as having rights to control the outcome, since he or she was the one who had suffered the injustice. Women apparently took greater cognizance of the promise-breaker's rights, since they were inclined to resolve the conflict if the promise-breaker apologized. The men's scripts reflected a more independent criterion, the women's scripts a more interdependent one. It is noteworthy in this regard that post hoc analysis of scripts in which the offended party escalated conflict suggested a similar difference in orientation. Specifically, of the 74 scripts in which conflict was escalated, 30 percent depicted the offended party dwelling on friendship implications of the broken promise (e.g., "If you can't make time for me, then I suppose our friendship isn't worth it" or "If you were my friend you would at least consider my feelings"). The remainder (70 percent) depicted the offended party threatening the promise breaker in other ways and/or blaming his or her dispositions (e.g., "Do you want me to start being as inconsiderate toward you as you are toward me?" or "You always break your promises"). Comparison of these two modes of escalation revealed that twice as many women as men who depicted escalated conflict made relational implications of the broken promise explicit (40.0 percent in contrast to 20.7 percent). Such results may suggest somewhat greater salience of mutual caring and responsibility among the women and somewhat greater salience of individual rights among the men. This interpretation would be in accord with differences in moral reasoning between men and women that have been described by Gilligan (1982).

Finally, the third research question concerned ways in which the subjects' conflict scripts might serve as guidelines for their behavior in conflict situations. Specifically, would there be statistically significant correlations between their conflict response preferences and the "goodness" or "badness" of their conflict scripts? These analyses suggested also that the men's behavior was guided more strongly by personal expectations for conflict than was the women's. The better their conflict scripts were, the less they preferred aggressive assertions and the more they preferred acquiescent responses. Thus, verbal aggressiveness was associated with "bad" scripts and acquiescence was associated with "good" scripts among the men. Among the women, only one marginally significant correlation was obtained between the "goodness" or "badness" of their scripts and their preferred conflict responses. The better were their scripts, the more they preferred tactful assertions.

The "goodness" or "badness" of the women's scripts was correlated significantly with their reported comfort and discomfort in the conflict situations. The less discomfort they imagined experiencing, the worse were their scripts. There was no statistically significant correlation between the reported comfort of the men and the goodness or badness of their scripts. Bad feelings about conflict, then, were associated with prosocial expectations among the women but not the men.

Although it is important not to forget the similarities in these conflict scripts, their differences in organization and correlation with conflict response preferences suggest somewhat different beliefs about interpersonal conflict among men and women. Outcomes and behavior for the women appear to have depended less on personal criteria and more on relational ones. Outcomes and behavior for the men appear to have depended more on personal criteria and less on relational ones.

REFERENCES

Abelson, R.P. 1981. "Psychological Status of the Script Concept." *American Psychologist* 36:715–29.

Bakan, D. 1966. *The Duality of Existence.* Chicago: Rand McNally.

Bem, S.L. 1974. "The Measurement of Psychological Androgyny." *Journal of Consulting and Clinical Psychology* 42:155–62.

Chodorow, N. 1978. *The Reproduction of Mothering: Psychoanalysis and the Sociology of Gender.* Berkeley, CA: University of California Press.

Fitzpatrick, M.A., and J. Winke. 1979. "You Always Hurt the One You Love: Strategies and Tactics in Interpersonal Conflict." *Communication Quarterly* 27:3–11.

Gilligan, C. 1982. *In a Different Voice: Psychological Theory and Women's Development.* Cambridge, MA: Harvard University Press.

Kimmel, M.J., D.G. Pruitt, J.M. Magenau, E. Konar-Goldband, and P.J.D. Carnevale. 1980. "Effects of Trust, Aspiration, and Gender on Negotiation Tactics." *Journal of Personality and Social Psychology* 38:9–22.

Miller, J.B. 1987. "Relationship Schemata and Responses to Interpersonal Conflict: Differences Among Men and Women." Paper presented at the 10th annual conference of the Organization for the Study of Communication, Language, and Gender.

Peterson, D.R. 1983. "Conflict." In *Close Relationships,* edited by H.H. Kelley et al. New York: W.H. Freeman.

Raush, H.L., W.A. Barry, R.K. Hertel, and M.A. Swain. 1974. *Communication, Conflict and Marriage.* San Francisco, CA: Jossey-Bass.

Rule, B.G., G.L. Bisanz, and M. Kohn. 1985. "Anatomy of a Persuasion Schema: Targets, Goals, and Strategies." *Journal of Personality and Social Psychology,* 48:1127–40.

Schank, R.C., and R.P. Abelson. 1977. *Scripts, Plans, Goals, and Understanding.* Hillsdale, New Jersey: Lawrence Erlbaum.

Shockley-Zalabak, P.S., and D.D. Morley. 1984. "Sex Differences in Conflict Style Preferences." *Communication Research Reports* 1:28–32.

Spence, J.T., R. Helmreich, and J. Stapp. 1975. "Ratings of Self and Peers on Sex Role Attributes and Their Relation to Self-Esteem and Conceptions of Masculinity and Femininity." *Journal of Personality and Social Psychology* 32:29–39.

Swap, W.C., and J.Z. Rubin. 1983. "Measurement of Interpersonal Orientation." *Journal of Personality and Social Psychology* 44:208–19.

Williams, J.E., and D.L. Best. 1982. *Measuring Sex Stereotypes: A Thirty Nation Study.* Beverly Hills, CA: Sage.

CHAPTER 22

Competition and Collaboration: Male and Female Communication Patterns During Dyadic Interactions

Mary-Jeanette Smythe
University of Missouri

Bill Huddleston
Central Michigan State University

In reviewing the second full decade of research on communication and gender, Thorne, Kramarae, and Henley (1983) noted that despite numerous studies from several disciplines, less is known concerning the actual language or nonverbal behaviors of men and women than might be expected. Much in these collections of literature is based on analyses of mixed-sex interactions in which questions such as "who asks the most questions," "who interrupts more often," or "who takes the longest speaking turns" are posed. Although useful, these studies are at best inadequate descriptors of the communication patterns of either sex, since a wealth of data suggest that the sex of one's conversational partner is likely to affect the communication behaviors in which one engages (Hall, 1984). What is needed is research that examines communication among women, and compares communication patterns with those that emerge during interactions among men, as well as the patterns characterizing mixed-sex conversations. The current study was undertaken to answer this need.

TALK AMONG WOMEN: SOME TENTATIVE HYPOTHESES

There is a dearth of literature on the characteristics of female-female interactions. Virtually no studies have focused on this type of dyad exclusively, but some studies have included female-female dyads in a broader research design. One of the general ways to characterize the results of these studies is to note that they appear to challenge existing frameworks of interaction analysis associated with research on language and the sexes. One point of departure would suggest that women engage in more collaborative patterns of communication (e.g., drawing out other speakers, using positive listening cues such as head nods, and emotional sharing) whereas men display a more competitive interaction mode (e.g., frequent interruptions, dysfluent speech forms, and low nonverbal expressiveness). Following are some of the specific findings about sex differences in communication. All must be viewed as largely conjectural and tentative. Taken together, they provide a foundation for the hypotheses in the current study.

1.   During conversations with another woman, women exhibit lower levels of dominance. Hall's work has revealed that women deal with each other in a more accommodating manner than they do with men (Hall, 1984; Hall and Braunwald, 1981; Hall, Braunwald and Mroz, 1982). Female- female interactions, argues Hall, contrast with male-male interactions due to a process of dominance-matching in which each male responds to the other's real or perceived dominance by behaving more dominantly himself. The possibility that the prototypic "feminine" behaviors are most obvious in same-sex interactions is a direct challenge to prevailing stereotypes of male-female interactions and to traditional concepts of complementary male and female roles. Research in this area could refine, even restructure many assumptions inherent in familiar analyses of sex roles and related behaviors.

2.   During initial interactions women talking to other women exhibit a unique pattern of relating (Martin and Craig, 1983; Hirschmann, 1974). Broadly similar to the ideas expressed in hypothesis one, the profile of behavioral cues supporting this hypothesis includes the volume of talk and degree of guardedness and relaxation that characterize female-female interactions. Women appear able to talk more easily to each other than to men, which is certainly consistent with ethological studies suggesting that in both nonhuman and human primates, same-sex clusters are more common than opposite-sex ones (Hall, 1984). Martin and Craig (1982) were struck by the pattern of low reciprocity in talk-time among female-female dyads in their study of initial interactions. Their interpretation was that women moved more quickly through the early phases of acquaintance and adopted a style of interaction characteristic of the later, more intimate stages of relationships.

3.   When talking to another woman, women tend to discuss more personal matters and focus on family, relationship problems, and men (Haas and Sherman, 1982; Aries and Johnson, 1983). That topic differences exist in same-sex and opposite-sex interactions is hardly startling. The motives or reasons underlying these behaviors are unknown. If Hall's (1984) argument that norms preclude competition in female-female conversations, this topic selection pattern may indicate rule-based rather than choice-based decisions. Or, these studies may support the concept of a gender-linked language effect that identifies emotional references in women's speech as a significant linguistic gender marker (Mulac, Lundell, and Bradac, 1985). What is needed are empirical data that indicate that women actually speak in this manner.

4.   During conversations, women talking to other women exhibit a high rate of verbal back-channel cues (Duncan and Fiske, 1977; Roger and Schumacker, 1983). Backchanneling, frequently referred to as listener responses, is most often seen as short verbal cues (e.g., "mmm-hmmm," "wow") that are spoken when one's conversational partner is speaking. Functionally, these cues signal the speaker that one is attending to, agreeing with, or comprehending the discourse. Analyzing language from a storytelling task, McLaughlin et al. (1981) report that one of the only story receipt behaviors that characterized women was expressions of appreciation (usually expressed as backchannels). Intriguingly enough, the behavior is most pronounced when women speak to other women.

5.   During conversations, women talking to other women engage in high eye contact (LaFrance and Mayo, 1979; Smythe, et al., 1985; Ellyson, et al., 1980). This principle reflects a pattern of results quite pertinent to this discussion of sex differences as a function of dyadic composition. The general rule is that women receive more of the same sorts of nonverbal cues that they themselves give off. In short, the findings indicate that women mirror one another's cues, resulting in higher levels of gaze in female-female dyads than in any other type. Thus, "typical" nonverbal sex differences tend to be most exaggerated when one interacts with one's own sex.

6.   Women report that the best aspect of talking with other women is empathy, followed by depth and ease of conversation (Haas and Sherman, 1982). To some degree, this final statement seems a global descriptor encompassing all those stated previously. It is, however, an empirically independent finding, although related conceptually to the other statements in this section.

    Taken together, the foregoing findings suggested the following hypotheses.

H1.   Dyads composed of two women will exhibit lower levels of verbal and nonverbal dominance cues than dyads composed of two men or of a man and a woman.

H2.   Dyads composed of two women will exhibit higher levels of interaction involvement and relaxation than dyads composed of two men or of a man and woman.

H3.   Dyads composed of women will choose different topics of conversation than dyads composed of men or mixed-sex dyads, and will discuss more topics.

H4.   Dyads composed of women will display a different pattern of nonverbal expressiveness (e.g., back-channels, eye contact, smiles) than dyads composed of men or mixed-sex dyads.

H5.   Dyads composed of women will exhibit a different pattern of specific language cues (e.g., questions, interruptions, fillers,) than dyads composed of men or mixed sex dyads.

H6.   Dyads composed of women will exhibit a higher level of interpersonal attraction between partners than dyads composed of two men or mixed-sex dyads.

METHODS

Sample. Sixty dyads composed of students drawn from the enrollments of several large basic communication courses at a large Midwestern university were used in this study. Twenty dyads were composed of women, twenty of men, and the remaining twenty were composed of a man and woman. None of the interactants had met his or her interactional partner previously. Assignment to dyad condition was randomized across subjects.

Experimental setting. Data were collected in a carpeted seminar room located in a laboratory suite. One small table and two chairs were located near the center of the room. Subjects were videotaped from behind a one-way mirror as they sat in armless chairs on either side of a small table.

Procedure. When both subjects were seated, the experimenter introduced herself and the subjects to one another, and explained that the study was a simulation of the acquaintance process. Subjects were told that the topic of conversation was left to their discretion, but if they had trouble getting started, a card listing possible conversational topics was located on the table in front of each subject.

After twelve minutes of conversation, the experimenter reentered the room and interrupted the interaction. The subjects were thanked and asked to complete a series of posttest questionnaires (e.g., interpersonal attraction measures) designed to tap perceptions of the encounter and of their partner. Posttest measures were completed by the subjects in separate rooms of the experimental suite.

Dependent measures. Each of the following dependent variables was chosen on the basis of earlier research suggesting the relevance of the behavior for sex-role display. Although inconsistent findings associated with these cues were common, the consensus of writers in the field is that these cues differentiate male and female discourse patterns.

1. *Talk time.* Duration of talk, calculated in seconds of continuous speech during the interactions.

2. *Speaking turns.* Defined as the number of different instances of speech an individual had during the course of the interaction, excluding minimal responses or fillers.

3. *Questions* were coded as units of discourse that by virtue of verbal content or intonation patterns, were designed to elicit a response from the listener in the dyad.

4. *Interruptions* were defined as the number of times the listener intruded into a speaker's talk before the last word that could signal a possible end or boundary of a sentence, question, or other unit of talk. Backchannels were not coded as interruptions, but overlaps, talkovers, and interjections were counted.

5. *Fillers* were defined as verbalizations made by speakers such as "um," "well," or "y'know."

6. *Qualifiers* were defined as softening, mitigating words or phrases used by speakers to blunt the impact of his or her remarks. Other forms of qualifiers include disclaimers, or introductory clauses that excuse, explain, or request understanding or forbearance from a listener.

7. *Topic initiations* were defined as the introduction of a new subject area in a conversation.

8. *Topics* were defined as the number of distinct subjects the interactants discussed during their conversations.

9. *Attraction* was measured by the McCroskey and McCain (1974) inventory. This 15-item instrument provides a global attraction score based upon three independent subscales measuring task and social and physical attraction.

ANALYSIS

Trained coders worked in various combinations of two, three, and four-person groups. Coders examined only one subject in a dyad and one measure at a time. Although the sex and dyadic pairing of each subject were obvious to the coders, they were kept blind to the specific research questions.

Interrater reliability estimates ranged from .87 to .94. These levels were considered more than adequate to warrant use of coder-generated data to test our hypotheses.

To assess the impact of individual and dyadic effects on the dependent measures, a series of two-factor analyses of variance were used.

Scores on disclosure within dyadic pairings were obtained through the use of trained coders, who rated the levels of disclosure on a five point scale. The attraction scales were tabulated for a global estimate of attraction as well as scores on the three subscales, task and social and physical attraction.

RESULTS

Significant differences emerged on a number of the dependent measures used in this study. Hypothesis one predicted differences in dominance displays across the three dyad types. Dominance displays were operationalized as floor-holding behaviors (speaking turns, talk time, filled pauses) and conversational control cues (topic initiation attempts and interruptions). Support for this hypothesis was marginal at best. As displayed in Table 1, no significant differences across dyads were observed on most of the dominance measures. A significant main effect for topic initiations, indicating that more topics were initiated during male-male interactions ($F = 3.46, p < .05$) was in the predicted direction, and some directional support, although nonsignificant, was noted in the means associated with interruptions and filled pauses.

Hypothesis two concerned the levels of interaction involvement and relaxation displayed within the dyad pairings. Variables associated with this factor included frequency and duration of eye contact, frequency and duration of smiling, questioning, disclosiveness, and postural shifts. Support for this hypothesis was substantial, and in the predicted direction. Dyads composed of two women engaged in significantly higher levels of smiling frequency and duration, ($F = 11.26, p < .05; F = 10.42, p < .05$), greater duration of eye contact ($F = 3.39, p < .05$), but significantly fewer eye contacts overall ($F = 5.23, p < .05$). Nonsignificant but directionally consistent support for the involvement hypothesis was observed on questions and postural shifts. Finally, no significant differences were detected in level of disclosure across dyad pairings.

Conversational topics were the focus of hypothesis three. Female-female dyads were expected to select different topics to discuss and to converse on more topics than male-male or female-male dyads. Content analyses of the conversations, however, failed to reveal many differences in the array of choices as a function of dyadic composition. Striking similarities

Table 1.   **Dyadic Means on Selected Behavioral Measures**

	MM	FM	FF
Total Talk	318 $_a$(sec)	319 $_a$	337 $_a$
Speaking Turns	55.7$_a$	55.2$_a$	54.6$_a$
Topic Initiations	7.0$_a$	6.6$_a$	6.2$_a$
Filled Pauses	2.7$_a$	3.6$_a$	2.0$_a$
Interruptions	6.2$_a$	6.8$_a$	5.8$_a$
Questions	15.4$_a$	15.6$_a$	16.9$_a$
Qualifiers	4.4$_a$	4.6$_a$	4.9$_a$
Eye Contacts	34.4$_a$	33.2$_a$	31.4$_b$*
Gaze Duration	442.7$_a$	469.0$_b$	513.6$_c$*
Smile (frequency)	18.6$_a$	23.9$_b$	25.7$_c$*
Smile (duration)	95.9$_a$	155.1$_b$	186.4$_c$*
Postural Shifts	4.0$_a$	4.6$_a$	4.9$_a$
Fillers	7.3$_a$	8.5$_a$	8.0$_a$
Topics	7.1$_a$	7.5$_a$	6.8$_a$
Disclosure	3.7$_a$	4.0$_a$	3.7$_a$

*Means with uncommon subscripts are significantly different

were instead the general rule. Moreover, the prediction that women would discuss more topics was not supported.

Means displayed in Table 1 revealed only partial support for the differential patterns of nonverbal expressiveness and language variables predicted for female-female dyads in hypotheses four and five, respectively. The display norms proposed by Hall (1984) appeared most consistently for nonverbal cues (e.g., smiling and gazing), although comparatively little significant support emerged on the language measures. Some trends within the means shown in Table 1 on language cues such as questions and qualifiers were in the predicted direction, suggesting some marginal support for the hypothesis.

Finally, hypothesis six predicted greater attraction as a function of dyadic composition. Means revealed a pattern that was counter to the one predicted. The lone attraction effect was on the dimension of physical attraction, and that effect was apparent only in the cross-sex dyads ($F = 4.68$, $p < .05$).

DISCUSSION

The results of the current study provide some empirical evidence concerning talk among women. It seems clear, however, that the predictions drawn from previous (largely self-report) studies were not especially well supported. Although correspondence between self-report and behavioral data is not uncommon, the pattern of findings reported here suggests some issues familiar to gender researchers. First, the differences among dyads were rather modest on most of the language measures. Differences in nonverbal displays were more robust. Taken together, these findings affirm a frequently observed pattern in the relationship between gender and communication behaviors. For whatever reasons, differences in the language behaviors of men and women rarely approach the levels anticipated. More internalized nonverbal behaviors, by contrast, appear remarkably consistent as signals of gender. Thus, when questions are posed about the gender and communication relationship, attention to differences in verbal and nonverbal display becomes important.

Much has been written about placing analyses of communication behaviors within their social context (Thorne, Kramarae, and Henley, 1983) and this perspective seems most appropriate to our data set. It seems reasonable to argue that the pattern of results obtained here reflects the primacy of context rules in shaping communication behaviors. Recall that subjects in this study were engaged in initial interactions, and were thus very probably concerned with matters of politeness, ingratiation, and impression management. Simply put, the etiquette of first encounters facilitates expression of some behaviors, such as questioning and smiling, while suppressing certain others, such as interruptions or excessive self-disclosure.

The implication for future researchers framed by the foregoing analysis poses a serious dilemma. Initial interactions between zero-history dyads have been the *sine qua non* for empirical studies of the gender/communication relationship. Relational histories among subjects introduce too much uncontrolled variance and render meaningful descriptions of behavior across groups virtually impossible. Perhaps more important is the argument that placing individuals into an unstructured situation with a stranger compels them to rely on secure, well-internalized, and thereby more "genuine" patterns of behavior. Now, researchers must begin in earnest to examine the impact of the contexts that frame interactions. Conceptual treatments of this issue are not hard to locate, but empirical efforts are sorely lacking.

Finally, a methodological note. The dyadic analysis used here seems quite plausible and consistent with the intent to search out behavioral differences corresponding to the collaborative and competitive constructs of interaction. In summing individual scores across partners to achieve overall comparisons on the variables of interest, much salient information is lost about the impact of individuals' behaviors. An alternative analysis that corrects for between-pair correlations, such as that proposed by Dindia (1987), might produce a clearer account of dyadic interactions.

Methodological options notwithstanding, the goal of this study was to examine empirically the claim that talk among women is in some fundamental ways distinctly different from talk among men or between men and women. The findings suggest that efforts to materialize metaphors such as "collaborative" or "competitive" communication styles are an essential and valuable scholarly enterprise. As an acceptable data base accumulates, more refined descriptions and predictions should become possible. In the meantime, however, attention should be directed toward the perceptual as well as the behavioral realm. Recall that differences in perceptions (both self and other) of male and female communication behaviors have been consistently more robust than empirical differences would seem to warrant (Smythe, in press). It may well be that the way women "feel" about the experience of communicating with another woman, as opposed to a man, is where the important differences lie. Exploring how and why individuals evaluate their own and others' communication behaviors differently may recast old assumptions about communication style in new and productive ways.

REFERENCES

Arics, E., and F. Johnson. 1983. "Close Friendship in Adulthood: Conversational Content Between Same-Sex Friends." *Sex Roles* 9:1183–96.

Dindia, K. 1987. "The Effects of Sex of Subject and Sex of Partner on Interruptions." *Human Communication Research* 13:345–71.

Duncan, S.D., and D.W. Fiske. 1977. *Face to Face Interaction: Research Methods and Theory.* Hillsdale, NJ: Erlbaum.

Ellyson, S., J. Dovidio, R. Corson, and D. Vinicur. 1980. "Visual Behavior in Female Dyads: Situational and Personality Factors." *Social Psychology Quarterly* 43:328–36.

Haas, A., and M. Sherman. 1982. "Reported Topics of Conversation Among Same-Sex Adults." *Communication Quarterly* 30:332–42.

Hall, J.A. 1984. *Nonverbal Sex Differences: Communication Accuracy and Expressive Style.* Baltimore, MD: The Johns Hopkins University Press.

Hall, J.A., and K. Braunwald. 1981. "Gender, Cues in Conversations." *Journal of Personality and Social Psychology* 40:99–110.

Hall, J.A., K. Braunwald., and B. Mroz. 1982. "Gender, Affect, and Influence in a Teaching Situation." *Journal of Personality and Social Psychology* 43:270–80.

Hirschmann, L. 1974. "Female-Male Differences in Conversational Interaction." Paper presented at the Linguistic Society of America, San Diego, CA.

LaFrance, M. and B. Carmen. 1980. "The Nonverbal Display of Psychological Androgyny." *Journal of Personality and Social Psychology* 38:36–49.

LaFrance, M., and C. Mayo. 1979. "A Review of the Nonverbal Behaviors of Women and Men." *Western Journal of Speech Communication* 43:96–107.

McCroskey, J., and T. McCain. 1974. "The Measurement of Interpersonal Attraction." *Speech Monographs* 41:261–26.

Martin, J., and R. Craig. 1983. "Selected Linguistic Sex Differences During Initial Social Interactions of Same-Sex and Mixed-Sex Student Dyads." *Western Journal of Speech Communication* 47:16–28.

McLaughlin, M., W. Cody, M. Kane, and C. Robey. 1981. "Sex Differences in Story Receipt and Story Sequencing Behaviors in Dyadic Conversations." *Human Communication Research* 7:99–116.

Mulac, A., T. Lundell, and J. Bradac. 1985. "Male/Female Language Difference and Attributional Consequences in a Public Speaking Setting: Toward an Explanation of the Gender-Linked Language Effect." Paper presented at the Speech Communication Association, Denver, CO.

Roger, D.B., and A. Schumaker. 1983. "Effect of Individual Differences on Dyadic Conversational Strategies." *Journal of Personality and Social Psychology* 45:700–05.

Smythe, M.J. 1991. "Gender and Communication Behaviors: A Review of Research." In *Progress in Communication Sciences,* edited by B. Dervin. Norwood, NJ: Ablex. 173–217.

Smythe, M.J., R.M. Arkin, S. Nickel, and B. Huddleston. 1983. "Sex Differences in Conversation: The Stereotype Revisited and Revised." Paper presented at the International Communication Association, Dallas, TX.

Thorne, B., C. Kramarae, and N. Henley. 1983. "Language, Gender, and Society: Opening a Second Decade of Research." In *Language, Gender, and Society* edited by B. Thorne, C. Kramarae, and N. Henley. Reading, MA: Newbury House 7–24.

CHAPTER 23

Enacting Feminism in the Teaching of Communication

Judith K. Bowker
Oregon State University

Pamela Regan Dunkin
S. Oregon State College

Integrating the feminist perspective with traditional viewpoints espoused in the field of speech and communication can be accomplished in several ways, two of which are modeling and instruction. In this paper we will outline one approach in which the teacher models the feminist perspective and, in so doing, encourages the students to investigate the course subject—whether that subject is public speaking, small group communication, or communication theory, for example—with feminist methods. We will cite examples from our combined twenty years' teaching experience in the classroom to illustrate procedures used to achieve our goals.

Before we describe those procedures, we will delineate what we mean by a feminist perspective. Given the developing nature of the feminist ideology, we choose to identify descriptors rather than assert a definition. The descriptors we have chosen reflect our own inventions as well as those of others (Bunch, 1987; Schuster and Van Dyne, 1985; Shrewsbury, 1987; Weiler, 1988). For our purposes, then, the feminist perspective is a way of being, knowing, and acting that intends empowerment rather than oppression by power; validation of race, class, and gender as dynamics that create valued difference but not oppressive hierarchy; and recognition of the meritorious complexities of various ideologies. In addition, our feminist perspective honors the personal as a way of knowing, giving credence to thought, feelings, and experience as purveyors of knowledge.

One objective of our procedures is to spend less time instructing or identifying the methods as feminist and more time enacting feminism in the classroom. The goals of this approach are several and are interwoven. One goal, for example, is to enable the instructor to practice feminism in a cooperative atmosphere, thus allowing the integration of feminism with the course subject material. Ultimately, such an integration will provide a more balanced teaching agenda for the communication discipline.

This balance further can be enhanced by a second goal, that is, encouraging students to effect feminism as a means of thought and a motivation for action. To facilitate those changes, our objective is the eradication of the competitive, stressful atmosphere of the traditional hierarchical structure of classes in rhetoric—particularly those in public speaking. Finally, achieving these ends will help raise students' awareness of the diverse means of instruction and ways of learning that are possible by introducing them to feminist ways of knowing (Friedman, 1985; Johnson, 1987).

Recognizing that these goals may be achieved in a variety of ways, we will discuss six procedures in detail: (1) creating a noncompetitive relationship for learning among class members and between the professor and her students; (2) establishing a norm of inquiring curiosity, rather than norms such as assaulting "Socratic" questioning; (3) introducing the personal as knowledge without sacrificing credibility; (4) promoting shared power by providing students with comprehensive syllabi and by teaching responsibilities/skills of small group discussion; (5) acting as intermediary between student and topic rather than as fountainhead of truth; and (6) facilitating particularly androcentric theories (à la Sandra Bem's Gender Schema Theory for alternative reading of male-centered stories to children).

The first procedure, creating a noncompetitive atmosphere among the students and between the students and the professor, is especially necessary in public speaking courses. Steeped in a tradition of opposition and rivalry, speaking in public has been reported as the greatest fear many American adults (41 percent) experience (*London Sunday Times,* 1973). Debunking the antagonistic nature of the course can be accomplished in at least these two ways.

Noncompetitive Relationships

First, the professor can use a section of the orientation lecture to express candidly her intention that such a competitive atmosphere not become the norm of the class. She can encourage students to approach the class with a sense of learning rather than a goal of achieving a grade. Judy's strategy to diminish the competitiveness is to explain that any student who earns a high grade will receive it. She emphasizes that students are not competing with each other for a prescribed number of top grades, but rather have the opportunity to engage other class members in pursuit of the course material. She encourages study groups and reciprocal editing of papers. She also points out the destructive aspects of "ambush criticism," peer criticism created by a selective listener who lies in wait for what he or she believes are the shortcomings of others.

In her public speaking courses, Pam establishes the prescription that no negative criticism be aired in oral discussions of the speeches. She directs students to voice only positive aspects of the presentations when the class members analyze each other aloud. Such a prescription eliminates the "I'm-better-and-I-will-tell-you-what-you-are-doing-wrong" syndrome so prevalent in lower division classes. She reserves the negative criticisms for written responses she delivers to the students, responses that begin with the positive and state the negative in concrete suggestions for change in the next speech. Being thus responsive to students' emotional reactions as well as cognitive reactions, Pam builds trust between herself and the student, while at the same time establishing her credibility as a constructive critic.

One last means by which to diminish the competitiveness between professor and student is the use of a personal response system. Useful for exams, papers, and speeches, this system establishes a way for students to have their individual voices in response to individual concern. If students wish to respond to a particular question on an exam or to an area of criticism on a speech, for example, they prepare a written document that includes their question, the perspective of the student, and explication that connects the student's perspective to the topic of the question. Students also outline a proposed grade adjustment.

The professor reciprocates with an individual response to the student. Exchanges between the student and the professor can be repeated. Judy has used this system for several years and has found that in classes of thirty students, she receives only three or four written responses a quarter. Not only does this system help her avoid what sometimes are power demonstrations by students in after-exam battles, but she also empowers students by creating this personal resource separate from their collective resources as part of the group.

A Norm of Inquiring Curiosity

The second procedure by which to enact the feminist perspective in communication classes is to establish a norm of questioning for the sake of discovery. The assaulting "Socratic" method, the roots of which are mired in the patriarchal tradition of rhetorical history, diverts the purpose of investigation from discovery to annihilation of opposition. Because of the multiple sources and myriad types of theories of communication, establishing a norm of open-minded questioning in undergraduate theory classes is particularly important. These feminist methods can allow both professors and students to value questioning as means for personal change and discovery rather than as means for competition and strategic annihilation.

Judy addresses this issue early in the course, explaining that questions can be critical connectors between experience and theory. She asks students if they recall classroom episodes when they felt questions were being used as weapons or means by which either students or professors accosted each other. Using students' examples of these episodes, she describes the use of questions in this class: to clarify, expand, or wonder.

The Personal as Knowledge

Such questioning often can lead to the third procedure: the introduction of the personal into knowledge without sacrificing the credibility or integrity of the source. For the discussion leader, integration of personal anecdotes or experience into conversations about theory can be challenging. Finally given the freedom to include their own inclinations as knowledge, some students clamor to express their particular stories. Other students, having been effectively indoctrinated by the American education system, scoff at personal data as nonknowledge.

Several means may be used to accomplish this objective of integrating the personal without sacrificing credibility or integrity. Judy announces her position as conversation moderator to her class. She explains that in order to accommodate the limited time frame of class meetings, she will exercise the responsibility to ensure each student has the opportunity to contribute. In such a position, she appears to retain for the initial stages of class development the figurehead of authority more familiar to students trained by the system to regard authority as credible, students who feel uncomfortable or who initially react negatively to such a cooperative structure.

As the course continues, Judy's use of methods outlined in this paper help her emerge as empowering manager rather than as authoritarian director; the time during which this emergence occurs allows for evolutionary changes in students' perspectives. The natural emergence of her system of management through classroom experiences provides students time to develop an ability to assimilate this unfamiliar style, a style usually quite different from that they have learned to expect in the classroom. Allowing the classroom management style to emerge from classroom proceedings—much in the same way that feminist research allows conclusions to emerge from the data—methodologically performs feminist ways of learning.

Judy relies on continued use of pointed narratives and connecting anecdotes to facilitate the student's increased understanding, familiarity, and pursuit of the personal as knowledge. She uses transcripts of dinner-table discussions with her children and film clips from movies familiar to students for examples in family communication. She has photographed students on campus and families in nearby, often-visited settings for examples of non-verbal communication. She also has used slides depicting sexism taken from area shopping malls, campus centers, local newspapers and current-release, best-selling magazines. Using such personal and familiar sources incites students both to (1) disclose and realize their personal experiences with the topic; and (2) receive the information in a form more likely to motivate personal affect than would more abstract examples.

In other ways to promote the personal as knowledge, Pam identifies and comments on provocative contributions made by students. She solicits students' narratives illustrating or negating the theoretical concept, using students' examples to guide such discussions as relationship development, disconfirmation, conflict cycles, and emotional expressiveness. Judy also makes overt her extended thoughts about students' experiences or in-class observations; she often returns to the next class session asking for others' reflective responses. Using student experience as the connector between class sessions and among students contributes to its importance as a way of knowing.

The last suggestion we have to offer in this discussion of introducing the personal as knowledge is that we both allow students to see us think. Judy often interrupts class presentations she is giving with questions she asks herself aloud. Having posed a question, she then asks for class collaboration to pursue other questions or answers or opinions. Such a model teaches students to infuse lectures of Truth they may hear in other classrooms with personal questions of their own and also to seek other opinions and perspectives for the various viewpoints possible.

Power as a Shared Experience

Such a focus on collaborative discussion brings us to our fourth procedure: to promote class discussion and the use of small groups and dyads for investigating theoretical concepts, discovering new perspectives, or finding as-yet-unrecognized connections between knowledge and experience. Using group inquiry rather than primarily a lecture format supports the objective to empower the student.

Providing students with a comprehensive syllabus is the first step in sharing power; adherence to that syllabus is the second. If students can rely on the syllabus for direction, they can feel less constricted by choices or changes made arbitrarily or otherwise by the professor. Using the first few minutes of each class period to solicit students' progress and to outline briefly the plan for the next fifty minutes is another way to free the students from guessing how (and if) the professor intends to interact with them.

In casting ourselves as moderators of small groups or dyads rather than authoritarian directors of the class, we have learned to expect confusion. The combination of the students being unfamiliar with having the responsibility of shared power and their lack of skills in group discussions can cause chaotic consequences. Judy uses a week of group discussion skill-building exercises (sometimes interspersed throughout two weeks of meetings) in her undergraduate interpersonal, family, and public speaking courses to teach students democratic leadership style, shared responsibility for group processing, and all-channel communication networking.

Pam focuses on problems with unintentional or neglectful nonverbal signals in small groups, emphasizing the power of such dysfunctional nonverbal communication as silence, withdrawal, or sarcasm. With the students' permission, Judy recorded a short meeting of a small group in her class, and she uses audio samples from that tape better to illustrate nonverbal dimensions sometimes difficult for students to identify in their own conversations.

Teacher as Intermediary

Using small groups, dyads, and class discussions as avenues to knowledge helps the professor enact the fifth procedure: to link the student *with* the topic rather than lead the student *to* the topic. Perhaps more than any other in our approach, this objective represents the enactment of the feminist perspective. The professor's position becomes one of connector between the student and, for example, interpersonal communication.

Rather than presenting herself as the fountainhead of knowledge in regard to interpersonal literature, the professor presents herself as well informed about academia and interested in discovering how she and the student may coordinate their mutual learning. Among their many contributions, the professor offers academic resources and established theories; the student offers insights into her or his own world view and creative, perhaps new, approaches to the topic. Both share personal narratives. Finding the ways in which theory and personal experience create a web of understanding becomes their shared goal.

Alternative Ways of Thinking

In the field of communication, some theories and models smack of androcentric bases, thus necessitating the final procedure: to facilitate students' generating alternative ways to think. Rather than omit or decry Altman and Taylor's Social Penetration Theory of relationship development (a theory which, in concept, has provocative implications but which, in presentation, embodies androcentrism), Judy fashioned an approach following Sandra Bem's Gender Schema Theory (Bem, 1983) and her suggestions for the telling of male-centered children's stories.

Bem suggests that after reading the story aloud, the parent take time to discuss the work with the child. Some appropriate questions at this time might be, "Isn't this an interesting way for this author to think? But people have many different ways to tell the same story. What are some other ways this story might have been told?"

Using Bem's model, Judy teaches the Social Penetration Theory as the students are likely to encounter it again, i.e., in its usual form and language. Then she asks students to devise other ways of describing relationship development according to their own experiences, avoiding such terms as "penetration" and "superficial self." Comparison and contrast among the various models produced by students often provide examples for the explanation of how a model or theory reflects the predisposition of its authors. This technique for examining Social Penetration Theory (or similar kinds of examples such as Orlofsky's intimacy research methods, in which only males were used until very recently) not only promotes discussions of the differences offered by the feminist perspective but also enacts one intent of that perspective, which is to embrace differences rather than oppose them.

Although the subject may arise spontaneously at any time, feminist teaching methods are not discussed by Pam until the end of the course. In a reflective, group discussion she asks students what they noticed that was different about their experience as a student in her course. Examples of the kinds of comments students make include that Pam listened to them more; that she seemed to value their input; that they found themselves changing their perspectives based on the contributions of other students; and that they felt freer to speak up, to think, and to generate ideas. Pam then inquires as to the value of those experiences. Using the students' responses, Pam briefly discusses feminist theories of pedagogy, citing the reasons offered by the students as the significance of the feminist theories.

Although we have offered six goals for educators wishing to implement a feminist teaching style within a traditional system, we do not propose that such an implementation will be either easy or always successful. Barriers abound, including the students' expectations borne of their previous training in education (particularly higher education); the historical, competitive precedent in oral rhetoric, particularly with regard to public speaking and debate; and the impulse to effect desired change by using the authoritarian power that is embedded in the position of professor in the American educational system. Our procedures, however, grounded in our own classroom experiences, represent methods we have found to be productive in achieving our goals and in helping students understand and enact feminism.

REFERENCES

Altman, I., and D. Taylor. 1973. *Social Penetration.* New York: Holt, Rinehart & Winston.

Bem, S.L. 1983. "Gender Schema Theory and Its Implication for Child Development: Raising Gender-aschematic Children in a Gender-schematic Society." *Signs: Journal of Women in Culture and Society* 8:598–616.

Bunch, C. 1987. "Not By Degrees: Feminist Theory in Education." In *Passionate Politics,* 240–53. New York: St. Martin's.

Friedman, S.S. 1985. "Authority in the Feminist Classroom: A Contradiction in Terms?" In *Gendered Subjects: The Dynamics of Feminist Teaching,* edited by M. Culley and C. Portuges, 203–08. Boston: Routledge & Kegan Paul.

Johnson, L. 1987. "Is Academic Feminism an Oxymoron?" *Women's Studies International Forum* 10:529–32.

Lucas, S.E. 1983. *The Art of Public Speaking.* New York: Random House.

London Sunday Times (October 7, 1973), cited in D.J. Ochs and A.C. Winkler, *A Brief Introduction to Speech,* 31–32. New York: Harcourt Brace Jovanovich, 1979.

Schuster, M.R., and S.R. Van Dyne. 1985. "The Changing Classroom." In *Women's Place in the Academy: Transforming the Liberal Arts Curriculum,* M.R. Schuster and S.R. Van Dyne, 161–71. New Jersey: Rowman and Allanheld.

Shrewsbury, C.M. 1987. "What is Feminist Pedagogy?" *Women's Studies Quarterly* 12(3 & 4):6–14.

Weiler, K. 1988. "Gender, Race, and Class in the Feminist Classroom." In *Women Teaching for Change, Gender, Class, and Power,* 125–45. Chicago: Bergin and Garvey.

CHAPTER 24

God's Wife: Some Gender Reflections on the Bible and Biblical Interpretation

John J. Schmitt
Marquette University

Ancient Israel is presented in the Hebrew Bible/Old Testament, according to some religious educators and biblical scholars, as the unfaithful wife of God, a wife who must be condemned for her infidelity. The story is familiar.

Although she was a whore, Israel was called by God. But after she became God's wife, the weakness of her nature led her into adultery and continued harlotry. Briefly faithful, she went awhoring after other gods, prostituting herself "upon every high hill and under every green tree."[1] She played the harlot rather than the dutiful wife. She is the inconstant woman who gives in to the weakness of her flesh.

This characterization of Israel is the way one might understand the Bible's honest presentation of the role of Ancient Israel. In this reading, Israel—chosen to be the wife of God, even though she was once a slut and a prostitute—became an adulteress rather than a submissive wife.

Why this feminine imagery for the people Israel? Why, when Israel, the chosen one, is to be condemned, does feminine imagery seem inevitable, as if condemnation and femaleness go hand in hand? Additionally, why do many biblical scholars tend to call Israel "she," although the Bible itself does not do so? Biblical scholars generally pride themselves on their fidelity to "biblical thought" or at least to the original biblical text. This idea is, indeed, the thesis of this paper: Israel is grammatically masculine, yet there flourishes among biblical scholars a proclivity to make Israel feminine. Depending on the significance people give to the Bible, this gender-changing can have considerable gender implications.

First, one should document the tendency. Three cases that involve the very text of the Bible or the printed comments below the biblical text illustrate this widespread openness among scholars to change the gender of Israel at will. The first example is from an annotation in *The Oxford Annotated Bible*,[2] a good study edition that contains the reliable translation called the *Revised Standard Version (RSV)*.[3] Psalm 130:7–8 reads, "O Israel, hope in the Lord! For with the Lord there is steadfast love, and with him is plenteous redemption. And he will redeem Israel from all his iniquities." The annotation reads, "Israel should take the same attitude [as the individual in verses 3–6] in her national difficulties." The annotator could not resist using the feminine pronoun for Israel rather than use the Bible's own masculine gender for Israel.[4]

This irresistible urge to make Israel feminine appears even in the very text of the Bible; that is, "she" is found for Israel in some biblical translations. In Jeremiah 2:3, a segment of Israel's history is described thus: "Israel was holy to the Lord, the first fruits of his harvest. All who ate of it became guilty; evil came upon them" *(RSV)*. The more recent *New International Version*[5] translates the second half, "all who devoured her were held guilty, and disaster overtook them." The Hebrew pronominal form (attached to the verb: "who-ate-him") is masculine, and can be translated into English as neuter, a gender which, although not existing in Hebrew, the *RSV* legitimately uses here. But should one use the feminine?[6] Since the original is masculine, is not the feminine an intrusion into the text?[7]

The third example of gender change, this one also in a translation of the Bible, is from the Christian Writings/New Testament. In Paul's letter to the Romans, at 11:7, Paul says, "What then? Israel failed to obtain what it sought" *(RSV)*. The *New American Bible*[8] translates, "What then are we to say? Just this: Israel did not obtain what she was seeking." Here, too, the change of gender is in the context of infidelity, or at least failure to meet expectations.[9] That urge to call Israel "she" is an ever-present reality. And the urge seems most compelling when Israel is unfaithful.

All three examples show scholars agreeing with commonly held assumptions rather than simply using the text in front of them.[10] Both in Hebrew (for the Old Testament) and in Greek (for the New Testament), Israel is grammatically masculine, and is legitimately translated into English as neuter, or—even better—plural. Why, then, do even biblical scholars automatically, as it were, choose feminine gender and imagery?

I suspect that a general backdrop for the stage on which many biblical scholars tend to call Israel "she," contrary to biblical usage, is the conviction that Ancient Israel was to be subservient to God, a position "she" sometimes rejected. Some scholars seem to want to make clear to the readers this rejection of subservience by continued use of the gender that recalls what "her" status should be. Thus, for some commentators, Israel's greatest sin lay in "her" acts of self-determination by which "she" decided to create for "herself" a future of "her" own. This behavior is epitomized in the creation of the monarchy. "She" chose for "herself" a monarchic form of government. Ancient Israel had existed in Canaan without a central governing authority. God was Israel's king. When Israel was threatened and needed a strong central government, an Israelite prophet, we are told (1 Samuel 8), objected to this innovation, which would seem to replace God's kingship over Israel by making a human being the king of Israel. This opposition to kingship is echoed by some modern commentators who view Israel's decision about its future mode of existence as a choice of a political existence rather than a purely religious one. Some writers on Ancient Israel seem to put it something like this: "Instead of remaining a people, she chose to become a nation."

Perhaps a second element of the background for people calling Israel "she" may be this: Many writers say that in the divine-human encounter, humans as related to God are always feminine—with the correlative that in that relation God is always masculine, the actor and never the acted upon, whereas the human being is the passive recipient. Sandra Schneiders describes the implications of this attitude thus: "Because God was imagined as a great patriarch in relation to a subordinate humanity, all people were imagined as feminine, that is, as weak, worthless, and sinful in relationship to God."[11]

The reason that most biblical scholars (who set the pattern for the less specialized Bible readers), when quizzed on this question of Ancient Israel's gender self-image, would give is that this practice simply follows the images of the Bible. The texts themselves depict Israel as a woman, so one has, I hear them saying, no choice, or at least perfect freedom, to call Israel "she."

Are they right? Is Ancient Israel feminine?[12] My answer is an emphatic "no." Israel is not feminine. My response is based, accordingly, on the text of the Hebrew Bible itself. The grammatical gender of the noun Israel is masculine. No one could question that.[13] But most who use "she" of Israel would respond that there are feminine images applied to Israel in specific passages. The resolution of the case depends, thus, on analyses of every biblical text that those people point to.

There are a number of such passages, too many to deal with individually here. I will give the results of my analyses by means of illustrative examples from the major prophets that Bible readers would give for this supposed marital imagery, namely from Hosea, Ezekiel, and Jeremiah. My basic observation is this: When the Hebrew Bible speaks of a wife of God, that wife is always a city. This imagery agrees with linguistic gender. In biblical Hebrew, the grammatical gender of cities is feminine, whereas the gender of peoples, as Israel, is masculine. My findings show that only masculine images are used of Israel. The city who is the wife of God is sometimes Jerusalem, sometimes

Samaria; and one time, in Ezekiel 23, both Jerusalem and Samaria are simultaneously the wives of God.

In Hosea 2, the wife of God is Samaria, the capital of the northern kingdom. The city is not named explicitly. Nor is the woman named.[14] The name "Israel" does not occur in that chapter at all. One can tell that a city is the referent by a simple comparison with prophetic passages that have some of the same ideas, e.g., stripping the woman to be divorced (Jeremiah 13:26–27, Ezekiel 16:39, 23:26, 29), and the clustering of the words "faithfulness," "righteousness," and "justice," (Isaiah 1:21–22). Each of these passages names the cities to which it refers. The lack of an explicit name of the city in Hosea 2 is not crucial. The audience of the prophet would know the identity of God's wife.[15] The usage is similar to that of a person speaking to New Yorkers, to whom one would not have to explain that "the Big Apple" is New York.

In Ezekiel 16, the wife of God is Jerusalem. In that chapter, the city is named twice. Again, "Israel" does not occur; the prophet narrates Jerusalem's history. (And yet this chapter is the one that people most often refer to as the best example of the marriage between God and Israel!) When Ezekiel does tell the story of Israel in chapter 20, the story has no marital imagery. Later, in Ezekiel 23, as already mentioned, God has two wives, Jerusalem and Samaria. They are the capitals of the northern and southern kingdoms. There both wives prove unfaithful; indeed, they vie with each other for the greater infidelity.

There are shorter passages where marital imagery is seen by some scholars, but where closer reading does not confirm the supposed marital image. The first example is an interesting case of some scholars ignoring both the linguistic usage and the context of the word. Jeremiah 31:31–32a in the *RSV* reads, "Behold the days are coming, says the Lord, when I will make a new covenant with the house of Israel and the house of Judah, not like the covenant which I made with their fathers when I took them by the hand to bring them out of the land of Egypt, my covenant which they broke, though I was their husband." This translation makes the people [Israel] feminine, the wife of God. But the other two times this Hebrew construction (*b'l b*) occurs in the Bible, Jeremiah 3:14 and 1 Chronicles 4:22, the *RSV* translates with the ideas of "be master of" and "rule in" respectively. The *New Jerusalem Bible*[16] reads the phrase in Jeremiah 31:32, "even though I was their Master." The *NAB* renders it, "and I had to show myself their master." There is nothing in the rest of the passage to suggest a marital relation.

In Isaiah 49–55, Zion is a major topic of discussion—sometimes addressed, sometimes speaking, and sometimes spoken about. Isaiah 54:5 contains the most explicit statement, "For your Maker is your husband." Despite those who would think of Israel here,[17] the addressee is clearly Zion/Jerusalem, as is evident in the feminine singular.

There is clear marital imagery in the Bible, but it is used with cities. Beyond those prophets who use marital imagery for cities, there is further feminine imagery for cities, conveyed in ideas other than wife. In Isaiah 40–66 the city of Jerusalem is often spoken of as a mother (perhaps the prophet's inspiration to compare God to a mother).[18] In Amos 5:2, the phrase "the Virgin of Israel" I take to be a reference to the city of Samaria.[19]

Part of the confusion among scholars who insist that Israel sometimes receives feminine imagery stems from those passages, especially in Jeremiah, where the text weaves together verses about Israel and verses about Jerusalem; that is, a masculine singular alternates with a feminine singular, as in Jeremiah 2–3 and 30–31. In those passages, a careful analysis shows that the prophet or, more likely, the editors followed a clear pattern, but not necessarily one that a poet today might choose. Thus in Jeremiah 2, verse 2 addresses Jerusalem in the feminine singular, verses 3–4 treat of Israel in the masculine singular, verses 5–13 speak of the people in the third person masculine plural, but masculine singular returns in verses 14–16, and feminine singular reappears in verses 17–25—all of it forming an artful chiasm. One needs to read very carefully the Hebrew text (in which these gender distinctions have different verb forms), with the conviction that the prophet or the editors ordered the words meaningfully. Thus, one can distinguish the Israel verses and the Jerusalem verses on the basis of the gender of the topic or of the addressee.

In biblical imagery, the people Israel, when personified as an individual, is a man, and Israel's relation to God is filial. Israel begins as the son of God in Exodus 4:12. The masculinity of Israel is reinforced and emphasized in Deuteronomy, where the father-son relation appears several times.[20] Even in the poetry in that book, Israel is God's son (Deuteronomy 32:6). At least one prophet speaks of Israel as the son of God (Hosea 11:1).

Regarding the origins of this marital imagery in the Bible, some scholars propose that such imagery goes back before Israel's existence in Canaan, and indeed to Ancient Near Eastern culture in general.[21] The city was the beginning of civilization, and many mythological ideas were connected with its self-understanding. Among these was the view that a city had both a Goddess and a God as patrons. The two were related as wife and husband.

In monotheistic Israel, however, this imagery appears, in this view, in a modified way: God is married to the city itself, not to its Goddess. And the prophets did not hesitate to use the familiar language when addressing their contemporaries in those cities.

Whatever the precise origins of this usage are, the focus here has been to see that marital imagery for cities has often been confused with imagery for the people Israel. Some people make much of this assumed marital imagery for God's relation to the people because they adopt the view of God as masculine and of human beings, in relation to God, as feminine.

But in my reading, there is no biblical (Hebrew Bible/Old Testament) conception of God's marriage with Israel. Some theologians find this supposed marriage to be very important for their theology. But when God is depicted as married in the Hebrew Bible, his wives are cities. Later Jewish tradition did develop a way to see a marriage between God and the people. Namely, some scholars in the Rabbinic Period of Judaism read the Song of Songs as a lyric about that relationship.[22] In order to use this image, however, they prefaced the term "assembly of" to the name "Israel," thereby producing a feminine image because of the gender of the noun "assembly," as in the Targum of the Song of Songs. The marital image has proven to be a popular one in later tradition.[23]

The Christian Writings/New Testament, of course, do speak of the marriage of Christ and the Church. My findings, however, show that that image is derived biblically, not from the God-Israel relation, but either from the Adam-Eve relation or from the ancient city tradition. Thus, 2 Corinthians 11:2 is followed by mention of Eve in verse 3, and Ephesians 5:23–32 quotes Genesis 2:24 in verse 31. The Bride of the Lamb in Revelation 21:2, 9–11 is explicitly the holy city which comes down from heaven.[24]

My concern for correctness in gender usage for Israel arises first from a simple desire to remain faithful to biblical imagery. One should not impose on a normative work (the precise way that Jews and Christians view their respective Bibles) a framework and a set of images that are extraneous to that work. For me, the imposition of feminine imagery on Israel is a significant distortion. The work must first speak for itself before one uses it for a purpose apart from the setting in which it was produced. Thus, all the more, biblical revelation has to be understood in and on its own terms before some system—philosophical, theological, social, or whatever—is applied to it in a later age.

I am convinced that the images of God as husband and of the people as wife of God is imagery from a male-superior cultural time.[25] When one applies such imagery in the modern world, that application can easily come close to an acceptance of the saying, "If God is male, male is God." Such a proposal is not just idolatry. It also imposes upon males the opportunity to vaunt their divinity (over females).[26] Perhaps worse for women, it suggests that women are to relate to men in the way humans traditionally relate to God. Humans ought to accept the divine word, acknowledge their sinfulness, worship God, and in general develop a spirit of docility toward the goals and desires of God. God is the infinite creator; a human is the finite, fallible creature. To apply this relationship to the male-female relation seems to adopt the standard image of woman as inherently valueless and contemptible.[27]

Grammatical gender is, indeed, merely a linguistic device for keeping together words that are meant to go together. Grammatical gender often has the benefit of allowing greater flexibility in word order. But in those languages that have grammatical gender,[28] gender has played a significant role and had undeniable influence.[29] Gender takes on a greater significance in religious language. Inclusive language in the translation of religious texts and in religious services has recently been widely discussed.[30] The exclusive use of the masculine for God, in gender and in imagery, has also caused some women much pain.[31] This phenomenon also must figure in an awareness of gender's importance in theological reflection.

It is not clear how much significance the Ancient Israelites saw in the feminine imagery their prophets used of cities. One can, of course, point out that the two notions of wife and of mother suggest the ideas of fidelity and nurturing. These seem to be positive and significant aspects of the choices women can make (choices—of being wife and mother—that were expected of them in antiquity). From a different perspective, one feminist biblical scholar has recently taken deep offense at this imagery, finding no reason to personify an inanimate (often sinful) city as a woman and taking this usage as an expression of a patriarchal culture.[32] For myself, I currently understand this language as a way of speaking without enormous significance beyond the utilization of traditional images and vocabulary. Thus we say, without thinking and, perhaps, with little attention to the gender, "Uncle Sam." Some prophets, however, seem to have expanded on the specific feminine image they chose to use. An example might be Amos's "Virgin of Israel" (Amos 5:2), which probably alludes to the sheltered, protected life that an unmarried woman in Ancient Israel received. In Amos's saying, now that Virgin's protection would cease, and the city would be totally vulnerable. "Fallen, no more to rise, is the virgin of Israel." (Amos 5:2, *RSV* with the "of" before "Israel" restored from the *King James Version*).

My point here has been not to deny the marital image in the Bible, but to show that this image is not the Bible's metaphor for the relation between God and Israel. There is no Hebrew Bible marriage of God and his people.[33] Marital imagery occurs only in God's relations to cities. As such, it hardly seems central to biblical theology. Moreover, the image is not of Israelite origin. When someone tries to use the marital image to describe the relation between God and Ancient Israel, that person ought to acknowledge that the image is not applied to Israel in the texts of the Bible.

NOTES

I thank Professors Alice Laffey, Phyllis Carey, Judette Kolasny, Bradford Hinze, and Roberta O'Hara Schmitt for reading various drafts of this paper. Their suggestions improved the presentation vastly.

1.   This phrase (or variations of it) occurs in Hosea 4:13, Jeremiah 2:20; 3:6, 13; 17:2; Ezekiel 6:13, Isaiah 57:5, Deuteronomy 12:2,1 Kings 14:23, 2 Kings 16:4, and 17:10. The phrase alludes, according to most interpreters, to the sexual practices of the Canaanites.

2.   Oxford University Press, 1962; 2d ed., 1973.

3.   Copyright by the Division of Christian Education of the National Council of the Churches of Christ in the United States of America; Old Testament, 1952; New Testament, 1946, 2d ed., 1971.

4.   Admittedly, contemporary English tends to use the feminine gender for countries. Even the United States, when not referred to as Uncle Sam, often gets feminine tags and pronouns. The question remains, however, whether or not Bible commentators should try to explain the Bible first in its own imagery, which includes the genders people thought in.

5.   Copyright by New York International Bible Society, 1978.

6.   The neuter might be used in English. Calling a group of human beings "it," however, is not standard English. Since the Bible often uses "they" as well as "he," in English "they" might be the best choice.

7.   The feminine is an intrusion only in that line, not necessarily in the whole passage, because the next verse, v 4, does have the feminine Jerusalem. The passage alternates masculine and feminine (for Israel and Jerusalem respectively). This phenomenon is mentioned again later in this paper.

8.   Copyright by the Confraternity of Christian Doctrine, 1970 (various publishers).

9.   The feminine occurs in copies of the NAB printed in the sixteen years before its 1986 revision of the New Testament. The feminine was dropped in this verse in the revision. This passage in Romans is an example of where the feminine came to the minds of the translators in the context of the sinfulness of Israel.

10.   To cite scholars who spontaneously call Israel "she" is easy. "By the rules of covenant logic, Israel had broken her vows to Yahweh..." James King West, *Introduction to the Old Testament* (2d ed; New York: Macmillan, 1981), 375. "Israel's religion, despite the fact that it came into being within this ancient, oriental, religious climate, stands out in complete contrast. Her religion was not merely largely adapted to...Her religion was at the same time both similar to and different from those of her neighbors." Henry Renckens, *The Religion of Israel* (New York: Sheed and Ward, 1966), 36. "...Yahweh's goodness to Israel was conditioned upon her obedience to the stipulations of the Horeb covenant." George W. Ramsey, *The Quest for the Historical Israel* (Atlanta: John Knox, 1981), 61. The scrutiny of authors' publications to see whether they call Israel "she" can warp one's personality, so I have stopped the practice. I have, however, noticed that this tendency to make Israel feminine is not an exclusively Christian phenomenon. I give two examples from highly respected Jewish scholars. "Israel and her adversaries..." Abraham Malamat, "How Inferior Israelite Forces Conquered Fortified Canaanite Cities," *Biblical Archeology Review* 8 (No. 2; March/April

1982), 26–27. "Israel, in preserving the message of the prophets, preserved wholesale a categorical denunciation of herself." Samuel Sandmel, *The Hebrew Scriptures* (New York: Oxford University Press, 1963; repr., 1979), 101. We should perhaps include our most distinguished universities. Frank Moore Cross (Hancock Professor of Hebrew and Other Semitic Languages, Harvard University) has in passing, "Moreover, such an epithet ['He who creates the (heavenly) armies'] lent itself to use not merely as a creation formula, but as an appropriate name of the god who called the tribes to form the militia of the League, who led Israel in her historical wars." *Canaanite Myth and Hebrew Epic: Essays in the History of the Religion of Israel* (Cambridge: Harvard University, 1973), 70. From a different camp, Brevard S. Childs (Holmes Professor, Old Testament Interpretation and Criticism, Yale University) offers, "Israel would understand who he [God] was by what he did on her behalf." *Old Testament Theology in a Canonical Context* (Philadelphia: Fortress, 1985), 39.

11. Sandra Schneiders, *Women and the Word* (New York: Paulist, 1986), 65–66.

12 Modern Israel is grammatically feminine in Israeli Hebrew. Note, however, that the official name of the country is *Medinat Israel* (the State of Israel), a feminine construction. See later in this paper how the rabbis developed a kind of female Israel by creating a grammatically feminine construction and image.

13. The noun "Israel" occurs 2507 times in the Hebrew text of the Old Testament. Twice "Israel" is treated grammatically as if it were feminine: 1 Samuel 17:21 and 2 Samuel 24:9. I am inclined to regard these two exceptions as errors (note how the latter is changed to masculine in 1 Chronicles 21:5 when repeated from Samuel) and not as deliberate shifts of imagery and usage.

14. The passage occurs within the narrative of the prophet's marriage to Gomer. The text compares God's marriage to that of the prophet. Gale A. Yee (*Composition and Tradition in the Book of Hosea: A Redaction-Critical Investigation* [Atlanta: Scholars Press, 1987]) proposes that the wife-of-God passage is earlier than the wife-of-the-prophet context. That is, the prophetic statement in Hosea 2:2–15 was spoken and existed before the surrounding material of Hosea 1–3 existed. My analysis takes the same approach: it studies the poetic/prophetic speech independently of the prose that surrounds it. For a comparable treatment of another eighth century prophet, in which the prophet speaks in poetic form and later editors add prose, see Robert B. Coote, *Amos Among the Prophets: Composition and Theology* (Philadelphia: Fortress, 1981).

15. For a fuller analysis see my paper, "The Wife of God in Hosea 2," *Biblical Research* 34 (1989), 5–18.

16. Copyright by Darton, Longman and Todd, Ltd. and Doubleday and Company, Inc., 1985.

17. For example, Claus Westermann, *Isaiah 40–66* (Old Testament Library; Philadelphia: Westminster, 1969), 273.

18. See my article, "The Motherhood of God and Zion as Mother," *Revue Biblique* 92 (1985), 557–69.

19.   The phrase recurs in Jeremiah 18:13, 31:4 and 21, once of Jerusalem and twice of Samaria. My paper on the topic, "The Virgin of Israel: Referent and Use of the Phrase in Amos and Jeremiah," *Catholic Biblical Quarterly. 53 (1991) 365–87*

20.   See Dennis J. McCarthy, "Notes on the Love of God in Deuteronomy and the Father-Son Relationship between Yahweh and Israel," *Catholic Biblical Quarterly* 27 (1965), 144–47. Also John L. McKenzie, "The Divine Sonship of Israel and the Covenant," *Catholic Biblical Quarterly* 8 (1946), 320–31.

21.   For the tie I see between Israel's usage and that in Mesopotamian culture, I am partially dependent on Jacob Klein's paper, "The Motif of 'The Lamenting Goddess' in Cuneiform Literature and its Assumed Biblical Parallel." A different study makes connections with Greece in the figure of Athens/Athena, the daughter of Zeus: Elaine R. Follis, "The Holy City as Daughter," in *Directions in Biblical Hebrew Poetry* (ed. Elaine R. Follis, *Journal for the Study of the Old Testament* Supplement Series 40; Sheffield: JSOT Press, 1987), 171–84. Another study relates the city as barren woman to the patriarchal traditions of Genesis: Mary Callaway, *Sing O Barren One: A Study in Comparative Midrash* (SBL Dissertation Series 91; Atlanta: Scholars Press, 1986). Still a different approach is to see the image of a woman in pain as a literary device, one chosen by the author and one which might allow for "the full and free acknowledgement of women as *persons*" (emphasis in original): Barbara Bakke Kaiser, "Poet as 'Female Impersonator': The Image of Daughter Zion as Speaker in Biblical Poems of Suffering," *Journal of Religion* 67 (1987), 164–82, citation from the last sentence of the article. In the light of the long Ancient Near Eastern tradition and of these varied proposals, it no longer seems accurate to say that the Israelites regarded countries and towns "as mothers and nurses of the inhabitants," as does A.E. Cowley, *Gesenius' Hebrew Grammar: As Edited and Enlarged by the Late E. Kautzsch* (Oxford: Clarendon, 1946), 391. Rather, any feminine idea was expected for cities, although each writer could expand on that basic feminine theme in a creative way.

22.   Some scholars claim Rabbi Aqiba (late first and early second century CE) as the first clear adherent of the allegorical interpretation of the song. None of Aqiba's sayings in the Mishnah, however, indicates what precisely his interpretation was. Those sayings only convey his conviction about the Song's canonicity and its sanctity. Rabbinical writings later than those of the Mishnah have sayings attributed to Aqiba that offer the allegorical interpretation, and the allegorical reading became the most popular.

23.   At least one Jewish biblical scholar insists that the Bible itself depicts the relation as marital: Jon D. Levenson, *Sinai and Zion: An Entry into the Jewish Bible* (New York: Winston, 1985) 75–80. Levenson places the wedding at Sinai.

24.   Among various other passages that are taken to be New Testament appropriations of the supposed Old Testament image of God's marriage to Israel is John 2:1–11, the episode of the wedding feast at Cana. But there the idea of marriage is not applied to something else. And even if there would be an allusion to an Old Testament text in the Johannine passage, the allusion would be to the

opening chapters of Genesis because of the way Jesus addresses his mother, simply "Woman." See Raymond E. Brown, *The Gospel According to John 1–11* (Anchor Bible; Garden City, NJ: Doubleday, 1966), 108–9.

25.   One can admit the existence of a different analysis. A. Neher ("Le symbolism conjugal: Expression de l'histoire dans l'Ancient Testament," *Revue d'Histoire et de Philosophie Religieuses* 34 [1954], 30–49) sees a marital relation between God and Israel but does not view it as patriarchal. Schneider (*Women and the Word,* 35) summarizes Neher's view well: "He suggested that the metaphor was so apt for the relation between God and humanity precisely because of the equality of the partners in marriage as two autonomous subjects who freely choose to relate to each other and because of the historical character of marriage which allows for mistakes and regressions, recoveries and triumphs, growth and deepening. In no other relationship do two free adults choose one another and bind themselves to one another in an eternal covenant which must take its shape from the historical experience they forge together." Neher surely has a beautiful view of marriage—a twentieth century one, perhaps. Not many readers can understand certain biblical passages from this perspective. One cannot forget that in Ancient Israel a husband could divorce his wife simply by putting his decision in writing (Deuteronomy 24:1–2).

26.   History and experience reveal an easy link between superiority and violence. "The twin assumptions of male supremacy—through self-identification with God—and women as male property constitute patriarchal order. Rationalized as loving protection of the ruled, the bottom line of patriarchal order is the use of violence toward and even murder of the ruled for their protection. Augustine's epic *City of God* provides the explicit connection between rule and protection that allowed patriarchal rulers in families and states to justify their rule to those subjected as 'for your own good.'" Margaret R. Miles, "Violence against Women in the Historical Christian West and in North American Culture: The Visual and Textual Evidence," in *Shaping New Vision* (Harvard Women's Studies in Religion; Ann Arbor, MI: UMI, 1987), 11–29, citation, p. 17. Miles's example from a novel by James Michener is telling.

27.   Joan Arnold ("Karl Barth's Theology of the Word of God: Or, How to Keep Women Silent and In Their Place," in *Women and Religion* [rev. ed. by Judith Plaskow and Joan Arnold; Missoula, MT: Scholars Press, 1974]) describes such an understanding in this way: "Thus it is woman who represents the creature, as in Barth's understanding of the Virgin Mary. She is subordinate and unequal, she must understand and keep her place. It does not seem to occur to him that male domination is the real *hubris,* the usurpation of the role of God with respect to women" (p. 67).

28.   One can note that Chinese, Japanese, Turkish, and Basque, among others, have never possessed grammatical gender. Persian, although belonging to the Indo-European language family that readily employs grammatical gender, once possessed it but subsequently jettisoned it.

29.   For the influence that grammatical gender has had on some writers, the following observations are helpful: "The Russian painter Repin was baffled as

to why Sin has been depicted as a woman by German artists; he did not realize
that 'sin' is feminine in German...but masculine in Russian. Likewise a Russian
child, while reading a translation of German tales, was astounded to find that
Death, obviously a woman...was pictured as an old man...*My Sister Life,* the title
of a book of poems by Boris Pasternak, is quite natural in Russian, where 'life' is
feminine, but was enough to reduce to despair the Czech poet Josef Hora in his
attempt to translate these poems, since in Czech this noun is masculine." Roman
Jakobson, "On Linguistic Aspects of Translation," in *On Translation* (ed. R.A.
Brower; Cambridge, MA: 1959), 237, as quoted by Susan E. Erwin, "The Connota-
tions of Gender," *Word,* 18 (1962), 249–61. Grammatical gender, although created
to keep specific lexical units connected, has clear psychological effects on those
sensitive to it. Ibrahim says of gender, "Once a grammatical category comes
into existence, speakers may utilize it in ways which had nothing to do with
the creation of that category in the first place." Ibrahim, *Grammatical Gender,*
p. 95. One might propose that sometimes the speaker is "used by" or influenced
by gender rather than the reverse. On a broader scope, Monique Wittig says,
"Gender is the enforcement of sex in language, working in the same way as the
declaration of sex in civil status." "The Mark of Gender," in *The Poetics of Gender*
(ed. Nancy K. Miller; New York: Columbia University, 1986), 63–73, citation, p. 65.

30.   Thus has appeared *An Inclusive Language Lectionary* (Philadelphia:
Westminster—and other publishers, 3 vols., 1983–1985). In addition, many translation committees are reviewing the current standard translations to assess their
use of exclusive language.

31.   The impact is described well by Carolyn Osiek: "The affront to one's
being that this one-sidedness represents can only be appreciated by someone
whose social identity is excluded from the divine imaging: an exclusively white
God with middle-class values is just as offensive for those whose identity is otherwise. The religious experience of one who has grown accustomed to the assumption that God is 'like me' is quite different from the experience of the one who
knows that God is 'like the other,' a being with whom I cannot identify according
to the analogy of my specific personhood." And more specifically: "If a woman
cannot find an 'I' mirrored in God or in Christ, what is left?" Carolyn Osiek,
Beyond Anger: On Being a Feminist in the Church (New York: Paulist, 1986), 19.
Not just the marriage image, but also the exclusively masculine gender for God
comes from a male-oriented society.

32.   "A woman may be understood to have much in common with a city
or a country: she may be more or less valuable, more or less beautiful, large or
small, a greater or lesser source of nurture, faithful or unfaithful. It is a compli-
ment to a city or a country to personify it; it is an insult to women that cities and
countries are so personified!" Alice L. Laffey, *An Introduction to the Old Testament: A Feminist Perspective* (Philadelphia: Fortress, 1988), 162. Perhaps Laffey's
discomfort comes from assuming that the physical city alone is being spoken of.
Biblical expression shifts quite easily among city as space, as ideal, as people.
When a city is condemned for its faithlessness, the focus surely is on its inhabitants. One can compare the biblical usage of Israel. The virtually exclusive mascu-

line gender and imagery for Israel indicate that the biblical writers thought of Israel as a people, not as a country (territory).

33.   The image that the Hebrew Bible most frequently uses for the God-Israel relation is covenant. Covenant/treaty language of the Ancient Near East, however, does not explicitly include marriage. It does use familial terms, and the familial terms that are used are "father" and "son." See Dennis J. McCarthy, "Notes on the Love of God in Deuteronomy" (note 20 above) and F. Charles Fensham, "Father and Son as Terminology for Treaty and Covenant," in *Near Eastern Studies in Honor of William Foxwell Albright* (ed. Hans Goedicke; Baltimore: Johns Hopkins, 1971), 121–35. Some scholars say that the prophets introduced marital ideas and terminology into the realm of covenant. But the texts that such scholars invoke are precisely the texts discussed above.

CHAPTER 25

Effecting Labor Reform Through Stories: The Narrative Rhetorical Style of Mary Harris "Mother" Jones

Mari Boor Tonn
University of New Hampshire

One of the most volatile issues in discussions surrounding gender is the challenge to traditional standards of evaluation based on the "masculine" as the "norm." Among rhetorical scholars, this debate usually focuses on two topics: first, the tendency for public address anthologies, textbooks, and courses to select speeches largely on the basis of the speaker's occupation, position, or prominence, and second, the exclusion of speeches by women because of their "feminine" or "unlogical" style. Although few women have been military leaders, Presidents, or prominent bureaucrats, many women have been active and effective social movement campaigners who merit scholarly attention.

Mary Harris "Mother" Jones, a turn-of-the-century labor union agitator, was one such woman. During her fifty-year involvement with the cause of labor, Jones was instrumental in organizing various labor groups including mill workers, brewery workers, streetcar workers, and most notably coal miners. Although the elderly Jones was neither a male nor a miner, her mesmerizing appeal to millions of workers was unsurpassed by any other labor activist of her day.

Although scholars have documented Mother Jones's remarkable popularity with the rank and file, many of those same individuals have dismissed her unorthodox rhetorical style as the catalyst for her success. Likewise, they appear to miss the significance of mobilizing the rank and file in order for any social movement to take flight and soar. The contradictory conclusions drawn by Dale Fetherling in the final paragraphs of his biography of Jones are representative:

Her forte was knowing how to arouse men to a fighting pitch, how to stir them to a realization of their plight and power...Her mild profanity was more colorful than productive, and it has been said with truth that she was closer to the heart than to the brain of the labor movement. She was not as effective as her retouched recollections would have us believe...Her rambling speeches made her an irrelevant, if revered, cheerleader...In starkest terms, she was a spectacular supernumerary. She was not important in the sense, say, of a Gompers or a Mitchell or a Debs...Thrust Mother Jones may have lent to the labor movement but not direction...[S]he may have been among the nation's most beloved figures at the time of her death...She was also extraordinarily effective in her limited field.[1]

Ironically, the stylistic element of Jones's rhetoric that Fetherling indicts as "rambling" is precisely what contributed largely to her incredible effectiveness in organizing workers, "the limited field" that was the heart and soul of the movement. Jones's dramatic and narrative rhetorical style found its force in shared experiences. Through loosely connected stories of the workers' separate struggles, Jones wove a potent personal message designed to build empathy and rapport among isolated individuals, convincing them that their oppression was politically motivated rather than personally based, and as such, required a political solution.

NARRATIVE AS A MEANS TO EMPOWERMENT AND ACTION

A narrative rhetorical style was uniquely suited to the social and psychological fabric of the working audiences Jones sought to empower.[2] Through acculturation, many workers had internalized the establishment's erroneous assumptions about themselves and others, embracing portions of the social credo that fostered oppression. Also hampering group action were the ubiquitous and debilitating fear of reprisals by owners and the divisiveness of racial animosity and multiple languages among immigrant workers themselves. Moreover, the controlled environment of workers, particularly miners, had retarded their capacity to make choices of any kind, a crippling liability to decisive action.

Because the workers themselves were the only channel for the social change they sought, rhetoric aimed at transforming such a people into a political force first had to forge individual workers into a personal collective. As Hans Toch explains, collective solutions to problems tend to arise when other solutions fail. Individuals must become convinced that the problems peculiar to them are sufficiently similar to the concerns of others to be jointly attacked and that "collectivation" would prove beneficial.[3] Additionally, rhetoric geared towards activating groups with low self-esteem first has to cultivate self-worth by encouraging personal decision making.

In accomplishing these ends, Jones necessarily accentuated the personal and generated self-persuasion, eschewing formal methods of argumentation used by the enemy to limit individual choice.[4] Because the establishment dictated society's major premises—social Darwinism and the Protestant work ethic—syllogistic reasoning entrapped workers, keeping them subservient by forcing them to reason that they were at fault. If America rewarded the enterprising and hardworking through wealth, and God punished the sinful through poverty, poor workers conditioned to reason deductively were offered only personal sloth or sin to explain their suffering.

In contrast to rigid syllogistic formulas, Jones's persuasive personal style was flexible, responding to situations, accommodating the experiences and conditions peculiar to the workers' special circumstance. Her speeches were pseudo-dialogues, resembling conversations between her and her listeners. She spoke to them directly about their concerns and the concerns of others like them, and she often openly asked them to verify verbally the observations she had made. Jones's narrative mode resembled the rhetorical style frequently used in recovery groups, self-change movements, and by rhetors addressing oppressed groups, a style popularly termed "consciousness-raising" by the contemporary woman's movement.[5]

As several scholars have noted, the structure of consciousness-raising rhetoric is inductive rather than deductive, moving from example to example, imitating the process by which individuals reason on their own. Unlike the linear design of traditional rhetoric, speeches in this mode are circular or weblike as the rhetor moves between first, second, and third person, simultaneously living the story as an active participant and telling the story as narrator. Audience participation is encouraged in several ways: through call-response or question-answer patterns; through metaphor and analogy requiring mental engagement of listeners; and by revelation of the speaker's personal reactions, which simulates a dialogue between the rhetor and the audience. The speaker relies heavily on personal experience and testimony and uses enactment as argument and evidence. The emphasis is on communion: reducing the experiences of all to one experience; connecting the relationships of any who share a social circumstance. The personal tone fosters acceptance and ego-gratification by allowing the audience to feel noticed; the style invites audiences to act, to make their own decisions and draw their own conclusions.[6]

As is characteristic of consciousness-raising rhetoric, Jones's style was highly personal, interactive, and communal. Because mobilization depends as much on favorable interpersonal contact as it does on a remote ideological appeal,[7] Jones's tone was intimate and her delivery was conversational. She addressed the miners as "boys" and insisted they call her "Mother." By speaking directly to her audience, Jones encouraged participation and commitment by allowing them to feel attended to as individuals. To foster camaraderie, Jones frequently moved from "I" to "we" to "you," often within the same sentence, enabling her to blur obvious distinctions between herself and her audience and among individual audience members. Also, by moving from first to third person, Jones subtly placed direct responsibility on her audience for action she wanted them to take: "*I* will give them a fight to the finish, and all *we* have to do is quit being moral cowards, rise up like men and let the world know that *you* are citizens of a great nation and *you* are going to make it great" [emphasis added].[8] By synthesizing their missions linguistically, Jones assured her anxious audiences that they were not alone in the actions she advocated: "*I* want to say my friends, in this age of ours, in this modern conflict *we* are going to prepare *you* to stop it" [emphasis added].[9] At times, Jones portrayed herself as surrogate for the worker's pain even more skillfully, merging her own voice with that of her male listener by using language that was clearly not her own: "*We* are law-abiding citizens, we will destroy no property, we will take no life, but if a fellow comes to my home and outrages *my wife,* by the Eternal he will pay the penalty" [emphasis added].[10]

Although Jones's rhetorical effectiveness hinged on her ability to speak personally to the individual needs of her audience, the union's success was contingent upon the power of the group. Jones regarded differences among people as trivial; allegiance to the union precluded loyalty to race, gender, or even union locals. The labor war was a class conflict, she argued, in which only *two* sides could exist. Significantly, the appeals she made to unity were always personal, and she discouraged resistance to collective efforts by singling skeptics out by name:

> *We are not brought up in contact with each other. Some of us are brought up in the mountains; some of us down in the hollows; some of us in the valleys; some of us in the canyons; and we cannot survey these things in the same way, and this thing of tearing each other up will have to stop.* I want to say to you, Duncan McDonald, *you haven't got one dollar in your treasury that belongs to Illinois. It belongs to the miners of this country; every dollar of it belongs to the working men, whether they are miners, steel workers, or train men. That money belongs to* us, the working class, *and we are going to use it to clean hell out of* the robbing class.[11] [emphasis added]

The import of enactment of personal example as argument in consciousness-raising rhetoric was particularly significant for Jones because of the incredibly high costs of labor agitation for most workers. To effect action against powerful forces at overwhelming odds required indomitable courage, which Jones herself demonstrated and the masses emulated. As a strategy, enactment was well suited to workers justifiably dubious of establishment logic and wary of change. Because many formal arguments require a "leap of faith" by audience members to believe that proposals will prove effective, the riskier the untested solution, the greater the resistance to it. By contrast, enactment removes much uncertainty, thereby promoting compliance even among those with much at stake. Whereas the power of syllogistic reasoning relies upon form and analytical precision, the rhetorical force of enactment is in the rhetor who embodies the argument, who *is* the truth of what is said.[12] In the person of Mother Jones, the remoteness of ideological principles became immediate, real, and validated; she herself became a vivid and stunning argument. Backing her boast that "I never was anywhere yet that I feared anybody,"[13] were thousands of witnesses and dozens of newspaper accounts to verify the legion of stories she told of her successful defiance of mine guards, politicians, and even death. By personal example, Jones called forth similar qualities in those who respected her:

> *The brave women from the northern Colorado fields came to me Sunday. "Mother, they have four machine guns, but if you will come down we don't care for their bullets." "I will come down," said I, "and we will give our lives that the workers of American shall furl the flag of freedom."*[14]

Because consciousness-raising rhetoric depends upon audience involvement, Jones used strategies such as metaphor and call-response patterns to encourage mental and actual engagement by her listeners and to facilitate action. Her vivid metaphors required intellectual participation from the audience, and she tailored them specifically to the workers' personal circumstances. She compared the worker's condition to slavery, charged that churches sacrificed mill children on altars of profit, drew correlations between the weapons workers faced and their own collective power, and likened the steel workers' anger to the boiling ore in the cauldrons they tended.

A key element in Jones's personal narrative style was her use of pseudo and actual dialogue. Frequently, she answered her own rhetorical questions, revealing her own reactions, inviting her listeners to concur in the process:

> *Don't blame the mine owners. I would skin you, too, if I was a mine owner—if you'd let me do it. They combine, don't they? Sure. Why? Because they realize that as individuals they could not do anything. The merchants, the clergymen, the doctors belong to the medical profession so they can give you a dose of pills.*[15]

She cultivated assent and involvement by liberally punctuating her speeches with questions inviting overt response: "How many of you fellows, when you pay your assessments, when you pay your dues—how many of you fellows after years have got enough money to buy your wife a dress— how many of you have?"[16] Occasionally, she actually engaged in extended conversation with her audience:

> *I will knock a few of these Senators down before I die. (Cries of: "Tell it, Mother, I heard it.") I will tell you. I want you all to be good. (A voice: "Yes, I will. We are always good.") They say you are not, but I know you better than the balance do. Be good. Don't drink. Only a glass of beer. The parasite blood-suckers will tell you not to drink beer, because they want to drink it all, you know. They are afraid to tell you to drink, for fear there will not be enough for their carcass. (Cries of: "The Governor takes champagne.") He needs it. He gets it from you fellows. He ought to drink it. You pay for it, and as long as he can get it for nothing any fellow would be a fool not to drink it. But I want you to be good. We are going to give the Governor until tomorrow night. He will not do anything. He could if he would, but the fellows who put him in won't let him. (Cries of: "Take him out.") I don't want him out, because I would have to carry him around.*[17]

Like paradigmatic consciousness-raising rhetoric, Jones's speeches were structurally episodic, with each vignette serving as an illustration of her thesis. Every incident was intended, in one way or another, to enforce a single conclusion. For rhetors, the power of examples is twofold: first, examples illustrate the kinds of situations and behavior that, when multiplied, give rise to generalizations. Second, examples can be used to illustrate and refurbish existing beliefs. As William Kirkwood argues, "[E]xamples...provide easily recognized, dramatic instances of familiar moral principles; indeed, they can revivify articles of faith grown too familiar."[18] Through numerous examples, Jones encouraged workers to reason inductively and to develop generalizations about their situation. By forcing workers to test the incidents she offered against their own experiences, she helped workers to realize the commonality of their condition and restored their belief in such moral principles as freedom of choice, freedom of opportunity, and the sanctity and dignity of all human life. In discovering that their oppression was universal, workers persuaded themselves that its core was political, enabling them to exonerate themselves from personal blame in the process. Frequently, Jones stressed to her audiences the importance of sharing in overcoming the workers' isolation and sense of futility, necessary for cultivating hope and vision:

> *Has anyone ever told you, my children, about the lives you are living here, so that you can understand how it is you pass your days on earth? Have you ever told each other about it and thought it over among yourselves, so that you might imagine a brighter day and begin to bring it to pass? If no one has done so I will do it for you today. I want you to see yourselves as you are, brothers and sisters, and to think if it is not time you took pity on yourselves and upon each other.*[19]

Interspersed with examples of the workers' desperation were crucial accounts of when group action had been effective in precipitating change. By synthesizing evidence of oppression with evidence of successful union efforts, workers came to believe that they could, indeed, effect social reform. Thus, Jones's consciousness-raising rhetorical style functioned like the enthymeme, forcing her audiences to use the evidence from various examples to complete an argument.

The most salient characteristic distinguishing Mother Jones's rhetoric from other examples of consciousness-raising and narrative discourse was her heavy use of the extended story as argument and evidence. Contributing to Jones's role as labor's muse was her assumption of two strategic personae: the archetypal mother and the prophet, both of whom are storytellers.[20] Just as mothers use stories with implied lessons to guide their children morally while letting them grow intellectually and responsibly on their own, Jones used stories to foster self-governance among workers. As Lance Bennett argues: "[T]he story form is clearly one of the most pervasive and powerful agencies of social and psychological organization...The most obvious characteristic of stories is that they build interpretations around social behavior."[21]

Although many of Jones's stories were actual incidents, others resembled fables or parables, metaphorical tales told with an implied moral. As with a metaphor, a parable requires listeners to see similarities between the principle or circumstances in the fictional story and real-life situations. Unlike formal argument, parables frequently contain multiple interpretations, allowing listeners to fashion responses depending upon their individual frames of reference. For example, in speaking of the parable of "The Good Samaritan," Robert Funk argues:

> *Since the metaphor gives itself existentially to unfinished reality, so that the narrative is not complete until the hearer is drawn into it as participant, the hearer is confronted with a situation in relation to which he [sic] must decide how to comport himself; is he willing to allow himself to be victim, to smile at the affront to the priest and the Levite, to be served by the enemy? The parable invites, nay, compels him to make some response. And it is this response that is decisive for him.*[22]

Like examples, parables can refurbish generalized beliefs that have become widely accepted and occasionally trivialized, twisted, or misunderstood over time.[23] For example, America's sacred belief in freedom of speech and assembly was born in the colonists' revolution against tyranny. As an agency to ensure the protection of the people, these first amendment rights later became twisted by public officials who, ironically, often justified revoking them in order to "protect" the country against revolutionary influences. To support her argument that the suppression of free speech was creating "more Bolshevism and I.W.W.ism than any other institutions,"

Jones told a story of a boat captain so intent upon winning a steamboat race that he forced an individual to sit upon the boat's steam valve. "What happened?" concluded Jones. "In a few minutes the steam blew the captain and all of them into the Mississippi River. Mr. Mayor, let [the nation's dissatisfied] blow off steam. You are a great deal safer if they do that, and so is the nation."[24]

The importance of these stories in Jones's rhetoric stemmed from her mission, as well as the psychological tradition and needs of her audience. For the union to flourish required action; for the workers to act for themselves and reject behavior that had been dictated to them depended first upon their ability to reason on their own and make their own decisions. A story Jones told in 1920 exemplified this process; her comments following the story clearly suggest her understanding of this process:

> *Now, if you had the brains of a little boy out in Chicago you would be all right. A fellow came along one morning and asked a boy, "How far is it to the B.&O. Station, do you know?" "Oh, yes, I know, sir. Go down to that corner, look up that way, you see a tower with a clock on it. It is the B.&O. Station." "Thank you, my boy. Let me give you a ticket to a lecture tomorrow night. You are a fine boy...I am going to lecture. I will show you the way to heaven." The boy said, "How in Hell can you show me the way to heaven if you don't know the way to the B.&O. Station?" The boy used the gray matter in his head. He knew nobody could show him to the way to heaven, and he had sense and wisdom. Nobody can show you the way to freedom, and I wouldn't free you tomorrow if I could. You would go begging. My patriotism is for this country to give to the nation in the days to come highly developed citizens, men and women...*[25]

In the narrative structure that characterized Jones's rhetoric, the people of her fictional tales or parables and those in the actual incidents she described became intertwined, connected in the shared moral principle each story represented. Mother Jones was and has been criticized, sometimes justly, for twisting dates and names and resorting to hyperbole to suit her purpose. To Jones, however, chronological accuracy and historical details and facts were all subordinate to the essential truths underlying the stories she told workers. Jones's merging of the actual with the invented was not unlike Christ's use of parables to illustrate or augment a lesson often prompted by an incident. For example, Jesus rebutted criticisms that he fraternized with sinners through using both parables and circumstances of actual events. On one occasion, he told those alarmed by his dining with the sinful the parables of the Lost Sheep, the Lost Coin, and the Prodigal Son. On another, he answered similar remarks concerning his attention to sinners by charging those without sin to cast the first stone at a woman accused of adultery. The lessons of forgiveness and the joy of a sinner's repentance were the same in the fictional stories as in the actual account. For both Jones and Jesus as storytellers, fact and fiction were often joined in the commonality of principle and purpose. As Northrop Frye explains, "Truth, by itself, cannot turn the will; poetry in alliance with truth, using the vividness and emotional resonance peculiar to it, may move the feelings to align themselves with intelligence, and so help to get the will moving."[26] Thus, Jones's tales, although occasionally embroidered, provided the crucial impetus for action that was the movement's lifeline.

SUMMARY

To create empathy among a diverse audience and foster identification between herself and her primarily male audiences, Mary Harris "Mother" Jones adopted a personal narrative style, similar to what contemporary theorists and critics term "consciousness-raising" rhetoric. Contributing to her personal conversational tone were detailed stories with specific characters and dialogue, language that merged her experiences with those of her audiences, and intimate terms of address. To generate self-persuasion and action among her listeners, Jones told fables and parables with implied morals, employed metaphors frequently, and used enactment as evidence. Additionally, Jones used structure that linked examples of actual incidents with fictional stories into one long narrative. Through poignant personal stories, workers shared and learned the truth of their oppression, prompting them to unite in order to effect a political solution.

NOTES

1. Dale Fetherling, *Mother Jones, The Miners' Angel* (Carbondale and Edwardsville, IL. Southern Illinois Univ. Press, 1974), 211–12.

2. For a discussion of the peculiar problems workers presented as audiences, see Mari Boor Tonn, "The Rhetorical Personae of Mary Harris 'Mother' Jones: Industrial Labor's Maternal Prophet," unpublished Ph.D. dissertation, Univ. of Kansas, 1987, 87–102.

3. Hans Toch, *The Social Psychology of Social Movements* (Indianapolis, IN: The Bobbs-Merrill Co., Inc., 1965), 71.

4. For a discussion of the general problem between traditional rhetorical theory and democratic principles, see Robert L. Scott and Donald K Smith, "The Rhetoric of Confrontation," *Quarterly Journal of Speech* LV (Feb. 1969), 7–8. See

also Karlyn Kohrs Campbell, "The Rhetoric of Black Nationalism: A Case Study in Self-Conscious Criticism," *Central States Speech Journal* 22 (Fall 1971), 151–60, for treatment of how contemporary black radicals viewed syllogistic reasoning as entrapment and rebelled against it.

5.   Toch, 79–80; for a discussion of the rationale for consciousness-raising in contemporary society, see Kathie Fairchild, "Consciousness-Raising: A Radical Weapon," paper, 1st Nat. Conf. of Stewardesses for Woman's Rights, New York City, 12 Mar. 1973; Barbara Deckard, *The Women's Movement* (New York: Harper and Row, 1975); Jo Freeman, *The Politics of Women's Liberation* (New York: Longman, 1975).

6.   For a discussion of consciousness-raising techniques used in rhetoric, see Karlyn Kohrs Campbell, "Black Nationalism"; "The Rhetoric of Women's Liberation: An Oxymoron," *Quarterly Journal of Speech* 59 (Feb. 1973), 74–86; "Femininity and Feminism: To Be or Not to Be a Woman," *Quarterly Journal of Speech* 66, No. 4 (Oct. 1980), 304–12; and "Style and Content in the Rhetoric of Early Afro-American Feminists," *Quarterly Journal of Speech* 72, No. 4 (Nov. 1986), 434–45. For discussion of similar strategies used in literature, see Josephine Donovan, "Towards, a Woman's Poetics," *Tulsa Studies in Women's Literature in Feminist Issues in Literary Scholarship* 2, No. 3 (Spring/Fall 1984), 99–111; Judith Kegan Gardiner, "On Female Identity and Writing by Women," in *Writing and Sexual Difference,* ed. Elizabeth Abel (Chicago: Univ. of Chicago, 1982), 177–92; and Jane P. Tompkins, "Sentimental Power in *Uncle Tom's Cabin* and the Politics of Literary History," in *The New Feminist Criticism: Essays on Women, Literature, and Theory,* ed. Elaine Showalter (New York: Pantheon Books, 1975), 81–104.

7.   J. Wilson, *Introduction to Social Movements* (New York: Basic Books, 1973), 131, as cited in J.F. Walsh, Jr., "An Approach to Dyadic Communication in Historical Social Movements: Dyadic Communication in Maoist Insurgent Mobilization," *Communication Monographs* 53 (Mar. 1986), 12.

8.   *United Mine Workers of America,* Proc. of 15th Consecutive and 1st Biennial Conv., Dist. 14, Pittsburgh, Kansas, 30 Apr. 1914, 219.

9.   Mary Harris "Mother" Jones, public meeting, Charleston, West Virginia, 1 Aug. 1912, George Wallace Papers, West Virginia Collection. Provided by Edward Steel, West Virginia Univ.

10.   Charleston, West Virginia, 1 Aug. 1912.

11.   *United Mine Workers of America.* Proc. of Conv., Indianapolis, 16 Jan. 1916, 956–68, in Philip S. Foner, *Mother Jones Speaks: Collected Speeches and Writings.* New York: Monad Press, 1983, p. 312.

12.   Karlyn Kohrs Campbell and Kathleen Hall Jamieson, "Form and Genre in Rhetorical Criticism: An Introduction," in *Form and Genre: Shaping Rhetorical Action* (Falls Church, VA: Speech Communication Association, 1978), 9–11; Paula Tompkins Pribble, "From Wage Slave to Model Union Member: The Role of Rhetoric in the Institutionalization of the United Automobile Workers," unpublished M.A. thesis, Univ. of Kansas, 1978, 29–30.

13.   *United Mine Workers of America,* Proc. of Special Conv., Dist. 15, Trinidad, Colorado, 16 Sept. 1913, in Philip S. Foner, *Mother Jones Speaks: Collected Speeches and Writings,* New York: Monad Press, 1983, 235.

14.   *UMWA,* Pittsburgh, Kansas, 30 Apr. 1914, 215.

15.   "'Mother' Jones at Jop[l]in," *The Workers' Chronicle* (Pittsburgh, Kansas), 17 Sept. 1915, 5, col. 3–4.

16.   *UMWA,* Pittsburgh, Kansas, 30 Apr. 1914, 208.

17.   Mary Harris "Mother" Jones, public meeting, Charleston, West Virginia, 15 Aug. 1912, George Wallace Papers, West Virginia Collection. Provided by Edward Steel, West Virginia Univ.

18.   William G. Kirkwood, "Parables as Metaphors and Examples," *Quarterly Journal of Speech* 71, No. 4 (1985), 425.

19.   To Tom Mooney, 21 Mar. 1913, in Edward M. Steel, ed., *The Correspondence of Mother Jones* (Pittsburgh: Univ. of Pittsburgh Press, 1985), 344.

20.   For a discussion of Mother Jones' use of mother and prophet personae, see Tonn, chaps. 5 and 6, respectively.

21.   Lance W. Bennett, "Storytelling in Criminal Trials; A Model of Social Judgment," *Quarterly Journal of Speech* 64, No. 1 (Feb. 1978), 3, 8.

22.   Robert W. Funk, *Language Hermeneutic and Word of God* (New York: Harper & Row, 1966), 214, as quoted in Kirkwood, 426.

23.   Kirkwood, 433, 435.

24.   *United Mine Workers of America,* Proc. of the 27th and 4th Biennial Conv., Cleveland, 9 Sept. 1919, 538. Provided by Maier Fox, UMWA National Office, Washington, D.C.

25.   Mary Harris "Mother" Jones, public meeting, Williamson, West Virginia, 20 June 1920, Army Intelligence Records, RG 165 10634/793/11. National Archives. Provided by Edward Steel, West Virginia Univ.

26.   Northrop Frye, *The Critical Path: An Essay on the Social Context of Literary Criticism* (Bloomington: Indiana Univ. Press, 1971), 66.

Appendix

AVOIDING SEXISM IN COMMUNICATION
RESEARCH: GUIDELINES FOR GENDER/SEX
RESEARCH AND PUBLICATION

A Statement Adopted by the Organization for the Study
of Communication, Language and Gender, October, 1990

In recent years, two fundamental conclusions have emerged from converging scholarship by feminist theorists in communication and a variety of other areas:

1. Sexist assumptions and values pervade the English language (and probably most other languages as well).
2. Sexist assumptions and values pervade the academic and scientific traditions.

These conclusions have led to the related discovery that much research in the field of communication, in both its humanistic and scientific traditions, has and continues to reflect a variety of forms of overt and subtle sexism. Because such sexism introduces inappropriate bias into conclusions drawn, its influence in communication research should be eliminated to the extent possible. To assist scholars and students in making their work as nonsexist as possible, the following guidelines were adopted October 9, 1990 by the Organization for the Study of Communication, Language and Gender. The Organization at the same date resolved to seek endorsement of these guidelines by other major organizations involved in the study of human communication.

Gender and sex biases pervade communication research at all stages. Effects of such bias pervade the language in which humans communicate the assumptions and values they hold about communication and their beliefs about goals and methods of research. Scholars should be explicitly conscious of that pervasive sexism and constantly alert to its effects in the formulation of research questions, the definition of what serves as evidence, the methods of data collection and analysis, the perception and interpretation of information, the phrasing of research reports, and the choice of scholarship for publication.

This document identifies some of the ways that such bias is manifest and suggests some means of eliminating it. The document is not exhaustive. Not all indications and effects of bias are included. One ongoing goal of the OSCLG will be to continue the process of identification, regularly adding to and updating this catalog of sources and manifestation of sexism. An ultimate, though perhaps unattainable goal, is to eliminate the necessity for such guidelines.

It should be clear that this document does not attempt to explicate guidelines for "good research," but is, rather, a set of guidelines for examining scholarship to eliminate gender/sex bias.

Whenever values and assumptions—whether related to sex, gender, ethnicity, race, age, disability, religion, sexual orientation or socioeconomic status—affect the research process, bias can (and usually does) operate. The guidelines articulated here relate specifically to gender and sex biases but the principles illustrated can apply as well to other forms of bias.

One problem that affects almost all research, especially that involving issues of gender and sex bias, is the absence of clear definition for the terms, sex and gender, with the resulting confounding in concepts and information. At the present time, measurement tools and state of consensus among scholars do not permit clarification of these terms and elimination of this problem. Therefore, throughout this document, the term gender/sex is used to denote the referent of either or both the words gender and sex.

Guidelines for Gender/Sex Fair Research and Publication

1. Scholars should be alert to gender/sex bias that inheres in traditional methodology. This will necessitate that they:
    a. examine the underlying gender/sex values and assumptions in all research and state them explicitly.
    b. encourage multiple research methodologies—those directed toward exploring issues, raising questions, providing detailed description, and generating theory as well as approaches designed for hypothesis testing.
    c. engage in ongoing debate about the strengths and weaknesses of *all* research methods and techniques insofar as these reflect and perpetuate gender/sex stereotypes.
    d. recognize that past research may have reflected gender/sex biases, both in content and methodology, when examining the state of "current knowledge" to determine what is known and what remains to be learned and tested.

2. Scholars should recognize that many consistently demonstrated gender/sex-related behaviors may result from physiological factors, pervasive cultural factors, situational factors, or some combination of these. Models may need to be developed that consider the complex relationships among the phenomena under study.

3. If post-hoc analyses of sex/gender are reported, it should be done cautiously. While unexpected findings can lead to valuable insights, researchers should be sensitive to the strength of these differences and should be careful not to make claims about the significance of these results in the absence of a theoretical or conceptual framework.

4. Researchers should operationalize clearly what is meant by labels applied to a gender/sex-related term or behavior such as "deviant," "mature," "rational" or "nurturant" and carefully consider the implications of using such labels. Avoid ill-considered or inaccurate labelling of any such characteristic or behavior as inappropriate or ineffective.

    a. attend to the situation in which the behavior occurs or the characteristic manifests.

    b. examine possible positive consequences of behaviors that differ from those that are traditional or expected.

    c. distinguish carefully between behaviors and interpretations of them.

    d. specify the context or population appropriate to the interpretation of normative labels or statements.

    e. avoid language that inappropriately implies gender/sex-related findings or bipolar characteristics.

5. To avoid gender/sex bias, communication analyses require that the investigation of some pattern of communication include appropriate descriptions and analyses of the situational context in which the communication occurred.

    a. context should be examined for overt or subtle forms of gender/sex bias.

    b. both messages and context should be examined considering differential salience, familiarity, relevance, and/or meaning of the task, stimuli, situation, etc. to male and female participants.

    c. in many circumstances, examination of communication context should involve learning from research subjects how they interpreted and evaluated the context and task and how they felt as events transpired.

6. Gender/sex-fair research requires attention to the status, communication behaviors, and role(s) of researcher(s) and all participants as they affect the situation and outcomes.

a. when appropriate, incorporate multiple researchers to permit analysis of researcher effects.

b. when relevant and appropriate, note effects of (or control for) numbers of and ratio of men and women among research subjects.

c. where possible, base conclusions about communication behaviors of males and females on research in multiple contexts.

d. when appropriate, involve participants in selecting topics and critique of results.

7. Research generalizations should be limited clearly to the population studied.

a. assess conceptual or theoretical frameworks for their relevance to both males and females or to females and males separately.

b. generate empirical support from both males and females for theories generalized to both women and men.

c. carefully examine the normative assumptions implicit in the choice of samples studied.

8. Scholars should engage actively in expanding the populations on which generalizations are based to include populations diverse in ethnic, cultural, socioeconomic and age composition.

9. Publishers and editors should give equal consideration to research regarding females and males as distinct groups as to comparisons between groups and to publishing findings of gender/sex similarities as well as to gender/sex differences.

10. Publication of studies in which the only significant finding is an unexpected gender/sex difference without conceptual or theoretical explication does not advance the cause of scholarship.

Typical Examples of Sex Bias

1. Failure to be alert to gender/sex bias that inheres in traditional methodology. Example: Aristotelian rhetoric and most rhetorical and persuasion research since that time was theoretically grounded in a male system. Speakers and audiences were predominantly male, but it was assumed that theories based on this population and tested in it generalized to men and women alike.

2. Failure to recognize that many consistently demonstrated sex-related behaviors may result from either biological factors, consistent and pervasive cultural factors, situational factors or some combination of the three.

Example: Studies that used only male voices when "authoritative" voices were required, based on a belief that women's voices are not "authoritative," thus both accepting and perpetuating a stereotype.

2a. Failure to develop models that consider the full complexity of relationships among phenomena being studied.

Example: Conclusions that women were more "persuasible" than men, conclusions based on models of persuasion that did not take into consideration all phenomena related to "being persuaded."

3. Failure to provide comparative analyses of males and females when justified by the theoretical framework, or (conversely) making such comparisons when not justified by theory.

Example: Measuring "effectiveness" of a speaker based on a composite response from both male and female listeners even though subject matter or other factors would predict men and women could be expected to react differently.

4. Failure to clearly operationalize what is meant by the labels applied to gender/sex related characteristics and behaviors.

Example: Kohlberg's theory of moral development, based on male population, when applied to populations of women resulted in most adult women being measured as having "arrested" moral development.

4a. Failure to avoid ill-considered or inaccurate labelling of characteristics or behavior.

Example: Using descriptive terms for the behavior of females placed in paradoxical situations that fail to consider the paradoxes as potential causatives in the behavior of women (labelling soft-spoken female public speakers as "weak" or women's indirect persuasive tactics as "manipulation").

5. Failure to adequately consider situation in analysis of communication patterns.

Example: Using self-report data to draw conclusions about propensity to communicate with hitchhikers that assume comparable responses of men and women to this situation.

Another example: Describing women as being less likely to "tell jokes" than men, or as having a less developed sense of humor than men without considering the situations in which jokes are usually told, the traditional content of jokes or the power implications of joke telling.

6. Failure to attend to the status, communication behaviors, and role(s) of researcher(s) and all participants as they affect the situation and outcomes.

Example: Studies of eye contact that failed to note such factors in finding (and explaining) differences in such behavior by men and women (or failure to consider cultural differences in similar studies/conclusions).

6a.   Failure to involve participants in analysis of findings.

Example: Much participant-observation research is conducted and analyses written with no conscious input or criticism from the groups observed or written about, explicitly excluding their perceptions from the conclusions.

7.   Failure to limit clearly generalizations to the population studied.

Example: The male-based theories of rhetoric and all related research are examples here, as are numerous studies that generalize from male college students to the general population, or from male and female, predominantly white, middle-class college students to populations that differ in age, socio-economic status, ethnicity, etc.

7a.   Failure to assess conceptual or theoretical frameworks for their relevance to both males and females or to females and males separately.

Example: Concluding that women speakers were less credible than men without regard to the salience of their topic to sex/gender of speaker.

8.   Failure to expand the populations on which research generalizations are based.

Example: In an effort to expand the applicability of generalizations derived from research, scholars have conducted much research in organizations without adequately noting that the conclusions are still largely limited to the male, white and middle-class populations studied. Another example: Many published rhetorical studies focus on little known male speakers while published studies of similarly unknown women are rare.

9.   Failure by editors to give equal emphasis to publication of findings of gender/sex similarities as to gender/sex differences, or to reports regarding females and males separately.

Example: Nonsignificant sex difference findings are usually considered as unworthy of publication as all other NSD findings. Another example: As recently as 1987, one researcher reported editorial rejection of a manuscript because she had compared two groups of women rather than comparing the women to men.

10.   Publication of studies in which the only significant finding is an unexpected gender/sex difference for which no conceptual or theoretical framework is provided.

Example: Many researchers divide their sample by sex/gender when considering variables such as credibility, loneliness, or communicator style, without constructing appropriate conceptual or theoretical rationales, thus supporting inappropriate, out-of-context conclusions about sex differences.

Index